HOT TIPS

FOR career
chicks

**Unlocking the
CODE to success**

HOT TIPS
FOR career chicks

Unlocking the CODE to success

Karen Adamedes

Abney Hall Pty Ltd

SYDNEY, AUSTRALIA

Hot Tips for Career Chicks®
Unlocking the CODE to success by Karen Adamedes

Abney Hall Pty Ltd
P.O. Box 189
Cremorne, NSW 2090 Australia
publisher@abneyhall.com

www.hottipsforcareerchicks.com

Second Edition 2010. International.

ISBN 1452833931

ISBN-13/EAN-13 9781452833934

Design and Typesetting by Mercier Typesetters Pty Ltd, Granville NSW, Australia.

This publication is to provide guidance regarding the subject areas covered. However, this is with the understanding that the author and publisher are not providing legal, financial or other professional advice.

To

Mum & Dad

for my foundations

&

Peter

who helps me build my dreams

TABLE OF CONTENTS

Chapter 1

Knowledge *Is* Power

"Be curious and ask a lot of questions and really be solid. Knowledge is power. It's a cliché, but it's true. The more you know, the more straight you can stand up for what you believe in"[1]

P!nk, singer and songwriter (in www.teenscenemag.com)

On the surface everything looks as it should for career prospects in the world of business. Men and women pursue their careers with equal vigor and the opportunities for career success are available to all. Men and women have the same access to training, roles, promotions and salaries. Rewards and success are based on merit and dependent only on the knowledge, skills, experience and effort that each individual applies to his or her role. However, all is not as it seems.

Over and over again, capable and ambitious Career Chicks find that their efforts are not recognized, the value they bring to a business or organization and their contributions are not appreciated and the success they aspire to is not realized. Often, they think, *"It must be me. I must be doing something wrong."* It seems the only rational explanation. Otherwise, why aren't Career Chicks getting ahead? The answer, as it turns out, isn't obvious because the workplace culture is full of subtleties and nuances in the way that men work that affect your success.

The more you know about what is really going on, the better equipped you are to work out these subtleties and positively influence your own destiny. As singer P!nk said in her interview with Chad Kennedy for *Teen Scene Magazine*, knowledge is power and you get this by asking lots of questions. When you come from a position of knowledge you can, as P!nk said, *"stand up for what you believe in."* What you know provides a solid foundation of information on which you can develop and base your opinions and beliefs. And it becomes the basis of the decisions you make and things you do in your life. Like whether you want to develop a career and how you'll go about it. And how you'll achieve the level of success you aspire to. However, not being aware of the subtleties and nuances of the work environment may just be holding back Career Chicks (like you) from achieving success. Knowledge of how the business environment works and what is required for success is the rationale behind *Hot Tips for Career Chicks*. Knowledge is the secret to the CODE for career success, but knowing what to do with that information is even more crucial.

Unlock the CODE To Career Success

Hot Tips for Career Chicks provides some key insights into how business works and reveals the CODE for career success. It also provides you with practical and tangible ideas to implement once you have this knowledge. The CODE has four key areas for women to focus on, which will build your knowledge about the subtleties and differences between men and women in the workplace. These are:

- *Communication*
- *Operating Style*
- *Career Development*, and
- *'Everything Else'* that you need to manage (while you actually do your job).

Each chapter contains Career Chick Hot Tips, which are relatively simple guidelines to help you make the most of your skills and knowledge. They will give you an equal chance of success based on your abilities, saving you from having to battle away simply because you wear a skirt (or have the option to anyway).

Communication is the mechanism for getting things done in organizations. It is how you build and manage your image, reputation and relationships, and how you demonstrate the value you bring to an organization. The importance of what you say, how you say it, how you present your ideas, what you write and how you write it, as well as the body language that you use are all discussed. *Hot Tips for Career Chicks* explores why these areas are important for your career, how to identify potential misalignments with the prevailing business culture and practical tips to make the most of your opportunities to communicate.

Similarly, we'll look at how you can develop a personal *Operating Style* that will support your career endeavors. This is another important piece of the CODE to help you achieve success. Your *Operating Style* encompasses the way you work, how you get things done and how you are perceived to conduct yourself. The Career Chick Hot Tips in this section cover how to:

- 'be seen' at work
- operate in meetings
- work in teams
- conduct negotiations
- resolve conflict
- demonstrate leadership, and
- handle the bad stuff and disappointments that are part of business.

All are vital to promote confidence in your abilities and ensure that your contributions are valued.

Career Development is another area for Career Chicks to prioritize. To realize success your career needs to be proactively and enthusiastically managed. You need to approach your career as if it were the most important project you're responsible for at work. And you need to apply the same rigorous (if not more so) process, which includes a plan, objectives, time-lines, milestones and measures of success. Your career needs to be supported by high-quality resources from the network you build and the mentors you identify. To support your *Career Development* you need the ability to recognize when it's time to move on, to know how to be successfully recruited and then negotiate the remuneration package that reflects what you are worth. You will learn the subtleties in these crucial areas, how they are important or different for women, and some practical and easy tips to implement.

Once you have mastered these three career focus areas – *Communication*, *Operating Style* and *Career Development* – all you need to do is manage '*Everything Else*' to do your job well. This makes up the final element of the CODE for career success.

There are a number of other important and challenging issues that impact Career Chicks that these Hot Tips will *not* cover. Like when to take a career break to have children, or how to find the Holy Grail that we all seek: work–life balance. Nor will it look at the broader issues of the role of women in society or the rights of women. These, and many other issues, are tremendously important and deserve significant debate and attention. It just won't happen here. *Hot Tips for Career*

Chicks is specifically focused on what happens (or doesn't) in the workplace.

What's more, as a matter of necessity, this book generalizes about the differences between men and women and their behavior at work. These generalizations won't apply to everyone or every situation. Different people have different styles. You'll recognize many situations and behaviors described in the CODE but others you won't. However, if you're looking to work smarter, be more effective or find answers to your questions, this book is one more way to add to your knowledge. Let's look at the mystery of how work works, then how to make it work for you! Keep reading to find out how to unlock the CODE so that you can achieve career success.

Girl Power

Women have come a long way since Napoleon Bonaparte reportedly said, *"Women are nothing but machines for producing children."* (Thank goodness he was defeated at Waterloo!). Many have since proved him wrong and made tremendous contributions to society, business, science, technology, politics and economics – as well as every other area of life. Women have been responsible for some of the most important and practical inventions in use today (not just for the exclusive use of women): Stephanie Kwolek invented the material used in bulletproof vests; Anna Connelly registered the first patent for a fire escape; and the windscreen wiper was invented by Mary Anderson.

Many other women are notable for being the first female in their field: Marie Curie was the first woman to be awarded a Nobel prize (for Physics in 1903); Margaret Thatcher was the first female British Prime Minister (1979); Katharine Graham became the first female chief executive of a Fortune 500 company in the US (The Washington Post Co. in 1973) and Barbara G. Stymiest became the first woman to be governor of the Toronto Stock Exchange (1999). In more recent times: Nancy Pelosi became the first woman Speaker in the US House of Representatives (2007); Julia Gillard became the first female Prime Minister of Australia (2010); and the University of Cambridge appointed Anne Jarvis as its first female University Librarian in 650 years (2009). Happily the list of female firsts is extensive and keeps growing.

Numerous women have forged successful careers in all sorts of areas, including business. Many women have made it to the very top of major corporations. Women who lead Fortune 500 organizations, like Indra K. Nooyi, the chairman and chief executive of PepsiCo; Irene Rosenfeld who holds the same position at Kraft Foods; Carol Bartz, the chief executive and a director of Yahoo! Women like Chief Executive at Alliance Trust, Katherine Garrett-Cox lead FTSE 100 organizations in the U.K., Financial Post 500 companies in Canada (like Karen Kinsley of the Canada Mortgage and Housing Corporation) and ASX 200 organizations in Australia (Gail Kelly, chief executive and managing director of Westpac Banking Corporation). These women are just as successful once they reach this pinnacle of business achievement.

There are many more women you haven't heard of, who are either successful or pursuing success in business. Their roles may not make it into the public spotlight, but they can still be a rich and rewarding experience for those women following their dreams. Millions of women around the world experience success in their careers every day. But there are many others who, although they work hard at their career, don't achieve the success that they deserve or desire.

The Numbers Tell The Story

There is strong evidence that women aren't succeeding as they should – and the trend is international. Very few females have made it to the top in business to become chief executives of major corporations. The numbers are low – very low. In early 2010, there were female chief executives in only 3% of Fortune 500 companies in the United States,[2] and in 2009 4% of FTSE 100 corporations in the United Kingdom,[3] 4.2% of Canadian Financial Post 500 organizations,[4] and in 2008, 2% of Australian ASX 200 companies.[5] *That makes a massive total of 44 women CEOs leading 1,300 of the world's major organizations.* Fifteen Career Chicks held the top jobs in the US, four in the UK, twenty-one in Canada and four in Australia. With combined populations of more than 422 million people in these countries, this just doesn't seem right.

In each of these countries women make up more than half the population: 50.6% in the US;[6] 50.9% in the UK;[7] 50.4% in Canada[8] and 50.2% in Australia.[9] There are plenty of women out there, so that's not the reason for there being so few at the top of the business world.

And it's not that they're not smart or well educated. In 2005-06, 60% of master's degree graduates and 57.5% of bachelor's degree graduates in the US were female.[10] Similarly, in the UK, women made up 57% of first degree graduates in 2007/08[11] and 60% of university degrees, diplomas and certificates in Canada.[12] In Australia in 2009, 54.3% of people with a bachelor degree, graduate diploma or certificate or post-graduate degree were women.[13] And women in Australia made up 51.7% of employed people with these educational qualifications.[14] So education is not the problem either. There's no lack of qualified women in these countries to account for the low number of senior female business leaders.

Neither is there a shortage of women in the workplace. Again, it's an international trend. In the US in early 2010, 47.3% of the employed labor force were women.[15] In Australia the number was comparable, with women making up 45.2% of the workforce.[16] And 46.2% in Canada (2009).[17] The numbers are similar when you look at the percentage of the workforce in 'professional occupations', the area, theoretically, where people will be promoted from into more senior roles. In the U.S. 51.4%[18] of people employed in management, professional and related occupations in 2009 were women. In the U.K. in the April-June quarter in 2009, 43% of people employed in professional occupation were women.[19] And in Australia in February 2010, 44.5% of managers and 'professionals' were women.[20]

So to review the stats so far: there are plenty of women in both the general population and, more importantly, in the workforce to be promoted to senior management. They're qualified and they work in professional occupations, yet very few achieve senior management status.

Compared to the number of women available in the pool of professional workers very few make it even part way up the ladder in the big corporations. In the U.S. in 2009 only 13.5%[21] of executive officer positions were held by women and in 2008 held 16.9%[22] of corporate officer positions in Canadian Financial Post 500 companies. It's a little worse elsewhere. In the UK, The Female FTSE Report 2008[23] revealed that women made up only 12.1% of FTSE 100 senior managers. In Australia, an Equal Opportunity for Women in the Workplace Agency

(EOWA) report found that in 2008 women made up only 10.7%[24] of executive managers in ASX 200 companies.

Looking in more detail at the Australian example, it gets worse when you consider the EOWA report's definition of 'executive managers'. The report splits 'executive management' into support roles and line-management roles. People in line-management roles are more likely to be promoted to more senior roles (chief executives, board members and the like) because they have either a profit-and-loss or direct customer responsibility. Surprise, surprise, the number of women in these roles in ASX 200 companies is lower again: women held only 5.9% of these line-management roles.[25] Little wonder then that the number of Australian female chief executives ends up as only 2%.

What's more, these Career Chicks don't earn as much as their male counterparts either. Female CEOs in Australia earn about two-thirds as much as men, and female chief financial officers (CFOs) and chief operating officers (COOs) about half as much.[26] In the last couple of years a U.S. study also found that female CEOs receive lower total compensation than men; about 85%.[27] Wait until you get to Chapter 19 for the full horror story of the salary gap between men and women to be revealed!

The Theories

There are plenty of women in the population, in the workforce in general and in professional occupations, and women are well-educated. The United States, Canada, the United Kingdom and Australia all have legislation that makes discrimination on the basis of gender illegal. In the United Nations' Human Development Report for 2009 the 'Gender Related Development Index',[28] which takes into account measures such as life expectancy, adult literacy rates, education and income. Australia was ranked 1st in the world, Canada 4th, the U.K. 17th and the U.S. was 19th. The United Nations also rated these countries highly on the 'Gender Empowerment Measure',[29] which looks at economic and political participation and decision making as well as power over economic resources. On these measures, Australia was ranked 7th, Canada 12th, the U.K. 15th and the U.S. 18th. Women in these countries are doing relatively well, very well, yet still limited numbers make it to the ultimate levels of career success. So what's going wrong?

There is the inescapable biological fact that women who want to have children need to physically take time off work, plus there are challenges for working mothers, and there are societal expectations of women to be prime caregivers. Excuses are also made that women are not up to the 'rough and tumble' of business and not capable of making the 'hard' decisions. Then there's the theory that there simply aren't enough women coming through the 'pipeline' of management ranks who are worthy of promotion.

This last theory has had considerable credibility for a long time. It stands to reason that in the interests of shareholders, customers and other employees it does not make sense to promote someone to a senior position who is not qualified or the best person for the job. The theory goes that as more women pursue careers in the business world, they will advance through the ranks and one day (hey presto!) there will be more women at the top. The problem with this theory is that over the last 20 years or so it just hasn't happened.

The argument has long been that because many women work part-time or take career breaks they exclude themselves from the business career path. While that is a factor (In 2010, 70%[30] of all part-time workers in Australia and 64%[31] in the U.S. were women), it's certainly not the whole story. Even when you exclude part-timers from the equation, in the United States 43%[32] of all full-time employees were women. And in Australia in 2010, 37.8%[33] of all *full-time* managers and professionals were women.

And many women do go back to work after taking maternity leave. In the United States in 2007, 55.1%[34] of all mothers with children under one year old were employed. Between 2000 and 2002, 79.4%[35] of women who had their first child and had worked during their pregnancy returned to work within the first year of having a child. Of these women, 83% returned to work with the same employer and of those that changed employers, 35% received a higher pay level than their previous position.[36]

A Parental Leave in Australia Study[37] conducted by The University of Queensland in 2006 reported that 70% of mothers who were employed prior to their child's birth returned to work within 15 months. Of this group, two-thirds returned to the same job with the same employer. So despite the fact that career breaks and part-time work do have an impact on women, there are still plenty of full-time working women, and those returning from leave, who are available for promotion. Yet the numbers tell the story. The number of women who make it to the top is not representative of the volume of women available in the talent pool.

Why Is It So?

From the 1960s to the 1980s, American scientist Professor Julius Sumner Miller hosted a science program for children and used physics to explain anomalies, like how it's possible to make a straw go through a raw potato. His stock phrase, *"Why Is It So?"* became synonymous with his use of science and experiments to rationalize astonishing happenings. The same question seems relevant to ask why the many women who pursue careers do not achieve the same level of success as their male counterparts.

The last 30 years have seen the Women's Liberation and feminist movements, affirmative action plans and many voices calling for women to have equal opportunities for success in all areas of life. Yet, clearly when it comes to careers, this hasn't been a complete success – to put it mildly.

And yet during this time, many intelligent, capable and talented women have worked hard, made significant contributions to business and aspired to achieve career success. Many companies have introduced family-friendly policies, programs have been implemented to help develop and retain female talent and, to a large extent, explicitly discriminatory practices have faded into (near) extinction. There are regular calls for quotas to ensure that enough women are considered for senior positions, but most Career Chicks don't want to be the 'token woman' in a team or be appointed to a role to help a business meet a diversity target. They (and you) just need an equal chance to get there on their own merit.

The reality is that regardless of all that has changed over the years, the culture and norms of business do not let Career Chicks achieve their potential. The prevailing culture of organizations – how people communicate and what behaviors are accepted and preferred – is male-oriented. Historically, there have simply been more men in business, particularly at the senior levels where decisions are made. Over time, the male culture has developed alongside the modern world to become the culture of business. In the more than 200 years since the Industrial Revolution began, men have dominated commerce, industry and government. How *they* work and how *they* communicate has become the norm. The culture of norms and expectations that men have established, and the nuances and subtleties within that culture, can trip up chicks in pursuit of their career goals. Rather than a glass ceiling holding women back, it's more like an invisible cloak hiding the intricacies of how to get ahead in business.

Day-To-Day Challenges

Men and women often find working together a confusing and frustrating experience. The differences can be considerable when it comes to both leadership and communication styles. Men often think women are unfocused, not strategic enough, soft and too preoccupied with the 'touchy feely' people/relationship stuff rather than the hard (and, therefore, more important) business decisions. Women often feel misunderstood, undervalued and taken advantage of. The root cause of these issues is that men and women approach how to do business on a day-to-day basis quite differently.

Of course, this is a generalization. Many women *have* figured out the environment and adapted to the predominant business culture. And many men display characteristics that are generally ascribed to how women work or communicate. However, what 'generally' holds true is helpful to understand and add to your knowledge. Like the inside information you need to understand a subtle joke, knowing what goes on in business will help you interpret what is happening in your career. Often the more subtle jokes are the funniest when you take the time and apply your knowledge to work them out. So too, your business career may be just that bit more rewarding when you work out the nuances, subtleties and fine distinctions of business culture.

Typically, men in business are hierarchical, task-focused and action-oriented. They take a problem-solving approach to issues. Men see themselves as strategic, focused and capable of making the 'hard' decisions. Their communication is often short and concise and they focus on the issues. They keep score (on everything) and take a competitive approach to their career. The male style dominates how business works, as a legacy of history. It dictates the language, rules and expectations of work.

Women work towards the same business goals, but with a different approach. They are more likely to adopt an affiliative, relationship-focused style. Women will spend time seeking opinions, considering options and ensuring that relationships are maintained. They'll spend less time keeping score, comparing themselves to others and explicitly focusing on their career as a part of their job. These differences in approach lead to many challenges for women in the workplace, ranging from confusion to exclusion.

The way that women approach doing business and developing their careers does not necessarily support their aspirations for success. This doesn't mean that women are overtly excluded from success due to an 'Old Boys Network' or 'Boys Club' culture (although sadly this is sometimes still true), but it does mean that men (and some women) expect to communicate and work with other people in the business environment, as they would with other men. There's a good chance that men don't even realize that this is the case. It's just 'the way that business is done'.

The reality is that there are simply more men than women in senior roles in business. Men have developed the language and rules about how they operate in business, and they are not particularly helpful about explaining to women what's going on. Largely because they don't realize that the way business works is more instinctive for them than it is for women.

Many women come into this environment and intuitively (or logically) work out what works, what doesn't and how to be successful. They adapt their communication and behavior accordingly. Often they can be criticized (by both men and women) for trying to act like men. That may be the case, but maybe they have just worked out that doing something one way didn't work, but doing it another way did.

If you ask men what women should do to be successful in business, half of them will say, *"Act more like a man."* The other half will say, *"Don't try and act like a man."* The truth is that men aren't sure about what's going on between men and women in the workplace either. Or how they want women to behave. Understanding that men and women work in different ways is the first step to developing a common understanding – and making it work better for everyone.

Better For Business

It makes sense for organizations (and the people who work in them) to utilize *all* the potential skilled, capable people who are available, rather than focusing on only half the people. As one senior executive of a large Australian corporation said, "Smart companies who value diversity will get the talent. Market forces, the simple laws of supply and demand, will sort which companies are successful in the long-term and which ones are not. If companies don't accommodate the talent pool (which is 50% women) then they will miss out and it will reflect in their business performance.

"It's really a matter of supply and demand," the executive explained. "If you limit your potential source of good people, someone else is going to snap them up. And the companies that miss out on good women will, ultimately, pay the price." The really pleasing thing about this view? The senior executive who said it is a man.[38]

The Choice Is Yours

Perhaps business should have already evolved to equally meet the preferred styles of both men and women. But it hasn't. This leaves Career Chicks with one of two choices ... struggle against the injustice of it all or accept where the business environment is right now and adapt to make it work for them?

Science shows that those species who survive and prosper (like the pesky cockroach) are those that adapt to their environment. If women can acclimatize to the business environment, they will not only survive, but also prosper. It's like the kids' joke: *"How do you eat an elephant?"* The answer is ... *"One bite at a time."* How do you change the norms of how to communicate and operate in business? The answer is ... One successful woman at a time!

The more women who have long-term, successful careers and use their knowledge to figure out the subtleties of business culture, the more they'll influence real and sustainable change. And it will be the culture that changes, not women. The culture of most organizations needs to evolve to take advantage of the fabulous resource that it's not making the most of ... Career Chicks.

The upside of having a successful career for women in general, and you in particular, makes the effort of learning and persevering worthwhile. Your career can provide you with the opportunity to be challenged and intellectually stimulated, fulfilled by your achievements and do some good. You don't have to be a humanitarian volunteer to make a difference (although those people work wonders), but you can make a difference by participating in business, even if it's in the way you work with and treat other people. Not to mention that a successful career also allows you to earn a good living and make a nice life for yourself (and others).

At its best, you can be doing interesting work, developing yourself, spending time with great people, contributing to something important, being appreciated for your efforts and earning good money. You may identify success as anything from becoming a senior executive, to working on projects that you are passionate about, to building a long-term career to provide you with a regular income (perhaps with enough leftover to regularly invest in a new pair of shoes!). Whatever your definition of success, the potential rewards can make it well worth the effort to develop the knowledge, work out the subtleties and unlock the CODE to achieve career success.

(After that we'll work out how to change the culture of business … one successful Career Chick at a time …)

Unlock the **<u>C</u>ODE**
for career success...

communication

Chapter 2

Choose Your Words

"Things do not change, we change"
Henry David Thoreau, writer & philosopher (1817–1862)

The first key to unlocking the CODE for career success is effective *Communication*. This chapter discusses the role of communication and its importance in business in general, and with men in particular. It also provides practical Career Chick Hot Tips to help you come out on top in the business environment.

The fact is, the workplace is dominated by a communication style that is more reflective of how men communicate than women. Traditionally, there have been more men in business and their natural style has dominated. But it can put you, as a Career Chick, at a disadvantage without you even being aware of it. Understanding and adapting your communication to the accepted business style can have a substantial impact on your career potential and success. Speak the language and you can more effectively demonstrate your knowledge, skills and how you can contribute.

The challenge for anyone when learning or speaking a new language is being understood. The business world has its own complex and unique language. Your ability to understand and speak the language of business will allow you to be more successful when working with both men and women. Clear communication is essential so that what you say is understood and valued. Your interactions and communications with others will determine your effectiveness, your reputation and the perception of how capable you are – and ultimately your success in the business world.

There are several elements of communication that significantly influence career success. These include:

- the words you use
- how you say them
- your ability to impress when you make presentations
- how well you write, and
- the messages you send with your body language.

Read on to see how these vital elements contribute to effective communication in organizations and, in particular, what significance they have.

A Little Effort Goes A Long Way

Think about France – any film you have seen set there, pictures you have admired or, if you are lucky enough, places you have visited. It is little wonder that the French have genuine pride in their country: with *haute couture* fashion, treasures in the Louvre, and countryside graced with vineyards and chateaus, France is unique. The French are proud of their country, culture and language, which have a rhythm that is passionate and musical.

The French also have a reputation for their aversion to speaking English, which often leads to accusations of arrogance. If you walk into a patisserie in Paris and order loudly in English, you may be ignored, glared at or even worse. Wander in with a smile on your face, start with a friendly *"Bonjour"* in the appropriate lilt and you will get a friendly response. A visit to a cafe is a lot easier when you order, say, *"Deux café, s'il vous plait" (Two coffees, please)*. The waiter, realizing you are making an effort, is more likely to help out by speaking English. It is worth making just that little bit of effort to speak the language. A few *bonjours*, *s'il vous plaits* and *mercis* (hellos, pleases and thankyous) go a long way to improving communication.

Likewise, adapting your communication to the language of the business world can be rewarding. And the benefits are potentially longer lasting than the coffee and croissant you willingly learned new words to order.

Career success can offer tremendous rewards. Think financial success, intellectual stimulation and job satisfaction to name just a few. All are great incentives to attract clever, capable and hard-working Career Chicks (like you) to the worlds of business, government and not-for-profit organizations. However, the success that you achieve, no matter how capable you are at your job, directly relates to your ability to communicate in the prevailing language of your organization. At this time, it is biased towards the way that men talk and interact with each other. Connecting with others, in the way they understand best, can make the difference between career success and just having a job.

Regardless of your skills or abilities, how you communicate impacts on what you achieve. In a French cafe you can refuse to adapt, insist the staff speak English, then find they don't have a clue what you are asking for. You may get the satisfaction of holding out and saying, *"If I'm going to spend my money here, they can speak English."* Alternatively, you can speak a little French and end up with your desired coffee much faster and with a lot less angst. You don't have to become French; just making a little effort and attempting to speak their language is appreciated and helps you get what you want. Similarly, for career success you don't have to become a man. But it will help if you understand, adapt and speak a little of 'their' language.

Career Chick Hot Tip: Learn the language of your organization, profession or industry.

Bridge That Gap

Communication between any two people is difficult enough. Different backgrounds, cultures, experiences, word meanings and changing contexts are just some of the factors that cause communication to be misunderstood, misinterpreted or just missed altogether! Regardless of the reasons, there are many differences between the way men and women communicate. This can lead to men undervaluing the contribution that women make in the workplace and women failing to achieve career success for reasons that have nothing to do with their ability. It can be a frustrating and time-wasting process when men and women struggle with this communication gap. Because men have dominated the working environment for so long their communication style has become the norm. It is in the interest of Career Chicks, like you, to understand the differences and bridge the gap.

In business, understanding the accepted style of communication will help you sell your ideas, report your successes, share your visions, negotiate what you need and help you reach agreements. It is vital to make sure that your abilities, the quality of your work and ideas, and the contribution that you make are appreciated on their merit. The last thing you want is for these to be diminished due to miscommunication or misunderstandings.

For Career Chicks, the difference between how men and women communicate is often a daily challenge that can be at worst frustrating and at best amusing. Of course, the variations between the sexes do not apply universally to every man and every woman, or in equal measures. However, generalizations about how men and women communicate can provide clues on how to improve the communication between them.

Career Chick Hot Tip: Understand the accepted style of communication to help your contributions be appreciated on their merits.

Say What You Mean

Have you ever thought that a manager or colleague wasn't interested in what you were talking about? Seemed impatient for you to finish what you were saying? Maybe didn't 'get' what you suggested? Or have you ever voiced a great idea that was ignored and then some guy came up with the same point and was praised as a genius? Career Chicks experience situations like these on a daily basis. It is unlikely that the problems had anything to do with the actual content of what was *said* but rather how it was *heard*. These situations are a result of the differences in communication styles between men and women.

So what are the differences? In general, men are often seen as being direct, authoritative and task- and solution-oriented. Women are often associated with a more indirect, subtle and relationship-oriented communication style. Men like to be known as 'straight shooters' who get to the point. Women are more likely to be seen as empathetic, softer and more interested in people. Where men will boast, women will play down their contribution.

One way men and women differ in their communication style is in the words they use. Words play a large part in influencing how well you are understood. Saying what you mean and being completely understood can be trickier than you think. English is a complex language with nuances and multiple potential interpretations of the same statement, question or even word. Look up 'set', 'run' and 'go' in a dictionary. These words have literally hundreds of definitions. With so many different meanings, is it any wonder that sometimes even the simplest conversations and comments are misunderstood? Have you ever been in the situation where you asked someone, *"How did you get here?"* only to receive a long-winded reply about their career moves or their journey through life, rather than what kind of transport they used to get there? Meaning what you say and saying what you mean can be very different things.

As the Hatter and the March Hare, in Lewis Carroll's *Alice's Adventures in Wonderland*,[1] pointed out to Alice:

> "Then you should say what you mean," the March Hare went on.
>
> "I do," Alice hastily replied; "at least … I mean what I say – that's the same thing, you know."
>
> "Not the same thing a bit!" said the Hatter. "You might just as well say that 'I see what I eat' is the same thing as 'I eat what I see!'"
>
> "You might just as well say," added the March Hare, "that 'I like what I get' is the same thing as 'I get what I like!'"
>
> "You might just as well say," added the Dormouse, who seemed to be talking in his sleep, "that 'I breathe when I sleep' is the same thing as 'I sleep when I breathe!'"

The characters of Wonderland were right! Words can have very different meanings in different situations. It is critical that you are aware of this to ensure you are understood. As there are hundreds of thousands of words in English you have an amazing variety to choose from. This also means that there's a wide margin for misinterpretation based on your choice of words.

The words you use can also determine whether others like what you are saying – and whether they like you. Psychology professor Albert Mehrabian[2] researched how words, tone and non-verbal communication influence whether others like what you are saying. He came up with the '7%-38%-55%' rule. This relates to the relative importance of particular elements to whether people like what you say: the words you use (7%); the tone you use (38%); and your non-verbal communication (55%). Although the first element is assigned a small relative weighting, Mehrabian's research supports that your choice of words does have an impact on whether others like what you are saying.

As big a challenge as it may seem, given the complexities of the English language, your objective is to select words that ensure that what you say is, in fact, what is heard. You can help this by understanding:

- your audience
- the context, and
- the meanings of specific words for certain groups.

For instance, a *"cookie"* has very different meaning depending on whether you are on your computer or in a kitchen!

How a listener interprets your words determines whether what they hear is what you meant to say. The difference in how men and women interpret what is said can cause misunderstandings and misinterpretations. For example, if you respond to a simple question like *"How are you?"* with *"I'm really busy"* or even *"Flat out, I haven't even had lunch today!"* you may mean *"I'm working really hard for you"* but a man may interpret it as *"I'm not coping."* Rather than admiring your industriousness, a man is more likely to be concerned about your ability to do the job, which undermines your diligence. Interactions like these happen many times a day at work, in elevators, lunchrooms and corridors, so there are numerous opportunities for women to inadvertently undermine themselves.

An alternative response to strengthen, rather than weaken, your position (no matter how busy you actually are) is to smile and joke, *"Actually I've got a bit of spare time on my hands. I'm looking for a few extra things to do."* In an appropriately light-hearted tone of voice, this will show that you have things under control enough to still have a sense of humor. However, don't do this if there's a chance you'll actually be given more work and you don't have spare capacity! Instead, you could stick with a simple, *"Great, how are you?"* or *"Good, things are going really well."*

In all your interactions it is vital that what you say reinforces that you are confident and in control. Even if you don't feel that way at that particular moment, you know that you will do what needs to be done. You don't need to create any doubts about your capabilities along the way. If you act self-assured and positive that is how you will be seen. This can only have a positive impact on your career prospects.

Career Chick Hot Tip: Say exactly what you mean, leaving no room for alternative interpretations.

Which Words?

If communication is the currency of an organization then words are the accepted legal tender. As notes and coins change hands in the economy, it is the trading of words in business that determines the value of the communication. Like spending money, you want to use the words that have the highest return for you. Your word selection not only increases the value of your individual interactions, but also contributes to your overall career worth. Fine-tuning your language to ensure men hear what you say means you avoid being judged on anything else. It is worth the effort to change some of the words you use, if it means being completely understood.

To make sure you are understood, choose words that:

- simplify what you are saying
- minimize the need for further explanation, and
- maximize the impact of your message.

Make it easier for people to understand just how talented you are and it will help you establish, or build, a successful reputation. The less effort others need to make to understand you, the more impressed they will be. Your choice of words should be the ones with the highest value – those that are most powerful in the business world. In general, the best choices are words that are:

- objective
- factual
- assertive
- positive, and
- action-oriented.

Choose words that are powerful and positive. Words that show you know what you are doing and that you are getting on and doing it; *'will'*, *'can'* and *'do'* all convey a more positive approach than, *'might'*, *'maybe'* and *'if'*. Women may subconsciously select these weaker words, often because they don't want to appear arrogant. But all this does is create uncertainty about your abilities. Whether you are successful or not, the doubt created by using weak words often remains.

Using strong, positive 'can-do' words creates positive expectations about your performance and abilities. When you do deliver (as Career Chicks do), you will reinforce that expectation and build your reputation. This is a much better strategy than creating doubt about your ability in the first place, then surprising everyone when you are successful. You don't want your success ascribed to good luck!

It is also best to use the simplest, most appropriate words. There is no advantage in demonstrating that you have the ability to write a thesaurus by using complicated or unusual words – unless your job is writing a thesaurus, of course! Simple, common, uncomplicated words help your listener understand exactly what you mean. The use of multiple polysyllables might make you feel intelligent, but it can cloud the other person's understanding or, worse, make them feel ignorant or at a disadvantage. This is unlikely to be a positive interaction for them (or you!).

In the business world, both men and women react positively when you use words that demonstrate you can do what needs to be done. That's what they want to hear. Everyone has accountabilities they need to meet. It helps to use words that are factual like *'think'*, *'is'* and *'can'*, rather than *'feel'*, *'might'* or *'maybe'*. Don't be wishy-washy by qualifying what you say with *'may'* or *'could'*. Also avoid *'but'*, as it undermines whatever you said before it. Use *'and'* to illustrate more than one point or issue for consideration. Be confident in what you say and demonstrate this with the words you use.

> *Career Chick Hot Tip:* Choose words that are assertive, objective, factual, positive and action-oriented.

What Not To Say

Saying what you mean, involves not only knowing which words to use but also whether to use them at all. For instance, it's best if you don't problem-solve out loud – at least, not around men. While women often solve problems by discussing them, men can interpret the process of weighing up alternatives as showing you are unsure what to do. It is much more efficient to discuss the options when you have reached a conclusion, even if it's not the complete answer. If you personally need to talk to think, find someone else who works in the same way to think out loud with – they will understand.

It is also preferable to have a solution to a problem before you complain about it. Expressing your frustration may give the (wrong) impression that you can't handle what is going on or that you're not 'up to the task'. Having the answer, or even a potential answer, to a problem demonstrates that you are solution-focused, clear thinking and action-oriented. All of which men appreciate.

They also like it if you get straight to the point. Don't take others on a long journey about why you are going to say what you are going to say. This can be frustrating and unproductive for everyone, cause misunderstandings and have people talking at cross-purposes. In business, men get straight to the point of a discussion with little or no preamble. Women, however, often use the beginning of a discussion to build rapport and position what they are about to say. Men may get frustrated by this and think, *"Why can't she just get to the point?"*, while the women wonder, *"Why is he so impatient?"* or *"Why isn't he listening to what I'm saying?"* The result is that judgments are being made and no one is really focused on the topic at hand.

To keep focused on the subject, the best place to start is at the end. Begin with the summary, punch line or request. If they want more detail, they will ask. If they ask, it means they are interested. If they are interested, they will listen. This is exactly what you want! If men don't know why they need to know what you are telling them, they may think you are wasting their time. Chances are, by the time you get to the important point and they are finally interested in what you are saying (if they listened that long), they'll ask you to repeat the details anyway!

Career Chick Hot Tip: Get to the point fast.

No Need To Apologize

Avoid saying "sorry" unless you have actually done something wrong. Really wrong. Women have a great propensity to say, *"I'm sorry"* at any opportunity – even when they don't know the other person. Someone wheels their supermarket trolley into you. A woman will say, *"I'm sorry."* (A man will keep going or bark *"Careful!"*) Someone accidentally steps on your foot in a crowd? A woman will say, *"I'm sorry."*

In the workplace, apologies are interpreted as, *"I was wrong"*, *"It's my fault"* or *"I've done the wrong thing or approached this the wrong way."* It isn't necessary for you to undermine your own reputation. (You can find plenty of other people to do that for you!) Instead of apologizing for everything, acknowledge the feedback and go into action-oriented, problem-solving mode. Others will think, *"Here's someone who can get on with things"*, rather than, *"It's her fault."*

The hot tip? Don't say *"yes"* when you mean *"no"*. Saying no, particularly to a superior, can be daunting. Women often fear putting a relationship at risk if they do. This can lead women to say, "yes" to a request, even if it impacts negatively on them. Women believe that saying "no" is not acceptable, and that they have to find a way to do what has been asked. *"They wouldn't have asked me if they didn't really need me to do it would they?"* rationalizes a woman as she cancels a networking appointment or gym class, or eats lunch at her desk (again). And, somewhere deep inside, a Career Chick feels valued because she has been asked.

This thinking is half right. If they ask you to do something, they want it done. But you know what? They don't necessarily need *you* to do it. This opens up your options because, rather than saying no, you can find alternatives. You don't necessarily have to do the task, but you can provide the solution. For instance, saying, *"I have to complete <<whatever you are working on>>, but I think Bob might be able to help"* won't be heard as *"no"*, but rather, *"I have a solution for you."* This positions you as a problem-solver, rather than a doormat. Alternatively, if you really are the only one who can do it, negotiate the time frame and amount of work that needs to be done, or ask for some help to complete the task.

Career Chick Hot Tip: Learn how to say *"no"*.

Be Clear

Women, generally, don't like to ask for help. Career Chicks don't want to reveal that they might not be able to do everything. However, in the complex world of business it is just not reasonable to expect that any one person can do everything. At times you will need to ask for resources, support or more time to complete tasks. Make no mistake, men do! So when you do, be direct. This will avoid ambiguity and demonstrate that you know what you are doing and what you need to get it done.

Whatever you are negotiating for, the rules of simplicity and clarity apply. When you ask for something, make your request clear. Don't talk around what you want, hoping the other person will figure it out. Chances are they won't have the time or the inclination to second-guess your requests.

Career Chick Hot Tip: Know exactly what you need and be very clear when you ask for it.

The Right Words Work

Communication in business exists to tell, share, delegate, ask and present. Communicating effectively showcases your ability. Getting it right means using positive, clear, action-oriented, solution-focused, problem-solving words that are brief and to the point. Using straightforward, commonly understood words and positioning important information at the start of a conversation has a huge impact on the effectiveness of your communication.

These tips apply whether you are talking to men or women. The prevalent communication culture of most business organizations is male-oriented because in the past, men have held the majority of senior positions. However, many women have adapted and learnt to work within the prevailing culture. When you are talking to other women, it's also appropriate to use a direct, clear, get-to-the-point style. There is no downside to being clear in your communication. Demonstrate that you are positive and action-oriented with everyone.

Saying what you mean and being understood is the first step to achieving the career success you want. Your choice of words can significantly impact the success you can achieve. Choosing your words carefully, to say what you mean, is the first key to unlocking the CODE. It's as easy as that!

Career Chick Hot Tips
to choose your words:

- Learn the language of your organization, profession or industry.

- Understand the accepted style of communication to help your contributions be appreciated on their merits.

- Say exactly what you mean, leaving no room for alternative interpretations.

- Choose words that are assertive, objective, factual, positive and action-oriented.

- Get to the point fast.

- Learn how to say *"no"*.

- Know exactly what you need and be very clear when you ask for it.

Chapter 3

Be Heard

*"Do you not know I am a woman? when I think,
I must speak"*

Rosalind in *As You Like It* (Act III Scene 2) by William Shakespeare, playwright
(1564–1616)

Whether gossiping over the back fence, or chatting on the phone, the stereotype that women talk for the sake of talking is alive and well. TV sitcoms, movies and comedians all get great mileage out of this theme. Studies that claim to 'prove' women speak more words in a day than men have been showcased by mainstream media to prove this long-held and popular view. Funnily enough, subsequent research that questions these findings doesn't get the same attention. Whatever the facts or the studies say, the reality is that women are commonly perceived as chatterboxes – a point of view that has not helped position women as serious business contributors.

This and other stereotypes of how women talk – too much, too emotional, too fast and too personal – can all undermine the importance of what women have to say. The next part of the *Communication* solution of the CODE for career success is to focus on how you communicate to be heard. This includes how you:

- use your voice – tone, pace, pitch and volume
- arrange what you say
- establish rapport, and
- portray your confidence by how you speak.

With some easy to follow Career Chick Hot Tips, you can improve your communications and overcome some of the stereotypes that may work against you.

What Men Think

(this is not an oxymoron!)

Generally, men think women:

- talk fast
- talk over the top of each other

- don't listen
- bounce from topic to topic, and
- are emotional.

In reality, a discussion between like-minded women can be a vibrant and energetic affair. Thoughts and ideas flow freely; one comment leads to a new topic and then winds its way back again. Several women might talk at once, and the volume will ebb and flow with the level of excitement. Is this ineffective communication? Absolutely not! It can be an exciting and productive environment where ideas are tabled, alternatives considered and decisions made. But throw a few guys into the frame and it's a different ballgame (to use a male sporting analogy!). A man, listening to women communicating in this way will think they are too emotional, unable to focus and impolite. This, as you know, is not the case, but that is their perception. And because of the sheer number of men in business, it becomes the prevailing view in this environment. The result can be a constant battle to overcome this stereotype and be heard on your own merit.

Career Chick Hot Tip: Develop your communication style to break the stereotypes and be heard on your own merit.

Find Your Voice

Be aware of your voice and how you use it. It is true that there are differences in male and female voices. The higher pitch and tone of a woman's voice can be melodic and attractive, but in business it can sound too fast and too emotive. This can distract men. Lower your voice if the pitch gets too high and allow men to focus on *what* you say, not *how* you say it.

Be conscious of your volume, pace, pitch and tone as you speak. A useful technique is to observe the style of communication being used in your business, or even in a specific meeting and adjust your style accordingly. Is it a high-energy, fast-paced meeting where ideas flow? Or is it a serious, formal reporting session, with everyone taking their turn to speak? You need to be a bit like Goldilocks and work out what is 'just right'. Too high a volume or pitch and you will be seen as too emotional; too soft and you will cast doubts about your confidence and your ability. Observing the style of others in a forum is helpful to figure out what is appropriate.

One At A Time

Often great ideas are stimulated by discussion and it is tempting to throw them into a conversation when you think of them, even if someone else is talking. Women will usually think nothing of it, but men hate it. When you talk over them they think you are interrupting them and being disrespectful. And with the male propensity to value their position in a hierarchy, this resentment increases, the more senior his position. Men interpret interruptions as an indication that you are not listening. They reason, *"How were you listening if you thought of the next thing to say?"* Little do they know how talented women are! The Hot Tip is don't do it! Easier said than done sometimes. It can be agony to keep quiet when you get a brilliant idea that seems vital to the conversation. However, the reality is that if you jump in when a man is talking, they will not hear what you have to say and your contribution will be lost anyway. Wait until you can get the idea across without offending anyone.

If you do find yourself talking over the top of someone, it is better to back out gracefully rather than keep going and compound the error. If you realize that you have interrupted someone just stop and say, *"Please continue, I didn't mean to interrupt."* They might be a little annoyed, but you won't have lost your idea or put them completely offside.

Bouncing around between topics is another challenge. Men interpret this as a lack of focus. If a conversation makes you think of another issue that needs to be raised, don't just throw it into the mix. Men will think you aren't paying attention to what they are saying. Without appearing distracted, make a note to yourself to make sure you don't forget your brilliant idea, and then focus on the original discussion. You can then raise it at the appropriate time without interrupting anyone. Alternatively, if your idea needs to be considered at that time, wait for the appropriate break in the conversation and say something like, *"I've just realized, this is going to have implications on some other things we are doing. Let's discuss this before we finish up today."* This approach is not only respectful of the current conversation but the use of *"let's"* also shows you are confident about the importance of raising the issue, rather than being apologetic or seeking permission.

It will also reinforce that you are listening and continuing to focus on the original topic.

Career Chick Hot Tip: Let others finish what they are saying; never interrupt.

Listen Up

Listening and demonstrating you understand what is being said is critical to successful communication. There's an old joke that people have two ears and one mouth because that's the appropriate ratio for listening and speaking (meaning you should listen twice as much as you talk!), which is pretty much right. You need to listen to ensure you really hear and understand what others say. To men it's equally important that you demonstrate you are listening to them. They see this as a sign of respect. As a result, this improves their confidence in you and your communication. Think about some famous TV interviewers, like Oprah, Barbara Walters and Sir Michael Parkinson. They all really listen to the answers to their questions, and adjust their next question accordingly. Many average interviewers (who don't jump so readily to mind) just ask the next prepared question, regardless of the answer to the previous one. Great interviews happen when interviewers listen.

Similarly, great communication happens in the workplace when people really listen. Demonstrating that you understand what has been said indicates that you have been listening. One of the best ways to do this is to use the good interviewer's technique and refer to what the other person has just said. You could ask a question to gain more detail or just restate what was said. Simply say, *"Can I just check my understanding of what you are saying?"* then rephrase what they said. They will think you are brilliant because you said exactly what they think! This technique allows you to demonstrate that you were listening and understood what was said. More importantly, you can be sure you actually did understand. It is better to clarify misunderstandings early, than talk at cross-purposes. Listening is vital to communicate effectively and to develop your personal credibility in the business environment.

Career Chick Hot Tip: Listen and demonstrate that you understand.

Making Introductions

As discussed in Chapter 2, the importance of choosing words that get to the point is vital for business communication. So, too, is the way you arrange what you say: how you make introductions, how you establish credibility and rapport, and how you present information. None of these is difficult; you just need to be conscious of the preferred style in the business environment.

Funnily enough, it starts at the beginning – with introductions! When men introduce themselves, or each other, they are quick to establish where they stand in the pecking order. They make sure the other person knows their qualifications, or their position in the hierarchy or their expertise – preferably, all three. The Hot Tip is to ensure you introduce men (and yourself to men) in this way. Here's a perfect introduction: *"I'd like to introduce you to Dr. Bob Smith (in this case, you are giving the title and qualification in one), the <<his position>>. Dr Smith is joining us today due to his experience in the field of <<his expertise>>."* Okay, this might be a bit over the top, but it's not far off!

Make sure that when you introduce yourself to others, you do the same thing: say who you are and establish yourself in the pecking order. Use your job title, department and area of expertise. Don't undersell yourself; let it be known who you are and why you are there. It is not showing off. Be proud of what you do. Others will appreciate knowing who you are, where you fit in and why you are there.

Career Chick Hot Tip: Provide details when making introductions.

Get Down To Business

A clear introduction like this meets the social needs of men who want to get down to business. Women, on the other hand, often start conversations on a personal level in the interests of building relationships. The rationale is that if you get to know someone and understand what is going on for them, it makes working together easier. You get a much better business outcome if you understand the issues that have an impact on another person. There is no point launching into a review of last week's action points if they are preoccupied with something else, is there? This is one of the attributes that make women effective, particularly in sales and managerial roles. Yet for others who just want to get on with business, it can seem like a waste of time to engage in chit-chat about the weekend. While men do take time to build rapport, it is usually in separate networking settings or at the end of a conversation or meeting (if there is time). Once the discussion is over, a comment like, *"By the way, how did your game on the weekend go?"* is often appreciated. Don't forsake the art of rapport building – just move it from the start of the conversation to the end.

> *Career Chick Hot Tip:* In discussions, get straight to the point after initial greetings; build rapport at the end of a conversation.

Set Meeting Expectations

Launching straight from *"Hello"* into a business discussion may seem abrupt, but people who are attuned to the business world won't see it this way. To make the transition, establish what you want to talk about and set expectations. This works whether it is a meeting with several people or a one-on-one discussion.

If you are chairing a formal meeting, start with the purpose of the meeting, the outcomes required and how long the meeting will take. Agreeing this information upfront can be a powerful way to boost your professionalism because it demonstrates your focus. It is efficient too, as it ensures that you all understand the purpose of the discussion. Even in regular meetings, start with something like, *"Thanks for your time, can I just confirm we have 30 minutes to review last month's results?"* This conveys your professionalism and gives everyone the chance to say if anything else needs to be discussed. Likewise, begin an opportune corridor conversation with, *"Glad I've caught you, would you have two minutes for me to fill you in on what happened at the meeting last Tuesday? Or should I set up another time? I just need to confirm you're happy with the approach we are taking."* This sets expectations and is more effective than launching into a discussion where the person has no idea of its purpose or how long it will last. An expectation-setting stage, between *"Hello"* and your topic, lays the groundwork for a positive and productive conversation.

> *Career Chick Hot Tip:* Set expectations upfront.

Start At The End

Start with the end of what you want to say first – it's critical to effective communication. Sara Jeannette Duncan, the first female editor of a major Canadian newspaper, put it succinctly: *"If you have anything to tell me of importance, for God's sake begin at the end."* And that pretty much sums up this Hot Tip. In fact, this could be the penultimate Career Chick Hot Tip and you can stop reading now (only joking!). The easiest thing you can do to have maximum impact is to put your punch line upfront.

If you need to ask for something, start with your request, then elaborate on why you need it. There's nothing like asking for an increase in budget or resources to capture someone's interest and get them asking questions! Always start at the end of the story: tell them if you've gained or lost a customer account, gone over or under budget, or any of the myriad of issues you need to discuss in the workplace. Knowing the end of the story makes the rest of the conversation more relevant. All communications should be 'front focused' so that their purpose is clear. Don't be concerned about positioning the whys and wherefores, what you did, and who said what. If these are relevant they will be uncovered later in the conversation. Getting to the point of a discussion quickly demonstrates that you are clear in your communication and focused on the issues. This translates into your professional reputation and you will be seen as being action-oriented and a problem-solver. This is exactly what you are trying to achieve!

> *Career Chick Hot Tip:* Start with the most important information first.

Find A Way To Speak Up

To demonstrate your professionalism and skills, you must find opportunities to speak. While keeping in mind the Career Chick Hot Tip to let people finish what they are saying, the likelihood is that whoever has the floor will keep talking, so it is often difficult for women to get the chance to speak in meetings.

Fortunately, there are a few Career Chick Hot Tips that can help you create the opportunity to speak up. One is to slightly raise your hand (not straight up in the air like you did at school). Keeping your elbow on the table, move your forearm only and point your index finger upwards (not at anyone). That way, it looks like you've just had an idea. Doing this as you start to speak reinforces visually that you have a point to make. Another Hot Tip is to wait for the person who is speaking to take a breath (they have to eventually or they will drop dead!) and take your opportunity. To grab their attention, use their first name as you start speaking. People like to hear their name and when they do, it creates a gap for you to start talking. On hearing their name, the speaker will usually look your way, which directs everyone's attention to you. Seize the moment and say what you have to say!

Another Hot Tip for breaking into a meeting or conversation is to address a question or comment to the most senior person in the room. If a meeting is going around in circles, or you really can't get a chance to say your piece, wait for the speaker to pause for a breath, and address the most senior person. Say something like, *"John, what is your view on …?"* Business etiquette dictates that on hearing the boss's name, everyone stops talking until he or she responds. This is your chance to get involved and take centre stage (or at least participate) in the conversation.

Career Chick Hot Tip: Create opportunities to contribute to a conversation.

Speak In Questions

When you are speaking, asking questions (rather than stating your view) is an effective way to communicate. Open-ended questions can help others make your points. These are questions that start with *"Why"*, *"What"*, *"Where"*, *"When"*, *"Who"* and *"How"*. Everyone loves the chance to say what they think, and they appreciate someone listening to them. On the other hand, anyone over three years old doesn't like to be told anything.

The most successful interactions often happen when you ask a few questions that lead the discussion in the direction you want to go. If the person you are talking to comes up with the answer you want, it is much more powerful for them to have said it than you. They will think you are brilliant because they agree with everything you said – because they said it originally! Asking well-thought-out and open-ended questions is one of the most powerful ways of saying what you want to say. And if the answers lead in a totally different direction, you may find out information you would not otherwise have known.

Career Chick Hot Tip: Ask well-thought-out, open-ended questions.

Use Analogies

When you want to make a point that can't be achieved by asking questions, a powerful technique is to 'paint pictures' by using analogies. Many people are visual thinkers and use pictures to process ideas. Creating pictures through a story or analogy can provide a common language or a reference point for comparisons, making it easier to explain something new. If you use analogies that people are familiar with, they can conjure up pictures that help them 'get' what you are talking about.

This is one reason why sporting analogies are common in business. Many members of the business community, who just happen to be men, are familiar with mainstream sports and this provides a common language. For example, you can compare someone's bad behavior with being given a red card on the field (soccer) or time in the sin bin (football); you can say a decision was line-ball (tennis); or that your successful presentation achieved a hole-in-one (golf). These provide visual clues for your listener, ensuring they understand what you are saying. Sport isn't the only analogy you can use, of course, but with so many men in business it is often a shared interest. Learning a little about some of the most common sports or other common interests gives you a library of analogies to use at the appropriate time.

You don't have to become a football, golf or baseball fan, but knowing a little bit about them can bring to life what you are trying to say. Being easily understood makes it simpler for others – and you!

Career Chick Hot Tip: Use analogies and paint pictures.

Just Say It

Some of the ways women communicate can undermine what they say and lead to misunderstandings. Women may soften what they want to say in the interest of building relationships, but in reality it only detracts from what is being said. These 'softeners' include the use of filler words, taglines, qualifiers and asking permission to ask a question. Filler words like *"maybe"*, *"sort of"* and *"probably"* can dilute your message, cost you credibility and make your listener wonder if you believe what you are saying. You can also undermine yourself by watering down your messages with taglines. If you are confident about the statement you are making: just say it. You don't need to add taglines like *"isn't it?"* or *"don't you think?"* It looks like you need agreement.

The use of qualifiers – *"sort of"*, *"just"*, *"only"*, *"kind of"* and *"just a suggestion"* – also weakens your statements. Using them regularly in your communication suggests that you don't have confidence in what you are saying. This can be interpreted as a reflection of your ability.

Career Chick Hot Tip: Know what you want to say, and say it!

Don't Ask To Ask

No capable Career Chick, like you, should undermine herself by asking permission to speak. Don't ask if you can ask a question. The minute you do, yoKnow what you want to say, and say it! ause you are giving the other person the right to grant or deny your request. Women often say, *"Could I just ask a question?"* as a way to break into a conversation without being disrespectful. However, anyone listening may misinterpret this politeness as deference. Assume you have the right to speak. Give others confidence in you by portraying confidence in yourself and speak up.

Be confident that what you say is worth hearing. Speak with confidence, and what you say will have credibility. Know your stuff and you will be well on the way to career success. Use the Hot Tips to help you communicate powerfully, then say what you have to say. It will be worth hearing.

Career Chick Hot Tip: Speak with confidence.

Career Chick Hot Tips to be heard:

- Develop your communication style to break the stereotypes and be heard on your own merit.

- Be aware of your voice and how you use it.

- Let others finish what they are saying; never interrupt.

- Listen and demonstrate that you understand.

- Provide details when making introductions.

- In discussions, get straight to the point after initial greetings; build rapport at the end of a conversation.

- Set expectations upfront.

- Start with the most important information first.

- Create opportunities to contribute to a conversation.

- Ask well-thought-out, open-ended questions.

- Use analogies and paint pictures.

- Know what you want to say, and say it!

- Speak with confidence.

Chapter 4

Present With Panache

"It usually takes me more than three weeks to prepare a good impromptu speech"
Mark Twain, American author (1835–1910)

You may not have quite as much time as Mark Twain to prepare a speech but the desire to present well is a widely held ambition. Studies regularly find that most people rank public speaking as a major fear. In fact, some claim that more people are scared of public speaking than they are of death. And yet, this skill is vital to showcase your abilities and contributions at work. So given you'd most probably rather drop dead than speak in public, it's worth looking at this critical area of career communications. This chapter provides Career Chick Hot Tips for making presentations that will, hopefully, bring your fear levels down to be comparable with a stubbed toe rather than a shark attack.

You may not need to address a meeting of shareholders or hold media conferences, but there are many other forums where you'll be required to make presentations. Even if you have made them since elementary school it can still be a nerve-wracking experience. There are many times when you will be called on to present – and many others when you should take, or make, the opportunity for yourself. These can range from small team meetings to large formal presentations. They may be presentations to people within your organization or to customers, suppliers, or people within your industry. No matter who you present to, how big the audience or the venue, all presentations require you to apply your effort and skills to show you in the best possible light.

Presentations can be to sell or to tell. Even if you are telling you are, on some level, selling the importance of your message. And you are certainly selling yourself and your capability. Presentations can be very formal or relaxed and casual, but either way you are still trying to achieve these objectives. Regardless, the basic rules of a high-quality presentation are the same. Whatever the occasion or style, a presentation is an opportunity to showcase your capabilities and influence the perceptions of others in your favor. Presentations can make or break careers and reputations. No wonder people are so terrified when the consequences are so enormous! It can seem much easier to curl up in a corner than to have to slink around the office because you made a bad presentation. The alternative is to develop your skills so you can use presentations to positively influence your career prospects.

You can use a presentation to demonstrate what you know, what you have done and what you are capable of. You can show how you think, approach issues and construct an argument. A well-executed presentation is one of the most persuasive tools to influence outcomes and create a buzz about you, your abilities and your potential. It can make the people who work for you proud or attract others who will want to work with you. It can raise your profile and make you a sought-after asset. The ability to make creditable presentations is seen as a key competency in an organization, a skill that is essential for your career repertoire. Career Chicks who want to achieve success need to make better than average presentations. You want to nail them and show exactly how talented and capable you are.

Career Chick Hot Tip: Present well to showcase your abilities and talent.

Grab The Spotlight

Women are often reluctant to step forward, take the spotlight and bring attention to themselves by presenting. When they do, they often hesitate or are indecisive. It's quite ironic really given the reputation women have as talkers! On the other hand, men are more likely to make sure they get the airtime that a presentation provides. When they do, they appear assertive and confident. That confident manner carries over into confidence about what they say. These are the opportunities that you need to create to grab the spotlight.

The communication style of women tends to be open, empathetic and intuitive. This helps many eloquent women be influential presenters. Many powerful women (think Oprah Winfrey, Hillary Clinton and Michelle Obama) are persuasive and capable speakers. Their reputations are linked to their ability to present and sell themselves, as well as their message. If you take and make opportunities to present, you will also have the chance to showcase your abilities and achievements. Actively seek out these opportunities whenever you can to advance your career.

Career Chick Hot Tip: Make and take the chance to present at every opportunity.

Where To Start

Like any big project it helps if you break a presentation into a number of stages. The place to start and the most important factor for the quality of your presentation is preparation. It's the most time-consuming and extensive phase of a presentation, but it can make the actual delivery seem like a piece of cake as opposed to a death-defying experience. More than likely, the best, seemingly off-the-cuff presenter you know has put years of preparation into developing their style. They may have attended public-speaking workshops, acting clinics or formal training programs (or all three). And you can bet your bottom dollar, every off-the-cuff comment (well, most of them) has been practised and rehearsed, several times. Reliance on your ability to 'wing' a presentation with no preparation is a potentially misplaced confidence in your ability that can backfire badly. To avoid this make your preparation for presentations a priority.

Preparation for a successful presentation requires you to:

- determine the purpose of the presentation
- understand your audience
- know your content
- decide on your style and structure
- choose your media and visual aids
- prepare how you will present, and
- rehearse.

Career Chick Hot Tip: Start with thorough preparation.

Have A Purpose

The first step, and one that's often missed, is to know and understand the purpose of your presentation. Just like you were meant to do in school or university exams: read the question and actually answer it. Many of us didn't, but we should have. For business presentations there are two things to consider: your business objective and what you want to achieve personally.

From a business perspective you need to understand the objective of the presentation. Aspects to consider are:

- the exact topic – or question you will answer
- the audience – and their needs, and
- the business outcome you want to achieve – to inform or ask for approval of something.

If someone else has asked you to make a presentation, consider why he or she asked you to speak. Your objective may well be to get the presentation over and done with and sit down again! But that would be your personal goal, not the business objective. Even if the objective is simply to provide an information update, being clear on the purpose and outcomes required will influence the rest of your preparation and delivery.

Your personal goals may include using the presentation to demonstrate your knowledge or to positively influence your image by confidently delivering a clear, concise message. Your goal may simply be to make the presentation and let people know you exist. Or it may be to demonstrate your expertise or logical thinking. Regardless of the objective, you should decide this before you put pen to paper (or fingers to keyboard) to provide you with a very clear focus for the direction of your presentation.

Career Chick Hot Tip: Set a business and personal objective for every presentation.

Know Your Audience

Once you know what you need to achieve it's time to think about your audience. Why do they want to hear what you have to say? What do they want to know? How will it help them? To gain these insights you need to research your audience and understand their needs. For instance, if you are presenting at your weekly team meeting, you know the people, the format of the meeting and the expectations about what you should present. You can then prepare your presentation accordingly. But you won't always be presenting in an environment you know. It may be in an unfamiliar setting, like a senior management forum you don't regularly attend, or to a customer or supplier at their premises. In these instances, you need to do further research. Find out who will be there, what their positions are, the purpose of the meeting and what they're expecting from your presentation.

To do this you need to judge each situation on its merits. You wouldn't ring the Chief Executive Office of a client to ask what they want to hear from you. But in most cases you'll have a contact who arranged your presentation and you can ask for their, and the audience's, expectations. This means you'll be able to address their needs – and involve the audience when you present. To demonstrate you have prepared, use references to relevant people. For example, *"As Susan and I discussed ..."* or *"As Greg asked me to cover today ..."* This is a powerful technique to connect with the audience. You demonstrate not only that you are linked to the people in the room, but also that you have researched your presentation. Excellent!

Career Chick Hot Tip: Understand the needs of your audience.

Content Counts

Now that you know the purpose of your presentation and who it's for, it's time to focus on content. Your subject matter needs to be accurate and relevant to the audience. And you need to know it forwards, backwards and any other way you can think of. A brilliant presentation can be completely undermined, if when asked you can't answer a question, it becomes obvious that your content was rehearsed but not really understood. If you know your content it will be obvious when you present, adding to the quality of your presentation. It will also give you added confidence. Attention to detail is a characteristic often associated with women, so it should be no stretch to apply your skills and knowledge to ensure your content is appropriate and interesting.

Career Chick Hot Tip: Know your content – forwards, backwards and in any other direction!

Begin At The Beginning

You need to structure your presentations so the material is logical, relevant and easily understood. One well-known method is to use the

'3 Ts': Tell them what you are going to tell them, Tell them, then Tell them what you told them. It's easy to remember, and effective. This and many other presentation techniques have a common structure: a beginning, a middle and an end.

Franklin D. Roosevelt, (the U.S. President during World War II) is often quoted as saying, *"Be sincere; be brief; be seated."* This is an example of another method in action: the 'Rule of Three'. This rule, which dates back to the Greek philosopher Aristotle, is based on the principle that most people can remember three things (like a beginning, middle and end!). Think of famous phrases, such as, *"Friends, Romans, Countrymen, lend me your ears"*, in Shakespeare's *Julius Caesar*; Thomas Jefferson's *"Life and Liberty and the Pursuit of Happiness"* and Winston Churchill's *"Blood, Sweat and Tears"*. The rule is used in movie titles, too, like *The Good, The Bad And The Ugly* and advertising campaigns, such as, *'Slip, Slop, Slap!'* They're all memorable and illustrate how the 'Rule of Three' can be effective. It's a simple method to give you a framework for your content and help you decide the most important points to cover.

Career Chick Hot Tip: Use a simple structure to support your content.

See And Believe

The next stage is to decide *how* you will present. A presentation can be brought to life with the clever use of pictures, diagrams and other media. For those in your audience who are highly visual in their learning style, 'seeing' truly is believing, so visual aids will support or illustrate what you want to say. On the other hand, busy slides that contain too many words can be the downfall of a presenter. Not only are they boring, but they can often make a presenter over-reliant on their slides. It also gives them an excuse not to be familiar with the content or rehearse properly. The overuse and reliance on slides can be tedious for your audience and certainly won't do your delivery any favors. 'Death by PowerPoint' may not actually be fatal, but it can feel that way to an audience.

What *will* help you stand out from the crowd is the clever use of visual tools. Australian mountain climber Michael Groom regularly presents to companies about how he successfully climbed the world's five highest mountains (he climbed four of them after losing the front third of both his feet on an earlier expedition). He uses a powerful PowerPoint presentation comprised of photographs. As Groom recounts his remarkable story, the photos take his audience on the journey with him. He leaves a lasting impression and, often, a room of teary-eyed listeners. You may not want to bring your audience to tears (unless it's from laughter!) but you do want them to remember you.

One technique to add interest in a presentation is to vary your visual aids or media every six to eight minutes, which is about the 'average' person's attention span. A variety of visual aids helps maintain the audience's interest. People like to see things other than slides, so you can show samples or examples that relate to your topic. If your subject is a report or a book … take a copy to hold up. If it is about an item you or your customer sell … take along a sample (tricky if you work for an airline, for instance, but you can use your imagination). The audience will appreciate and remember your creativity.

If you use slides, make sure they are of a high quality. It can be tempting to rely on slides to tell your story but there are some simple rules to follow. You need to use:

- dark backgrounds
- a few bullet points – 5 or less
- no more than 14 words per slide
- large fonts
- high-quality graphics
- pictures and other media, and
- charts that are easy-to-read – even from the back of the room.

And don't, whatever you do, use a slide where you need to say, *"It might be a bit hard for you to read this slide but …"*. If it's hard to read, put it on a handout to distribute to the audience. If this level of detail is required, a handout is respectful to the participants (they won't get eye strain reading your slides); it provides them with somewhere to take notes about the (no doubt) interesting points you make; and it gives them something to take away to remember what you said. Above all, don't put everything you want to say on your slides or handouts. *You* need to be essential to the presentation. It is the information, insights or recommendations that can't be read that adds to your worth. The value that you bring to the content needs to be you; what you say and how you say it.

Career Chick Hot Tip: Be creative with your use of visual aids.

On The Stage

Whether you're on a stage or presenting at a team meeting, the focus of your presentation will be on you. When you plan your presentation think about how you want to present. Even in a small team meeting consider standing up to make a formal presentation. This is a powerful way to ensure you have the attention of the room and that you come across as a professional. If you will be on a stage, think about how to use it. Plan your moves and practise them in your rehearsal (yes, rehearsal!). If you aren't tall enough to play basketball, think carefully about the use of a lectern. While it's a great safety blanket to hide behind, and a handy spot for your notes, if you're vertically challenged a lectern will cut you off. Think about what the audience can see. If they can only see your upper body and head, you may look more like a puppet than a statuesque, confident speaker! If this applies to you, get out from behind the lectern – no matter how tempting it is to hide behind it.

Whatever visual aids you plan to use, or venue you end up with, doing some preparation will make them work for you. How many potentially excellent presentations failed before they began because the presenter couldn't get the technology to work? Don't lose your credibility before you even start. Visit the venue beforehand and test the technology. Work out where you'll stand and how you'll use the room. Consider using a remote mouse, remote microphone and small, easy-to-hold notes. Practise with the microphone before you need to use it. If the presentation is not in a room you are familiar with, find out what equipment is available. If you can't test the equipment, take your own and make sure that it is compatible with the system you'll connect to. Always take two copies of your presentation (you never know, a page could fly away) and more handouts than you think you'll need.

Before you finish your plan (yep, this is all still the preparation phase!) think about your own appearance. Men have it easy! All they have to do is choose their suit and the color of their shirt and tie. Women have more choice (yippee!), but their appearance must still be appropriate for the environment. A good rule of thumb? Be the best-dressed person in the room – in the appropriate style of course (a ball gown, even at head office, is likely to be a little overdressed).

On one level it shouldn't matter how you dress, but the reality is that people make (quick) judgments about how capable someone is from their appearance. And they'll use your appearance to decide how capable you are.

In most business environments a well-fitted suit and favorite pair of shoes does the trick. It's appropriate, looks great and will give you confidence. If you need a bit more of a confidence boost, wear something new or get a manicure. The men in the room may not notice, but it will add polish (literally) to your look and give you courage.

Career Chick Hot Tip: Be the best-dressed person in the room.

In An Emergency

This is a direct contradiction to all the other Career Chick Hot Tips, but if for some (unavoidable) reason you haven't been able to do all the preparation you need for a presentation, head to the Hair Salon for a wash and blow-dry. 'Winging-it' is not a recommended presentation technique, but sometimes, in an absolute emergency, you may have to. Reschedule your meetings if you can or get an early morning start and head to the nearest Hair Salon. The hour you spend won't be wasted either; it will give you time to think through the three things you are going to say. It's a classic case of killing two birds with one stone. And neither of them is your career! You'll look good and have something to say. (This doesn't mean of course, that you can't be well prepared *and* also spend the time to look stunning.)

Career Chick Hot Tip: In an emergency, if you need extra help – head to the Hair Salon.

It's Showtime (well ... almost)

You look sensational and you have the appropriate content for the audience, organized in a clear structure with powerful visual aids.

You know exactly what you want to achieve, have all your support materials organized and are familiar with the venue and technology. Now, there's only one more thing to do before you get on with the show: rehearse.

No matter how experienced you are as a presenter, it's essential to rehearse. It helps you clarify what you say and how you present. If something doesn't make sense to you when you say it out loud, it won't make sense to anyone else. A rehearsal, even for the best presenter, is a necessity. It's like putting a coat of polish on your shoes and it will help you shine. If you haven't made many presentations in the past, practising will also help with your nerves.

Practise your presentation initially by reading it to yourself. Then read it out loud. You may be a bit surprised when you stumble a bit or find it doesn't sound as smooth as you thought. That's the point of a rehearsal. You will be presenting out loud, not reading something to yourself. Keep practising until you can get through it and sound the way you want – at least once.

Don't overdo it though. Give yourself time for a break between your last rehearsal and the presentation. Have a cup of tea, go for a walk or share a joke with someone. Take time to clear your head before you do it for real.

If you take shortcuts in the preparation … you might make a half-reasonable presentation. And that's exactly what your presentation will be … half-reasonable. It certainly won't have been presented with panache or enhance your reputation or career prospects. It won't do you any favors to do less than your best. In fact, if you're like most Career Chicks you'll probably beat yourself up mentally about how you could or should have done so much better. So put the energy in *before* the presentation and have something to pat yourself on the back about afterwards: the great job you've done.

Career Chick Hot Tip: Prepare, prepare, prepare! There's no substitute!

It's Time!

Once you've finished your preparation, you're finally ready to present. There are several tactics to make sure all goes well. These allow you to control any nervousness you may have and involve the audience in your presentation. To control your nerves while you present, use some of these techniques:

- take a sip of water – to give you time to think
- shift your body weight between your feet – it stops your knees wobbling, and
- pace your breathing – it makes you sound in control.

To involve your audience you can make eye contact, smile, be animated and modify the tone of your voice. Try to avoid filler words, like *"feel"*, *"might"* or *"maybe"* (they diminish the impact of what you're saying), jargon (don't assume everyone will understand what you mean), and *"umms"* and *"ahhhs"* (they are distracting).

Because you already analyzed your audience, you'll know how formal you need to be and how the audience will perceive what you have to say. Involve them with the use of words such as *"we"* rather than *"I"*. And refer to people in the audience by name by acknowledging their achievements or the previous discussions you've had with them. This will keep their attention (and that of the people who know them). Apply these, and numerous other techniques, to make your presentations the very best they can be.

Career Chick Hot Tip: Involve your audience and control your nerves.

Be Yourself

Most importantly, be true to yourself and present in your own style. Use whatever works and is comfortable for you. If you are not a comedian and don't feel comfortable telling jokes, don't. If you don't feel comfortable walking amongst your audience, don't. Find other ways to keep your audience interested. You may have a wry wit, high-energy delivery or just know your stuff so well that your presentation is compelling. Be you. Just make sure it is the best 'you', you can be.

Take time to review your performance each time you present to develop your presentation skills. Don't be too critical … Career Chicks can be far too hard on themselves. If someone tells you, you've done a great job – take the accolades (as a man would!). You deserve it.

Say, *"Thank you"*, and ask what they liked about your presentation. When you get down to specifics you learn to know what worked and what to replicate in your next presentation.

If you aren't offered any feedback then ask for it. Talk to your manager or a trusted colleague for specific feedback to help you uncover what worked or what didn't. If you ask, *"Did I do okay?"* and get a positive response, you won't know specifically what worked. Generally people are kind and don't like to say negative things. This might make you feel good, but it doesn't give you any guidance on what you can improve next time. Instead, a question like, *"Is there anything you think I could do differently next time?"* opens the door to some gentle, helpful suggestions rather than criticism.

Presenting is one area where your employer may offer you formal training or coaching. If you get the opportunity, grab it! Even if you think you are pretty talented, take whatever development is on offer. As they say, practice makes perfect. Attend any courses you are offered, read books, watch and observe the presentation styles of others, and ask your manager or mentor for their tips.

If you prepare and deliver a presentation to the best of your ability you have the right to be proud of yourself. If you achieve your goals, take time to acknowledge your success and reward yourself. Perhaps with a new handbag? Or a new pair of shoes? Essential items for the next time you present with panache!

Career Chick Hot Tip: Be true to your own style and learn from each experience.

Career Chick Hot Tips to present with panache:

- Present well to showcase your abilities and talent.

- Make and take the chance to present at every opportunity.

- Start with thorough preparation.

- Set a business and personal objective for every presentation.

- Understand the needs of your audience.

- Know your content – forwards, backwards and in any other direction!

- Use a simple structure to support your content.

- Be creative with your use of visual aids.

- Be the best-dressed person in the room.

- In an emergency, if you need extra help – head to the Hair Salon.

- Prepare, prepare, prepare! There's no substitute!

- Involve your audience and control your nerves.

- Be true to your own style and learn from each experience.

Chapter 5

Write Well

"The letter I have written today is longer than the usual because I lacked the time to make it shorter"

Blaise Pascal, French mathematician and philosopher (1623–1662)

The ability to write well provides you with the opportunity to demonstrate the very best of your knowledge, skills and expertise without any preconceptions about who you are. It allows you to be persuasive, table your ideas and justify your recommendations. Written communication is, theoretically, an even playing field for women and men in the workplace. However, women often don't leverage this opportunity or they undermine their own impact by being hesitant or non-committal in their prose. The art of writing, and it is an art, as Blaise Pascal observed several centuries ago, takes time. Achieving excellence in the area of written communication is another of the not-so-secret necessities for career success.

Although there should be little differentiation between men and women when it comes to written communication, there are a couple of areas for Career Chicks to be mindful of. These align with the other Hot Tips for successful communication covered earlier: say what you mean, be front-focused, specific and action-oriented. And don't dilute your writing by being hesitant or using ineffectual words. This assertive approach lets you demonstrate your confidence and capability. This chapter looks at how to apply and demonstrate your abilities as a strong, focused, problem-solving, intelligent (and as many other positive adjectives you can think of) Career Chick in everything you write.

The Power Of The Pen (or keyboard)

Writing has moved on a long way from the pen (and definitely the quill), but whether you communicate with a keyboard on a laptop or another electronic device there is considerable power in the written word. The trick is to understand your method of communication, the intended audience and the appropriate style to apply in the circumstances. This gives you the opportunity to say exactly what you want to say, and to reduce the risks within other forms of communication that can lead to misunderstandings between the sexes.

For anyone who uses the written word there are some hidden dangers. When you write, there is no opportunity to add detail if something isn't clear to the reader. You also don't usually get to judge the comprehension of your audience while they read your document. And there is always the danger that you'll come across differently to how you intended. A jokey retort in an email may come across as inappropriate or sarcastic to the reader.

There are many and varied types of written communication used in business. They range from formal proposals and presentations, to everyday interactions, such as emails, memos, letters and even old-fashioned 'With Compliments' slips and thank you cards. Then there are the very informal, modern forms of written communication, such as text messages, blogs and message boards, just to name a few. All of these provide you with the opportunity to positively (or negatively) influence your business reputation. With a well-written report, you can be a hero. Send an inappropriate text message to the wrong number, and your credibility can be zero (with a long road in front of you to recover it). The goal is to use every opportunity you can to present yourself in the best possible light.

Career Chick Hot Tip: Understand your audience and use the appropriate writing style.

Pick Your Words

The words you choose when you write are every bit as important as those you use when you speak. You want the reader to understand exactly what you mean. The best words to choose are those that are simple, easily understood and business-like. Avoid long, complex or wordy sentences. Unless the purpose of your document is to show how many syllables you can fit in a sentence, choose clear and concise words. That way, what you want to say will also be clear and concise.

Winston Churchill, the British Prime Minister during World War II, once said, *"Broadly speaking, the short words are the best, and the old words when short are best of all."* Given Churchill is remembered for his memorable speeches, with lines such as, *"Never in the field of human conflict was so much owed by so many to so few"*[1], his advice is credible. Short, simple, easily recognized words help convey your meaning.

However, even if the words you use are well known, slang should be avoided. By using slang, or even company jargon or acronyms, you run the risk of confusing or even offending your reader.

Another thing to consider is that written communications are easily circulated, sometimes far beyond the audience they were intended for. Reports and presentations can be handed around, and emails can be forwarded at the click of a mouse. The influential person reading what you have written may not be the intended reader or have the level of knowledge you assumed. As a rule of thumb, ask yourself, *"Would someone who didn't know anything about the topic be able to understand what I have written?"*

Your objective is to choose words that create and support what you mean. The beauty of writing is that you can make drafts, reread and refine them until you have said what you really want to say. Unlike the many times you finish a conversation thinking, *"I wish I'd said ..."* if you invest the time to write well and revise, you can write like you wish you could speak!

Career Chick Hot Tip: Use simple, business-like words that say what you mean.

The Basics

Your credibility and competence will be tarnished if you don't write well. For instance, there is no excuse for incorrect spelling. Misplaced apostrophes may be forgiven, inappropriate semicolons may be excused, but spelling never. Sure some people in your potential audience won't even notice, but there are others who won't even try to see past your spelling mistakes to understand what you have written. No excuses: use spell check and proof read your work!

Grammar is also important. You may, at times, want to get into an all-out argument with the grammar program on your software, as they can be very opinionated. Frequently the recommendations of these programs are reasonably accurate. But if you're in doubt, say the sentence out loud. That should give you a pretty clear indication if it makes sense or not.

Proficiency in the basics of writing is essential to establish your credibility. These include not only spelling and grammar, but also layout, the font and size, and your use of white space to help readability. Also consider the length of your document or email message. In the busy business world, if a document looks easy to read, it's more likely to actually get read. You don't want the blood, sweat and tears you put into crafting an important document to go unnoticed because it intimidates the reader. How you do this varies considerably depending on the type of written communication.

Career Chick Hot Tip: Be proficient in the basics of writing (spelling and grammar).

Start At The End

Whether you write a policy paper, customer proposal or a couple of lines in an email – put the most important thing first (as discussed earlier in the Career Chick Hot Tips to be heard). Everyone's busy, so to break through the time-constraint barrier and over-abundance of available information, your written communications need to be easily understood and relevant. Putting exactly what you want or the purpose of the communication at the beginning does both. It will be clear to the reader exactly what they are reading and why it is important to them.

Your beginning should be clear, specific and actionable. It does not need to be positioned or contextualized. If the reader wants that level of detail they will keep reading. They may stop without going any further than your well-written opening. It may be because they 'get it' quickly. Excellent. Or they may get interrupted or distracted by other priorities. This is less likely to happen if you captured their interest at the start.

The challenge is how to be concise and say what you need to say. One technique is to write the entire document (or email), then go back to the beginning and rewrite your opening. Writing gives you the luxury of being able to go back to the beginning and be specific. Once you have finished writing something it's much clearer to see what you need to highlight. For example, you could start a report with, *"The purpose of this report is to request the additional resources required to continue the <<XYZ project>>."* If the reader has any interest in either the XYZ project or resource allocation there is a reasonable chance they will keep reading. Similarly, an email can also make its purpose abundantly clear with an opening such as, *"I'd like to ask for your time to discuss ..."* It's so much clearer to tell the reader why they have the email than to make them read a dissertation on whatever the issue is and then request even more time to discuss it. When the reader understands why and what they are reading they will be much more receptive.

Career Chick Hot Tip: Be specific and action-oriented. Start at the end.

Quality Not Quantity

With the sheer quantity of communications that are now a part of everyday life, it's a challenge to achieve the quality that you want to be known for. Emails and texts can seem to attack from a million different directions at once. Some days, just getting through your Inbox may be your objective, rather than taking the time to redraft or review what you send out. Appropriately managing dreaded email is one of the many challenges of business life – and it's no different for chicks or guys.

Email can be the best thing to help fast, instant communications ... or a nightmare to manage. It can get you instant answers to business problems and give you access to people you don't know. On the other hand, it can be time-consuming, distracting and conceal unwelcome surprises. By applying some simple rules to your email communications, making them clear and focused, they will be appreciated. It may not improve the quality of the ones you receive, but you never know, you could start a trend! Quality emails. Imagine that. That would certainly enhance the reputation of a Career Chick.

Here are some rules of thumb for email:

- Make sure your subject is clear, concise and explains what the email is about.

- Keep your emails short, preferably to one page that can be seen on the screen.

- Use lots of white space and a font that is easy to read. Start a new paragraph for every new idea, and add a line of white space between paragraphs.

- Start your emails with the most important information first.

- Use an auto signature that has your name, title, division and other contact details so your recipient can choose how to contact you.

And use "cc" 'courtesy copies' with care! If you have been asked to copy someone, do it. If you haven't – don't. Copying half the world on an email can be disrespectful – both to the person that the email is for, and the people who are copied. Generally, it's excused as a way to keep people informed. In reality, it's often used to protect the sender by spreading the responsibility or pressuring the recipient into doing something they'd probably rather not. An email, copied to others, gives the addressee no chance to respond directly. Not only does the topic in the email need to be dealt with, but now everyone who has been copied needs to be communicated with. It also invites everyone in the email to have their say, which means you can get into an incredibly time-consuming email chain, a real time waster. Email is not an appropriate way to shift responsibility for an issue. Copying in more senior people, so that the recipient has no choice but to do what you want, may work once or twice, but it won't earn you any friends or favors in the long term.

If you are the recipient of emails that have been copied to the equivalent of a small village, don't feel obliged to play the game. Respond directly to the person who sent it to you. Better yet, ring them and discuss the issue directly with them. If they felt the need to copy half the world, there is probably something else going on that you'll never find out if you get into an email war. You may also need to contact all the people who have been copied on the issue. This can be time-consuming, but it can also be an investment in your reputation.

Like emails, text messages are being used more and more in business. This is another minefield of potential issues. If it is someone you know really well there should be no problem. But if someone you don't know texts you to say they are running late for a meeting, don't assume you now have a new casual relationship because they sent you a text.

They're probably just being considerate. Think about the relationship you have with the person before you start regularly sending them text messages. When you do send them be brief and appropriate and avoid text shortcuts that may be misinterpreted. Your goal is to be appropriate and understood.

Career Chick Hot Tip: Communicate for quality not quantity.

The Personal Touch

Other methods of communication, like the phone call, allow you to add a personal touch. Then there are handwritten notes or even 'With Compliments' slips or memos. These aren't quite as prevalent as they once were, but they are still quite useful to position a report, an interesting article you have seen in a business magazine or other documentation you leave on someone's desk or send through the mail. Funnily enough, the rules about high-quality written communications apply here too: be clear, concise and to the point. *"Dear Bob, Thought you might be keen to see what the market is saying"* on a magazine article about a topic of interest is perfect. Sending something through the mail is likely to keep you on the radar and bring whatever you have sent to the top of the pile (or at least ahead of all those emails!)

There is still a place for person-to-person interactions like thank you and special occasion cards. People love them. While it's polite to send an email and thank a group of people who have worked with you on something, there is nothing like receiving a personal thank you card. Even at home when you go through the mail, a handwritten envelope will stand out from the bills and bank statements. The same applies at work. It is important to acknowledge people as individuals and thank you, birthday and other special occasion cards (like anniversaries with the company or team) are a great way for people to feel valued. Think these are too 'girly' for a serious Career Chick? Would men take the time or trouble to send personal notes? Or even think about it in the first place? Not many. But the ones who do are admired for it. And if a chick can't be a chick who can? Women are recognized as being skilful at the relationship, empathetic, people-side of business. Take advantage of that reputation. If this comes naturally for you, do it.

Career Chick Hot Tip: Don't be afraid to apply a personal touch.

Too Much Information

While cards, emails, memos, texts, blogs, pokes, walls and virtual hugs are abundant … there is nothing quite like the old-fashioned approach of actually talking to someone. The danger, particularly if you feel more articulate in writing, is to fall back on written communications rather than making, say, a difficult phone call. Don't overly rely on your written prowess. Pick up the phone and remember to talk to people.

The recent explosion of technology means you can showcase your eloquence with the written word to the world through blogs, Wiki's and social-networking sites like MySpace, and Facebook to name a few. Consider for a moment, if your senior management, a prospective manager or a recruiter did an internet search on you. What would you want them to see? Make sure anything about you on the internet aligns with your business image. Be conscious that what you write out of work is out there for anyone to see. As you've heard before: if in doubt – don't!

To make the most of your abilities and achieve career success you'll need to be skilled in all forms of communication. The ability to write well will help you demonstrate your strengths and proficiency, to get things done and, most importantly, build your image and reputation. Your capability to communicate in writing is a necessity for every Career Chick. As the 18th century English poet Samuel Johnson said, *"What is written without effort is in general read without pleasure."*

Career Chick Hot Tip: Make the effort to write well.

Career Chick Hot Tips to write well:

- Understand your audience and use the appropriate writing style.

- Use simple, business-like words that say what you mean.

- Be proficient in the basics of writing (spelling and grammar).

- Be specific and action-oriented. Start at the end.

- Communicate for quality not quantity.

- Don't be afraid to apply a personal touch.

- Make the effort.

Chapter 6

Speak With Actions

"When the eyes say one thing, and the tongue another, a
practised man relies on the language of the first"
Ralph Waldo Emerson, American philosopher and poet (1803–1882)

The most powerful communication can happen without needing to speak or write a word. The right words in the right order won't work if your body language says something different. You want others to 'see' what you mean, not just hear what you say. Your non-verbal communication has a significant influence on your credibility and ultimately your career success.

When your body language aligns with what you say and how you say it, it reinforces your message. However, if there is a disconnection, not only in meaning but also in the apparent confidence you project, your body language can completely undermine you. Mismatched messages can have a pretty big cost. In this case, to your credibility or, at the least, how seriously people will take you.

Fairly or not, others will interpret your body language to make assumptions about your knowledge and how truthful you are being. While your body language is often a reflection of your confidence or personal style, it will also be used by others to measure your capability. There's an opportunity here for you to take control of your facial expressions, posture, movements, gestures and other non-verbal methods of communication.

A Little Knowledge

A lot of people are self-taught 'experts' when it comes to diagnosing the body language of their friends and colleagues. When someone looks to the left when they talk to you, does that mean they're lying? Or that someone walked by and distracted them? Maybe someone you're talking to has his or her arms crossed. Does that mean they are closed and resistant to what you are saying? Or that they are cold? And if they shift their weight uncomfortably from side to side … is that because they are uncomfortable talking to you. Or because they have sore feet? Of course, it could be either! If you try and become a closet expert you can get a bit too clever and misinterpret what you see … or be so preoccupied second-guessing what's going on that you don't pay attention to the conversation.

You don't want to be preoccupied with what others are doing. Other people may not have this same knowledge or awareness, so don't be too quick to judge what they think solely on non-verbal cues. But *you* can focus on how you optimize your own body language. For the Career Chick, it's not a matter of how to become a body-language expert but rather how to use your own body language to backup what you mean. You want it to support and reinforce what you say and your desired persona, rather than send mixed or contradictory signals. This is, in many ways, the same for men and women, however, there are some instances where women can, unwittingly, convey the wrong impression or end up with an unintended consequence. An understanding of how to use non-verbal communication can help you avoid these pitfalls and use it to support what you say. This final chapter of the *Communication* part of the CODE for career success looks at some of the general rules of body language in the business environment and some specific tips for Career Chicks.

Career Chick Hot Tip: Align your body language with what you want to say.

The Basics

There are a number of 'rules of thumb' for body language that apply to everyone. These are relevant in business, as well as socially, and to men and women equally. There are many non-verbal signals that we don't mean or intend. The what-not-to-do list includes:

- crossing your arms
- fidgeting
- avoiding eye contact
- putting your hands on your hips
- standing too close, and
- pursing your lips, raising your eyebrows and other inappropriate facial expressions.

Even if you have made up your mind about something, don't cross your arms. If you do it may be interpreted that you are closed, resistant or even that you disagree with what has been said. You may just be chilly and want to keep warm, but the other person won't know that. If you're cold put on a jacket, and if you do disagree with what is being said, consciously make an effort to keep your arms by your sides and wait until it's appropriate to have your say. Effective listening means letting the other person have their say and not interrupting with either your words or other signals.

If you tap the table or fidget, people can take it as a sign that you are bored, impatient or uncomfortable with what is being said. If you find that you are doing this, stop. Find something else to do, like taking copious notes about the topic. If you are busy writing, you can't be fidgeting. Don't look out the window into the distance, as this sends the same kind of negative message.

If you are in discussion with others and you avoid eye contact this can indicate that you are untruthful or at the very least uncomfortable or lack confidence. If you make eye contact when you look at another person you will appear confident and demonstrate that you are paying attention.

How you stand is also an important part of non-verbal communication. Avoid the hands-on-hips stance, unless you are about to give a hula demonstration. In most other circumstances, it will be interpreted as a judgmental or aggressive stance. Standing too close to others and invading their personal space can also make them feel uncomfortable. In the worst cases it can be interpreted as intimidation. Always keep an appropriate distance from others.

Whether you are standing, presenting, listening or even on a videoconference, watch your facial expressions. The other person doesn't need to be a world-class poker champion to figure out what you are thinking if you raise your eyebrows or purse your lips. Think about your facial expressions to ensure they are not giving away what you're really thinking. Bite your lip if you have to. Listen to what is being said and keep your expressions under control.

There are many examples of how body language can be misinterpreted. Meanings vary by culture and by country. There may also be health reasons behind why people use different gestures, have a different posture or send different signals. Without being an expert it can be very easy to get this stuff wrong. The key is to be aware of how you move, stand, sit, gesture or express yourself and the impact that it has on your communication.

Career Chick Hot Tip: Be conscious of your body language, so you don't send negative messages.

Show Your Confidence

Imagine a graceful swan gliding down a picturesque, tree-lined stream – calm, serene and elegant. Yet underneath the water, the swan may be paddling like crazy just to keep moving. Like the swan, regardless of how you actually feel or how confident you are, you can use your body language to present a positive, confident image to the world. It may take some conscious effort, but you can control what you say with your body, as much as you can with your words.

You have command of your posture, your facial expressions and your gestures. There are many successful techniques that apply for both men and women. You know them. You just need to make sure you use them. *"Stand up straight"* is something you probably heard throughout your childhood. Parents, teachers and relatives would all chime in if you slouched around. And with good reason. Apart from any spinal benefits, an upright posture portrays confidence and enthusiasm. Hold your arms and legs relatively straight, put your shoulders back and hold your head high. No, you're not in the army, just demonstrating your confidence.

You may have heard of communication techniques from models like Neuro-Linguistic Programming (NLP) that talk about mirroring or matching your body language to other people. When people talk to each other, they often adopt the same body language, either consciously or unconsciously. You'll often see that when a meeting's going well, everyone involved leans forward and is animated. Or people who are really relaxed and having a casual conversation lean back in their chairs. This often happens quite naturally. The theory goes that matching your body language to others helps establish rapport. This includes things like posture, head tilts, gestures and facial expressions, as well as speaking rhythms. Be aware of your body language in relation to other people. Have a bit of fun in your next meeting to see how it works. If everyone is leaning forward in their chairs ... do the opposite and see if anyone adopts your position. You may be surprised what influence you have on others. If you demonstrate with your body language what you want to say, others will 'see' what you mean.

Career Chick Hot Tip: Be confident with your posture, facial expressions and gestures.

Specifically For Chicks

While there are numerous examples of how to use body language in the business environment there are a number of things that chicks need to be aware of so they are not misinterpreted. Women often use body language to convey empathy for others, demonstrate that they are listening and develop relationships. Some of the signals women use to do this are:

- smiling
- nodding
- tilting their head, and
- patting or touching others during a conversation.

Too much smiling and nodding can make you look like a laughing clown in a sideshow alley, but it's more than how you look: it's about the wrong message you send. When you're smiling and nodding to say, *"I am listening to you,"* it can often be misinterpreted to mean, *"I agree with you."* It can be quite a shock to someone if you smile and nod through their presentation, then disagree with them at the end. They thought you were enthusiastically agreeing to everything they said. The risk is that not only will they be confused by your change in approach, but they may also perceive you as being inconsistent and contradictory.

Smiling and nodding too much can also be viewed as 'girly'. This can have connotations of immaturity, meaning others may not take you seriously. Another potentially 'girly' move to be aware of is tilting your head sideways when you're listening to someone. Women often use the head tilt to signal that they are paying attention and listening. But it can also be interpreted as boredom. Not a message you want to send, even if you are!

Frequently touching or patting other people should also be avoided. Some people touch to make a connection. But it can make the other person very uncomfortable and infringe on their personal space. Worse still, a pat can seem 'motherly' or be associated with other female roles – appropriate if you are their mother or little sister, but not in the business environment. You don't want to take on any female role or stereotype other than that of a confident, successful career person.

Career Chick Hot Tip: Limit your smiles, head nods, head tilts and touches.

Fear Of Tears

Overt displays of emotion should also be limited in the workplace. Men often view women as being overly emotional, less stoic and even-tempered than men. An unemotional, clear head is what they believe is necessary for business. And the fear of having to deal with emotions in the workplace often scares men away from wanting to work with women. Tears or even watery or red eyes can make others, particularly men, very uncomfortable. (And even the possibility that they may get this reaction can scare men, and some women too.)

Managers with a 'fear of tears' may avoid giving female employees honest feedback about their performance or career prospects, or from recruiting or promoting them in the first place. Not all managers are capable of providing feedback in a positive and constructive way. But not getting it at all won't do you any favors. You can't improve or work on aspects of your performance if you don't know what is required. Just because a man doesn't know how to handle your possible reaction doesn't mean you shouldn't receive feedback. And if a man is worried that you'll get watery-eyed that's exactly why they'll avoid the conversation that they would have had if you were a man. This automatically puts you at a disadvantage. The only way to avoid this possibility is to keep tears for outside the office.

For business issues, work must be kept a tear-free zone. However, if you receive unfortunate personal news, then all rules go out the window. No one whose opinion means anything will form a negative opinion about you in those circumstances. But in regards to work-related issues, 'no tears' is the policy.

This may be easy for you. On the other hand, you may be one of those people who are very expressive with your emotions and get watery eyes with little prompting. You may regularly get misty-eyed watching the news or movies or when you feel criticized. If that's the case you may want to look at some strategies to stay dry-eyed. For example, you could focus on something else or temporarily remove yourself from a situation to get your emotions under control. Disappointing news about a promotion or unexpected negative feedback about your performance may trigger an emotional reaction. In these circumstances, it's acceptable to say, *"Okay, this is a bit of surprise/ disappointment. I'd just like to think this through,"* and excuse yourself for a couple of minutes or reschedule another time to meet again.

Most managers would prefer to reschedule than work out how to respond to tears. For a manager it can be difficult to know how to react. Do they acknowledge the tears? Keep talking? Pass over a box of tissues? Anyone will respect that you may need to take a moment (or longer) to remind yourself that whatever is being said is not personal. And give you the time to be able to respond in a business-like way. Because it is business, not personal. Sometimes though, you just need a few minutes to remind yourself. A reputation for controlling your emotions will ensure that you get treated the same as the men.

If you are a chick in management, keep a box of tissues on hand for such occasions. Don't be afraid to offer it if the person you are talking to does tear-up. There's no reason that you can't make it easier for others and rewrite some of these rules. And you'll find that it won't only be women who get watery-eyed! The fact that guy do sometimes get emotional at work is a big guy-secret. But for chicks, it's best avoided.

Career Chick Hot Tip: No tears at work.

Business Rituals

A handshake can help women establish parity with male colleagues. Where it was once used to bind a contract, nowadays a handshake is an accepted business formality. It is used as a greeting, a farewell, to express congratulations and as a sign of goodwill when an agreement has been reached. Men, unless they see each other every day, often greet each other with a handshake. Even in a social setting, a handshake is the accepted convention and establishes rapport. Men don't think twice about this ritual. It's an accepted business practice. When women don't shake hands this sets them apart. Many men aren't quite sure whether to offer their hand to a woman. If they have to debate with themselves whether to shake or not to shake, before you even started talking, the gender difference will be unsaid but on the table, loud and clear.

To avoid this situation, offer your hand in all situations where men would shake hands. Do this with both men and women. For men, it takes away the guesswork. With women, it establishes business rapport. You'll present yourself as confident and professional. Be the first to offer your hand when you meet others, so that there is no time for confusion.

The other benefit of a handshake is that it can fend off the unwanted greeting kiss. It has become more common, particularly when work colleagues meet at social occasions, for men to greet women with a kiss. You really need to make an assessment on the appropriateness of this based on the situation, who the person is and your relationship with them. If you are comfortable, this is fine in a social environment. But it's a little bit icky when it happens in the office and you're not comfortable with it. A polite, confident outstretched hand should avoid this situation.

Career Chick Hot Tip: Shake hands and offer yours first.

It's In The Cards

Another business ritual that women often shy away from is the exchange of business cards. This exchange at the beginning of a meeting provides a little time to establish rapport, helps with remembering names and lets everyone know who everyone else is. The hierarchies are easily established and the meeting can progress appropriately. Having their business card means that you have phone numbers, email addresses and other contact details for the future.

If you don't swap cards it just reflects that you are a little less professional. Or even that you are less comfortable being in the type of situation where cards are exchanged. If you are eligible for business cards with your company make sure you order them. Don't think you won't need them. If you are still on your way up the career ladder and your position doesn't qualify for a business card, get a personal card with your name and personal contact details to use when you are networking. There are many places where you can get extremely professional cards that are virtually as cheap as chips.

Career Chick Hot Tip: Offer and exchange business cards.

Common Courtesies

More confusion arises in business, for both men and women, when common courtesies are misinterpreted as chivalrous behavior. Men often don't know whether to hold open a door or walk through it first. Women don't know whether to barge through first, expecting it to be opened or to hang back and wait their turn. Sometimes there is no problem. An elevator door opens and it's every man or woman for themselves. Or a man takes a step backwards and signals you to move. It may or may not align with your views of the modern world, but it's a polite gesture. In the interests of not spending all day arguing at the elevator or outside a door, it's appropriate to just say *"Thank you"* and get going.

The tricky part is if the body language is unclear and you don't know whether you should go first. For example, what if you are in a elevator with a more senior, older man who is talking on his cell phone? Is he going to stand back and wait for you to exit first because he always lets women go first? Or is he going to barge out without looking sideways at you? This quandary can leave you with a Mexican standoff or a potential collision. If in doubt, politeness always pays dividends. Deferring to a more senior person is never the wrong thing to do and is often appreciated as an indication of your respect for their position in the hierarchy. A man would defer to a more senior man in the same situation. And other people don't have to be more senior than you for you to be polite.

Career Chick Hot Tip: Extend and accept common courtesies.

Presentation Moves

When you make a presentation, whether it is to three people or 3000, your body language determines a large part of your success. As discussed in the earlier, 'Present With Panache' chapter, you should stand up to make a formal presentation. Make sure there's nothing blocking the space between you and the audience, like a podium, a table, a pile of electronic equipment or chairs. Be conscious of your body language and use it in a positive way. To do this, you can:

- use hand gestures to emphasize a point or refer to your visual aids

- maintain an upright posture to indicate confidence, and

- move around the room or stage to involve the audience.

Another technique is to choose a couple of people in the room to make eye contact with during the presentation. In a large room, your audience can't actually tell who you are looking at and a large group around your chosen person will think you are looking at them. Australian filmmaker Eva Orner was a surprise win for Best Documentary Feature at the 80th Academy Awards. Afterwards she said that she had been given the advice to focus on one person while she was speaking. She chose George Clooney. If that's an option for you – go for it!

If you do get nervous when you present, your body language is likely to betray you. Using techniques to help you manage your anxiety can make the difference between a presentation that's successful and one that's not. You can either enhance your image and achieve your business objectives or be so nervous you distract your audience to the point that it impacts their confidence in you and what you say. Too many nerves can cause you to shake or your knees to knock. They can raise the pitch of your voice and turn some helpful adrenalin into a serious loss of confidence. There are many techniques you can learn to help manage your nerves. Preparation, practise and control are the keys. Learn techniques to manage your body language so that you deliver a knockout performance.

Career Chick Hot Tip: Show you are confident when you present.

Communication
Is The First Part Of The CODE

Aligning your body language with what you want to say and how you want to be seen is important for your business credibility and reputation. This needs to be combined with all your communication skills to optimize each interaction and achieve success.

The secrets of effective communication are not so secret at all. They are the norms of business. They are just the unspoken rules and behaviors in the prevailing culture of the business world. None of the Career Chick Hot Tips are rocket science, witchery or sorcery. You are not trying to manipulate or trick people into what you want. You also don't need to become a man and talk and act differently. But you do need to ensure that your communication skills and style align with the environment and reinforce your ability to be successful.

As you have read through the *Communication* Career Chick Hot Tips you may have thought *"Oh yeah, that does happen"* or *"I know that, I must remember to do that more often."* Or you may have thought of examples where the generalizations about male and female attributes and behaviors don't apply to every person, organization or situation. And you are entirely correct. People are individuals and should be treated that way.

For Career Chicks being able to unravel the characteristics of male communication (in the workplace anyway ... once you get home you're on your own!) provides you with knowledge. It won't apply to every person or every situation, but having an insight into the prevailing business culture gives you some techniques to ensure that you are not misunderstood or misinterpreted.

If you communicate with people in a way that they understand, they'll appreciate your value and unique contributions. As many of the people you work with happen to be men, understanding the 'general' characteristics of their communication approach and style won't compromise you or who you are. But it will give you techniques to improve your communications with them. This is the first element of the CODE to ensure you work effectively and achieve career success. It's not secret ... it's just information you need to know. And use! The Career Chick Hot Tip to communicate for career success is to practise and apply the Hot Tips, then see how everyone suddenly notices how effective you are!

Career Chick Hot Tip: Help others see what you mean.

Career Chick Hot Tips to speak with actions:

- Align your body language with what you want to say.

- Be conscious of your body language, so you don't send negative messages.

- Be confident with your posture, facial expressions and gestures.

- Limit your smiles, head nods, head tilts and touches.

- No tears at work.

- Shake hands and offer yours first.

- Offer and exchange business cards.

- Extend and accept common courtesies.

- Show you are confident when you present.

- Help others see what you mean.

Career Chick Hot Tips to _Communicate_ for career success:

- **Choose words** that say exactly what you mean

- Develop a communication style to help what you say **be heard**

- **Present** with panache

- **Write** well, and

- **Speak with actions** to help others see what you mean.

operating style

Chapter 7

Be Seen

"The obvious is that which is never seen until someone expresses it simply"
Kahlil Gibran, philosopher and writer (1883–1931)

In the first *Shrek* movie, the ogre was looking for a guide to help him find Lord Farquaad, who had banished all the fairytale creatures to Shrek's swamp. Millions of people around the world laughed at the donkey when he jumped up and down in front of Shrek, yelling out to be picked. Although the donkey was, quite literally, making an ass of himself and was the last animal Shrek would have chosen, Donkey was eventually rewarded when Shrek gave in and said he could go with him. Despite his annoying behavior the donkey got exactly what he wanted.

Ever see anyone like this at work? You know, those people who are always with the boss, volunteering for extra assignments or telling anyone they think is important how good they are? When you see overt behavior, like the donkey's, do you cringe and ask yourself, *"How can they be so obvious?"* But have you also seen that that those people often get what they want? It isn't usually seen as an admirable trait, but 'sucking up' to the boss often gets results. Even when it is said in jest there's often a feeling that this is the underlying reason for the success of the self-promoters – those who get the good project, the promotion or some other benefit over their colleagues. Often a lack of subtlety, like the donkey's approach, seems to work.

Many people, but particularly women, see the company donkeys in action, but they can't reconcile this behavior with their own style, preferring instead to keep their heads down and get on with their work. It can be even worse when the person getting ahead is either as capable as you or, perhaps, even less so. Chicks think, *"My good work will be noticed."* Often it's noticed, but you won't receive recognition. *"Hard work is its own reward,"* they console themselves. This may be true, but often the 'reward' is to be given even more work. *"My results speak for themselves,"* say optimistic Career Chicks. The truth is they don't. The reality is that those who make decisions, potentially about your future, need to know who has the knowledge, skills and attitude to do what is required – who will help them and the business be successful. Managers often work in stressful situations, under tight time frames that don't allow for a full review of who is 'the best person for the job'. Don't hide in the background; make it easy for your managers and make yourself and your accomplishments known.

Career Chick Hot Tip: Make your accomplishments known.

The Best Choice

So, what's a girl to do? Learn some techniques (that won't make your skin crawl with embarrassment), so that you are the best, easiest and obvious choice for promotion, a pay rise or whatever your heart desires. Making sure you're seen in the best light is one of the core skills you need to be successful in business.

In fact, there's a whole range of skills you need to succeed in an organization, but they are not necessarily the skills you need to do your job well. You need to ensure that your efforts and results are noticed and appreciated, enhancing your reputation and maximizing your opportunities for career success. These skills are the basis of your personal *Operating Style* – the second part of the Career Chick CODE for career success. The O stands for the *Operating Style* you develop that will come to be identified with your credibility and reputation.

The key components of your *Operating Style* include being seen and how you:

- behave in meetings
- work in teams
- negotiate
- resolve conflict, and
- handle the 'bad stuff' that happens at work.

These skills are essential to success at work, yet they aren't often taught or even talked about. Many successful people are instinctively good in these areas or have learnt by observing others. There are specific skills that you can develop in these areas and there are plenty of Career Chick Hot Tips in the CODE for success.

These are not techniques to trick people into thinking you're good at your job if you're not. The assumption is that as a Career Chick you are already capable and have, or are developing, the skills, knowledge and attitude to be successful in your actual role. What you need are some specific and tangible tactics to optimise your time, your energy and your potential for career success. Your *Operating Style* is the expertise underlying how you behave and interact, which is fundamental to business success.

Your *Operating Style* allows you to showcase what you have achieved, what you can contribute and your value to an organization, all of which make you a more valuable commodity and help you achieve your business objectives. When you have a reputation for being successful, and the credibility that goes with that, you'll find it's easier to access the support and resources that you need to do your job. Success really does breed success.

Career Chick Hot Tip: Develop your *Operating Style*.

Be Top Of Mind

For your career to develop, it's essential that you are visible. Women often don't want to be seen 'playing the game', and they think that their work will stand on its own two feet. However, it's important to be visible in your organization or industry, so that you receive acknowledgment for your achievements. It allows you to build your profile and reputation to assist your business and career objectives. Being visible keeps you 'top of mind' with time-poor managers who must make decisions in a hurry and under pressure. If they know about you, what you do and what you are capable of, there's more chance that you'll be on their radar when decisions are being made about resources, promotions or bonuses. Your reputation is your most valuable career asset. To build it up, you need to let others know you exist.

So how do you step out from behind your excellent work to build your profile and be seen? When you have successes, you need to share them. Develop tactics to make them visible and incorporate this activity so it's a regular part of what you do. Some proactive, appropriate self-promotion is a basic activity that should form part of your career management.

Career Chick Hot Tip: Share your successes.

How To Gloat (without being sickening)

When you want the world to know about your success, you need to decide on your key messages. They should be clear, concise and factual. And, most importantly, they should be quantifiable. It's extremely powerful to be able to relate your achievements directly to numbers and business results. Numbers are tangible evidence of your success and generally understood by people in business.

You should always have a 'one-liner' ready in answer to the perennial *"How are you?"* question you're asked about 20 times a day. Make it a quick response that tells a positive story about what you are doing. For example, *"I'm doing well, did you hear that the new sales campaign our team designed brought in 20% more sales last month? We're all pleased it's going so well. I loved developing the strategy behind the campaign."* Or, *"Good, I'm writing up the report on the new IT project. Looks like we've reduced expenses by about 15% with the new system."* Or here's another version, using questions to show you're interested in what they're doing too: *"I'm doing great ... And you? Have you seen any of the benefits in your area yet from the new employee incentive plan we introduced? I'm really pleased with how well the promotional material I developed turned out. It looks like it's helped because we've had feedback that 70% of staff are going to take up the new offer!"*

These are just some examples and you can develop your own. The key is to use simple, factual and quantifiable messages that will help build your profile. It won't sound like you're bragging if you have real data, give specifics of your role and share the glory with others involved. It's always worth remembering that nothing gets done, particularly in a large organization, based on one person's efforts alone. Even the CEO needs other people to implement their plans. Your standing will be enhanced when people know you always share the glory because people want to work with (and for) people who acknowledge their contributions.

Take a minute to think about your contribution to a recent accomplishment and write down the answers to these questions:

- What did you achieve?
- What did it deliver?
- What was the benefit for the business?
- What was your specific contribution?

Now turn your answers into a couple of brief sentences and say them out loud. What do you think? Sounds pretty impressive doesn't it? And it's not that hard to do. Do this each time you have a success. It could be at the end of a project, or at the end of a month or quarter. Start using these one-liners in your casual conversations and you'll soon find you're more comfortable about 'being seen'.

You need to tell people about your successes because chances are, no one else will. You can't assume that people know or even remember what you did in the past, or even what you are doing now. You need to pick an appropriate time, be ready with your clear, quantifiable message and speak up with the facts. Don't wait for them to present themselves; give them a helping hand by putting them on the table.

Career Chick Hot Tip: Quantify your achievements into positive one-liners.

Speak At Meetings

Meetings are another opportunity for you to positively influence your profile. In this forum, women often take a back seat, letting themselves be overshadowed by those who are more domineering. How you operate in meetings can determine how you and your abilities are perceived. Be careful not to allow yourself to be interrupted or cut off when you speak. This can make you look weak. If someone tries to cut you off, be polite, hold your ground, acknowledge the other speaker, and say something along the lines of, *"... to continue my point ..."* or *"... to conclude ..."* then pick up from where you were interrupted.

Don't attend meetings and sit there like a wallflower. If you don't have anything to contribute don't go. Use meetings to 'be seen' and say something, anything! Well not just anything, but anything that's relevant and makes sense. You can just agree with someone or summarize what they said by saying, *"Can I confirm that we have agreed to …?"* These techniques demonstrate that you are engaged and have understood the topic under discussion.

You can also proactively demonstrate your leadership skills by calling your own meetings. This allows you to set the agenda, as well as showing your knowledge and leadership skills. How to operate in meetings is discussed in detail in the next chapter. For now, to be seen, just remember to have something worthwhile to say.

Career Chick Hot Tip: Say something that demonstrates your knowledge or skills at meetings.

Spread Your Wings

Many people are capable at what they do, so it's often what they do outside of their usual role that is recognized. This could be a one-off business project, an inter-department initiative or getting involved with a sporting or charity activity that your organization supports. The more people who know about you and your capabilities, the more opportunities might come your way! One way to do this is to volunteer to participate in cross-functional activities or projects. Apart from increasing your visibility, working on new projects allows you to meet new people, which builds your network. They also provide you with the opportunity to learn new skills and knowledge about another part of business.

Don't be afraid to ask if you can participate in other roles or projects. What's the worst that can happen? If they say no, are you any worse off than before? Not at all. Even if it's not right for the business at the time, they'll know that you are keen to contribute and develop. If you don't tell anyone you're interested, they'll never know!

Career Chick Hot Tip: Volunteer for activities outside your job description.

How To Be Seen

To increase your profile, look out for opportunities where you can be seen. For example, make sure you attend company events and be on the lookout for public-speaking opportunities. There are all sorts of ways to do this. You could volunteer to chair a meeting, present to staff or customers at a forum, or you could seek opportunities to be an expert speaker or to represent your company at industry or trade conferences and associations. Giving a knowledgeable, articulate presentation that is relevant to the audience will do wonders for your profile – and not only with the people you present to. You and the impression you make will be discussed by others.

Another way to get 'your' message out there is to contribute to company or industry publications. In the world of the internet there are plenty of ways to do this, such as company intranet stories and blogs (you can participate with your own insightful comments or write about your area of expertise). And then there are the 'old fashioned' methods, such as contributing an article to your company or department newsletter. You could write about the results of a project, a significant anniversary for your department or a customer story. When you do get your name and accomplishments in print take advantage of the opportunity. Send the paper or the web link to colleagues or people in your network, and point out the business reason that makes it relevant to them. That way you remove any likelihood (or guilt) that you are showing off.

You can also send people who matter information that you know will interest them, such as copies of articles you find in publications or on the web, or a relevant report. Take the time to drop them a quick email or, even better, attach a hand-written note to the document – it will help keep you 'top of mind'.

Career Chick Hot Tip: Find ways to be visible.

Show Off (just a little bit)

If you win an award, get recognized with a certificate, or even receive a thank you letter from a customer or other department put them on display around your desk. They show people that others have recognized your contributions. Even if you get a certificate when you become a member of a professional organization display these too, as they will reinforce your credibility. When you do this, you may be surprised at how often visitors to your desk remark on an award or certificate that's on show. Others won't comment, but they will notice. Awards, certificates, and letters of commendation … they all provide credibility and show that other people have recognized your work. Let your successes speak for you – and they will, loudly!

Career Chick Hot Tip: Show off your successes (a little bit).

Your Image Is Everywhere

At the same time, be a little bit cautious about the personal items you display on your desk. There is absolutely nothing wrong with being yourself and having some photos or your favorite mug on display. Just think about what they say about you, and ensure that the items are consistent with the image you want to portray. If you want to be seen as professional and efficient, you may not want a whole lot of the pink girlie items you love on show. On the other hand, if you are confident in your image and want to hang a calendar with pictures of handbags or dogs to show people the 'other side of you', that is your choice. Just make it a conscious decision.

The other place to be careful of your image is on the web. More and more employers, and nosy colleagues, use the internet to find out about you. You may not Google yourself but others will. Be conscious that what you post on social-networking sites aligns with your desired career image. Your hilarious antics on the dance floor on Saturday night might not be quite as hilarious if your boss is viewing them from the comfort of his or her office on Monday morning. This doesn't mean you can't have a life or be yourself. Just make sure that when your business and personal worlds crossover they align.

Career Chick Hot Tip: Present the image you desire.

Don't Doubt Yourself

Have you ever had a nagging feeling that maybe you're not that talented at what you do? That there's someone who is better than you? Knows more than you? You're not the only one. When women feel this way they tend to keep their head down and not make a song and dance about what they're doing. By keeping a low profile, you may feel you can avoid the risk of being 'found out' in case you aren't actually that good at what you do. This approach may seem safe, but it won't advance your career.

If you do your job to the best of your ability and continually strive to improve your skills and develop, then don't doubt yourself. Be realistic when you compare yourself to colleagues and others who are doing a similar role, but don't be overly hard on yourself. And don't set yourself impossibly high standards that you can't possibly live up to until you have more experience. If you are doing well, be proud of yourself and don't let self-doubt stop you from sharing your successes.

Career Chick Hot Tip: Don't doubt yourself.

It's A Big World

As you share your success and build your profile within your organization you should also look further afield. If you can build credibility and respect, as well as make a name for yourself, outside of your organization, it can actually enhance your reputation inside your current organization as well. Sometimes that outside reinforcement raises your credibility. People think, *"If other people think she's good, she must be."* External views are sometimes seen as more credible than those of the people who know you well. A strong external profile also provides a platform for future opportunities. You never know where the next opportunity will come from or when you might need it.

To build your external profile, you could:

- participate in industry events and forums
- get involved in professional organizations and associations in your field of expertise, like university alumni
- meet with people in other companies who have a role similar to yours – you could start with suppliers to your company or customers
- visit local business events and forums for your town, city or state, and
- join sports and community activities – you never know who you will meet.

You don't have to become a keynote speaker at events or volunteer to help out for hours a day to build your profile. Just go to events and be seen! Have your one-liners ready to tell people who you are, what you do and how well you do it.

Career Chick Hot Tip: Spread the word about who you are, widely.

On The Grapevine

People often worry about what others think and say about them. But this can be very powerful, especially when people start spreading the word about your talents. People will talk. Even those who don't know you are likely to have an opinion about you or something you have done. Sometimes people who don't even know you that well will offer their opinion on you. They might recommend you for a role or mention some achievement you have made, often because it reflects well on them or the business. Many times you won't even know that you have been spoken about, or that someone has helped influence a decision about you or your future. These people, who speak well of you, are known as sponsors. Your job is to be seen positively so that you are recruiting favorable sponsors.

A sponsor may be a mentor, your manager or someone from your network. Then again, it may be someone you don't even know who knows about you. This could be a senior manager who sees you speak or hears about the work you have been doing. The people who can influence your career progress and work results are everywhere. So the more you are seen and the more you build your credibility, the more people you'll have working on your behalf to help you achieve your career objectives. Ultimately the better you are at your job and the better your business results, the more sponsors you will have.

It is possible to give yourself a 'helping hand' to get the positive discussions about you underway. If there is something you're hoping to achieve, like a new role, you might want to ask a trusted advisor, who you know will have some influence on the decision, to have a word in the ear of the decision-maker on your behalf. It might be a senior manager you have worked with before or a colleague, but it is important that the 'trusted' person will act in your best interests. You might approach them with a brief, front-focused explanation of what you want to achieve and why. Ask, *"Would you mind mentioning in the meeting that I have experience in this area?"* You're not asking them to do anything untoward. This is just another way of building your profile so that you have the chance to benefit from your achievements.

Career Chick Hot Tip: Ask for sponsorship.

Don't Hide ... Shine!

Many women work hard, achieve magnificent results and wait to be noticed. Most of them are still waiting. If you've done well, let people know. When you make a big sale – let it be known! When you bring a project in under budget – tell people! When you get an email of thanks from someone about the terrific job you did – send it on to your manager! Career Chicks need to make opportunities out of their success and take advantage of the chance while it is relevant. Don't wait to become yesterday's news or tomorrow's fish wrappings. You need to shine while in the glow of your successes. It may feel more comfortable and safer to hide away and avoid jealousy and self-doubt, but when you are fabulously successful don't be afraid to be the golden girl and shine. Where everyone can see. You deserve it.

Career Chick Hot Tip: Enjoy your success and shine!

Career Chick Hot Tips to be seen:

- Make your accomplishments known.

- Develop your *Operating Style*.

- Share your successes.

- Quantify your achievements into positive one-liners.

- Say something that demonstrates your knowledge or skills at meetings.

- Volunteer for activities outside your job description.

- Find ways to be visible.

- Show off your successes (a little bit).

- Present the image you desire.

- Don't doubt yourself.

- Spread the word about who you are, widely.

- Ask for sponsorship.

- Enjoy your success and shine!

Chapter 8

Meet Successfully

"Opportunity is missed by most people because it is dressed in overalls and looks like work"

Thomas Edison, American inventor (1847–1931)

Not all meetings happen around a table. Some happen over the phone by teleconference, others are via video, cell phone or web collaboration. However they happen, meetings have a reputation as being time-consuming and the downside of business life. It can be hard to find anyone who's positive about all the time we spend in meetings. What people miss is that even though meetings can seem boring, frustrating and non-productive, they can also be a great opportunity to advance your career.

The opportunities that can be gained from them can be lost in the day-to-day drudgery of participating in bad meetings. How many meetings have you attended where the major action item at the end is to hold another meeting or for some of the participants to meet again separately? These are just some of the outcomes that cause meetings to get a bad rap. However, there are lots of others: they can be too long, involve too many people, be disorganized or dominated by one person, have no agenda or clear outcome … the list goes on. But despite these problems, meetings are a fact of business life and play an important role in career success.

Once upon a time, not that long ago, and not in a galaxy far, far away, women were thankful to have 'a seat at the table' of important meetings. The idea was that if you were in the meeting where decisions were being made, you were privy to what was going on and could, potentially, influence the outcome. But there is no point having a seat at the table if you don't do something with the opportunity. Being at meetings gives you the chance to achieve business outcomes and further your career. Playing the role of wallflower, or silent witness, doesn't fit with the image or aspirations of today's successful Career Chick. Your conduct in meetings is a skill for you to develop as part of your *Operating Style*.

The Value Of Meetings

We discussed earlier that communication can be likened to the currency of organizations. In that case, meetings are like an ATM: where deposits and withdrawals are made on business reputations, rather than bank accounts. There are many types of communications in companies, but meetings are highly visible forums where decisions are made and opinions are formed. And like the ATM you can choose whether you use them to boost your personal assets or whittle away at your bank account. Think about how you look after your cash. You only carry what you need, it's safe in your purse (which you have with you at all times) and you always know where it is. You don't consciously think about the security of your cash, but you develop sensible habits as a safeguard. When you have your purse in your hand and stand in front of an ATM to withdraw cash, you're a bit more exposed and vulnerable. You tend to be more conscious of your security and take a few extra precautions: making sure no one sees you put in your PIN, looking around you and quickly putting your cash into your bag. You are also a little bit more visible and exposed when you attend meetings for the exchange of business communication. Like standing at the ATM, you need a few techniques to make sure you safely complete the business you want and enhance your reputation.

Career Chick Hot Tip: Use meetings to enhance your business reputation.

Meeting Skills

Knowing how to manage meetings effectively and efficiently is a skill you need as part of your *Operating Style*. The truth is, many people don't know how to conduct meetings well. This is the key reason why meetings are often seen as a waste of time. By developing your skills to run effective meetings, you can use them to positively enhance your credibility, reputation and, consequently, your career prospects. You will earn respect by doing the basics well.

To lead an effective meeting, you need to:

- have an agenda
- record (and later circulate) the minutes

- keep meetings to time
- ensure that everyone has the opportunity to contribute, and
- assign actions and follow them up.

Perception is reality and reputations can be made or lost on the ability to communicate effectively in meetings. As well as having an impact on your career, performing well in meetings is necessary to advance your ideas, make progress in your job and meet your accountabilities. That's why it's worth learning the core organizational skills required to survive and thrive in meetings.

Career Chick Hot Tip: Develop the skills to lead effective meetings.

Meeting Traps

Women often find that they are not taken seriously or don't get the opportunity to properly explain their position in meetings. If you are undermined or can't get across your key message, it can lower people's opinion of you. And not just the people in the meeting itself – word spreads.

Not only is your reputation at risk, but going back to resolve issues after a meeting can cause you a lot of extra work. People may wonder why you didn't raise an issue or express an opinion when you previously had the opportunity – even if you felt you couldn't get a word in edgeways. Worse still, meetings sometimes become a forum for inappropriate or bullying behavior.

When women find themselves unable to express themselves, marginalized or undermined in meetings, it tends to reinforce the stereotype that women are not as assertive and resolute as men. This creates doubt about your ability to be effective in business.

Career Chick Hot Tip: Be assertive and resolute in meetings.

Prepare, Prepare, Prepare

If you want to succeed, you need to have a plan. When it comes to meetings, the first issue to understand, or decide on, is what your role will be and how you'll play it. Start by determining the meeting's objective. Is it to:

- deliver information?
- make decisions?
- learn or teach?

Knowing the objective of the meeting helps you decide on your role. For instance, will you lead, actively participate or observe during the meeting? Will you be vocal or only speak occasionally? How will you position your role with other attendees? What results do you want from the meeting? And what preparation do you need to do? For example, you may need to prepare an agenda or presentation, or even engage in some 'stakeholder management', by talking with other participants before the meeting to provide them with information or canvass their views on the topic.

Career Chick Hot Tip: Prepare for meetings.

The Best Seat

One part of your preparation is to put yourself in the best position, literally, in a meeting. Power and influence can be assumed or given away by the simple act of where you sit. In a traditional, face-to-face meeting at a rectangular table, the positions of power are at either end or in the middle of the table. If you will lead the meeting, or are a key contributor who is presenting, make sure you are in one of these positions. If you want to be an active participant but are not the meeting lead, place yourself next to the positions of power in the middle of the table. This ensures you can make eye contact with the senior managers or leaders of the meeting and speak to all the participants relatively easily.

The other advantage of these positions is that you'll also be able to see what the senior people write down. You need to look discreetly, of course, but it will help you pick up on the points they think are important. If for some bizarre reason you're being forced to go to a meeting and need a place to hide, the corner seat at the end of the table is the place to hang out; other people will block the view to you, you won't be able to make eye contact and it'll almost be like you're not there. However, let's assume that you go to meetings to be effective in your job, so make sure you get to meetings a little early to get the pick of the seats.

Career Chick Hot Tip: Pick the best seat.

Introductions

Regardless of the technology used or the type of meeting, make sure you introduce yourself, say where you are from and what your involvement in the meeting will be. This knowledge helps other meeting participants understand who you are and why you're there. It can also ensure you're not marginalized as the meeting progresses.

Introducing yourself in meetings is a business norm but one that women often hang back from. Often they politely wait to be introduced to others. Men are not backwards in making themselves known. You need to be proactive and establish yourself in the same way as your male colleagues and let others know who you are. Be proactive in your introductions. When you walk into a meeting always introduce yourself to anyone you don't know. Or at least one person you don't know if it's a large meeting. And make sure you offer your hand first to shake. It's polite and professional. If the meeting is over the phone or video it is still important to introduce yourself and let others know why you are there.

The other introductory technique, which men often use, is to identify yourself early in a conversation. Say who you are, where you're from, your qualifications or what your role is in the meeting. For example, *"Hi I'm Sally, from the Finance department. I'm the accountant allocated to this project."* Position yourself so that everyone understands why you are there.

When women sit back and don't introduce themselves or explain who they are, it adds a level of uncertainty that needs to be worked through as the meeting progresses. With the amount of work that people have to get through, this can be, at best, annoying, and at worst, a waste of time. Your risk is that if no one has time to do this, you'll be marginalized. Other people will not take the time to work out who you are and the meeting will forge ahead without you.

Career Chick Hot Tip: Introduce yourself, your position and your role.

Introduce Others

Likewise, when you introduce people to each other (which you should if you called the meeting) make sure you identify them. You could give a brief explanation of their expertise, accomplishments or their position in the company. For example, *"Peter, this is Helen Smith, who just led the launch of our new product line. Helen, this is Peter Jones. Peter just started with us as the new finance manager."* Remember, too, that you should always address the first introduction to the more senior or important person (such as a client). In the example above, it would be assumed that Peter is the more senior of the two. Once you've made easy and simple introductions, you can get down to business.

Career Chick Hot Tip: Identify others when you make introductions.

Get On With Business

Getting down to business is exactly what you should do in a meeting. Women often like to ease into business discussions by establishing relationships. They'll ask, *"How was your weekend?"* or *"How are the kids?"* and so on, but men can find this frustrating and conclude that you are not sufficiently focused on the business. So it's best to get straight into the meeting. If you are the meeting lead, make sure all the introductions have been made, then set expectations for the meeting. Make sure you include:

- how long the meeting will last
- the exact purpose or topic of the meeting
- the meeting's objective – what needs to be achieved
- how the meeting will operate, and
- a run-through of the agenda.

Career Chick Hot Tip: Get straight down to business.

Resist Volunteering

A common trap for many women is to 'volunteer' to take on actions (that they shouldn't) from meetings. The motivation is admirable: you look proactive, it helps you build a relationship with the person you offer to assist and, after all, the work does need to be done. Just think about your motivation and the implications of volunteering for more work. There may be many justifiable reasons for you to do so. For example, perhaps your work can't proceed or be approved until the action is completed, it's a fantastic opportunity for you to improve your profile or maybe no one else has the skill set or time to do it. Of course, there really is no question about it if it's your job and part of your responsibilities. But, and this is a big but, do not volunteer and take on extra work simply because no one else offers or it's expected that you always 'pitch in' and take on extra work. Women have the reputation as the doers, the workers, which is very noble. But your career value is enhanced when you are recognized as a thinker.

Sit on your hands. Count to ten or 10,000. Step backwards when there is a request for volunteers. Don't let the peer pressure or silence get to you. Those extra tasks may prevent you from doing your own job, meaning you'll need to work longer hours. Worse still, you may come across as being gullible or a bit of a sucker. Men can be masters at sitting back and waiting for someone else to volunteer. Women often just can't help themselves. Don't be one of them.

Unless it's your job, hold back from volunteering to take the minutes or be the whiteboard scribe in meetings, too. You may have the neatest handwriting or know the most logical way to present information, but having a chick play the 'secretary' role in a meeting, especially if it's male-dominated, only reinforces male–female stereotypes. There is nothing wrong with it, if that's your job, but if you have a different role, don't take this one on. The power, control and ability to influence the meeting direction is with the people who speak, not the one trying to write fast enough to keep up with the conversation. You just can't do both. When the call goes out for a volunteer, keep quiet (unless it's your job or turn).

Career Chick Hot Tip: Participate as an equal.

Make A Contribution

Ensure that you contribute during a meeting. You should speak early and at least once, but make sure you have something worthwhile to say. Even if it's just a summary of what has been said to demonstrate that you understand the topic at hand. People love hearing you repeat their ideas. And they'll tend to agree with everything you say! One technique is to phrase your summary as if you are seeking clarification Ask, *"Do you mean …?"* or *"Is my understanding of what you are saying correct that …?"* They agree, you demonstrate you've been listening and your presenter is happy because they know they were understood.

In your effort to participate in a meeting, be careful that you don't give away your killer idea. You know, the most brilliant thing you've ever thought of (or it seems that way at the time). When an awesome idea is raised in a public forum, people often forget who brought it up. It becomes the property of the meeting. If something amazing occurs to you when you are in a meeting, write it down. Wait until you have time to think it through or talk it over with a trusted colleague. If the idea is really as stupendous as you thought, then raise it one-on-one with the relevant person, either in person or by phone or email. That way they'll remember it was your idea. On the other hand, don't be reluctant to come forward in meetings (just not with your idea of the century!).

Men are often more assertive in meetings, so they are seen as more confident and, consequently, more competent. You need to ensure that you don't get interrupted and that you finish what you want to say. If you wait your turn to speak in most meetings, the only chance you'll get will be when everyone else has left the room. A little bit of assertiveness is needed to ensure you get your turn.

Do not ask for permission to ask a question. No matter how forcefully you say, *"Do you mind if I just ask …"* (or words to that effect), you'll be seen as less powerful and confident than the person you are asking the question. Acknowledge the previous speaker, but just get in and say what you need to say. Try something like, *"That's an important point, Bill, and we need to take into account …"* You'll come across as polite yet knowledgeable.

Career Chick Hot Tip: Speak up.

Be Clear

Use your meeting 'air time' wisely. Save your interruptions for what is important. How often you speak in meetings will vary, depending on your position in the organization, your role in the meeting and what you plan to achieve from it. Remember, you don't need to have an opinion on every single thing that is discussed. If you get a reputation for always having something to say, people can switch off when you start talking. On the other hand, if you have a reputation as a measured, insightful participant, who speaks when they have something worth saying, you are more likely to get the attention and interest of the other participants.

And be clear when you talk. Moderate the pace of your speech. Be slow and deliberate. Modulating your voice will show you're in control and reinforce the facts. Talking too fast, or being overly emotive, can distract from what you say. Unfortunately, this can lead some people, like men, to write off what you're saying without listening to the content.

Another tip is to use people's names when you speak or refer to them. People love to hear the sound of their own name and what they said acknowledged. This applies in many situations, but it's particularly powerful in meetings. It has the extra advantage of making people feel valued because they are being acknowledged in front of their colleagues. When you make that acknowledgement it reflects well on you, because everyone loves a team player, but that's another chapter …

Career Chick Hot Tip: Make your point clearly.

Read The Room

Be aware of the mood of a meeting and gauge when to stick to your argument and when to back off. Watch for body language and other non-verbal communication. Pick up on the visual clues and work out the best course of action. You may need to get to your point more quickly or ask questions to draw out concerns.

If things get a bit heated, as they sometimes do, you may need to make a decision about how rigid you should be about your position on an issue. Provided you have done your work and know your facts you should be prepared to stick to, and defend, your argument. But don't make it emotional or personal. Remember you are discussing a business issue, not your worth as a person. Remain logical, know your facts, be empathetic and respectful. Agree to disagree if need be, or acknowledge that others have different views. But don't concede you are wrong if you are right. If you cave in, you run the risk of appearing weak and not confident. If you need alternative tactics, you can find a way to defer the discussion, suggest actions to gather more information or recommend that other people be consulted. Stick to your argument but not at the expense of your reputation or relationships.

Career Chick Hot Tip: Gauge and adapt to the meeting's mood.

Use Meetings Well

Meetings are an excellent opportunity to be seen. They are where business gets done. They also provide a forum for you to build and enhance your reputation, develop relationships, exchange ideas, gain credibility, share information, obtain approvals and, last but not least, get some work done. With all these positives, meetings aren't really so awful. And they are a fact of business life. Make the most of the opportunities they present so that they can make the most of you.

Career Chick Hot Tip: Use the opportunity to be seen.

Career Chick Hot Tips to meet successfully:

- Use meetings to enhance your business reputation.
- Develop the skills to lead effective meetings.
- Be assertive and resolute in meetings.
- Prepare for meetings.
- Pick the best seat.
- Introduce yourself, your position and your role.
- Identify others when you make introductions.
- Get straight down to business.
- Participate as an equal.
- Speak up.
- Make your point clearly.
- Gauge and adapt to the meeting's mood.
- Use the opportunity to be seen.

Chapter 9

Work In Teams

"Sticks in a bundle are unbreakable"

Proverb

People will judge your performance at work by looking at how you work in and with teams. Successful teamwork is central to achieving your objectives in the business world, plus being seen as a team player is of value to your career. Being able to work successfully as part of a team is another skill set that you need to develop as part of your *Operating Style*.

Think of any of the TV shows you love to watch. Getting them to your TV screen involves many skilful people, including writers, actors, editors, publicists and production staff. Take the gaffer, for example, who heads up the electrical department of a production and is responsible for the lighting. Although this job doesn't have much of a profile, it's integral to the show. An actor could give the most impressive performance of his or her career, but there isn't much point if the set wasn't lit and no one saw it. Everyone involved in a project can be an expert in their area, but they all need to work together for a successful result.

So, too, in the business world: the complexity and expertise required mean there's little room for any one person to play the role of the actor, and take centre stage, without the rest of the team to help them succeed. Whatever your role, whether you're leading a team or supporting it, working successfully with a team will help you achieve business goals and contribute to your career success.

Sometimes, it may seem easier to do something yourself, rather than work with a team. Many people find teamwork frustrating, and you've probably heard people muttering, *"When you want something done properly, do it yourself."* Particularly, if they're fixing someone else's mistakes or making up for those who don't pull their weight or deliver work to a good standard.

Unfortunately, as appealing as it is to do it all yourself, the reality is that in business, it's just not possible. Why? You need to work with other people to share the workload and gain access to their organizational expertise and specialized skills. In the business world, this translates to working in teams. No matter how proficient you are at what you do, to be a successful Career Chick you need other people with their skills to help you achieve your best. To do this you need the skills to work well in teams.

Career Chick Hot Tip: Work in teams to be successful.

Teams Work

A team is simply a group of people who work together to achieve a common purpose or goal. Teamwork is beneficial because it can:

- motivate people who want to belong to a group and contribute

- give a sense of pride in team membership and results

- create a productive work environment, which stimulates and promotes engagement and collaboration, and

- provide business outcomes that are superior to those that individual team members could have achieved.

To enjoy these benefits, and the success that comes with them, you need to learn and incorporate the skills that make you a successful team player into the way you work. Whether it's making a TV show or achieving business targets, the purpose of any team is to work towards a common goal or outcome. You can achieve more with a team than you can by yourself.

Even the best team members in the world, like sports stars, have to learn this. Michael Jordan has been described as the greatest basketball player of all time, but his success was tied to his ability to play with a team. No matter how many baskets Jordan could sink, he had to learn to pass the ball to become a champion. If you let the other people in the team do their part, you get to focus on your area of expertise. Michael Jordan focused on sinking basketballs and playing defense. What would you do if, instead of doing everything yourself, you focused on what you are good at and what you enjoy?

Career Chick Hot Tip: Trust the team and concentrate on your area of expertise.

The Team Difference

Working in an effective team can help you realize your business or personal goals and objectives. Plus, when your team achieves superior results, you get to share in the reflected glory. Much easier than struggling on your own, achieving an average result and shouldering all the responsibility! Being associated with successful teams improves your credibility. Others may not know the contributions of each individual, but they'll view everyone positively, if the team was successful.

On the other hand, being associated with an unsuccessful or dysfunctional team that hasn't achieved their objectives can reflect badly on your individual performance. Sometimes, no matter how hard you work in a team, the result doesn't get delivered. This can be an unfair reflection on you. The only way to reduce this risk is to focus on the success of the whole team and the required business deliverables. Don't get worked up about others who aren't pulling their weight. Essentially, there's only one person's behavior you can have an impact on: your own. As much as you'd like to change other people's behaviors or make them do some work, the only person you can really control is you. So do your best: the team will have a much better chance of success than if you don't.

Career Chick Hot Tip: Focus on your contribution to a team.

Team Types

As you know there are many different types of teams in all areas of life, for sport, social, community and business activities. They can be permanent teams or ones where the membership changes regularly based on the ability of its members, such as sports or project teams. In a business environment, teams can be formal or informal, project-focused or based on formal reporting lines. They are a way to organize people, generate ideas, collaborate and solve problems.

Teams can be seen negatively when people get caught up with processes, don't have a clear purpose, have team members who are at odds, or all of the above. Your opportunity is to influence what happens in a team to ensure its success. If you understand the needs and dynamics of a team, you can identify how you can provide assistance.

According to research, teams are more successful when their members have a broad range of team behaviors or *Operating Styles*. Dr Meredith Belbin,[1] a management consultant who is a Visiting Professor and Honorary Fellow at Henley Management College in the UK, is well known in the business world for his work on team roles, that is, the different roles that make up an effective team. The research came about following the outcomes of mixed feedback on the effectiveness of certain business 'games' involving teams, which were part of the college's business program. Some teams had beneficial learning experiences, while other teams were ineffective. The feedback had the potential to negatively impact the reputation of the business program.

Dr Belbin conducted a range of psychometric tests on the participants and concluded that while they were all intelligent, successful and able to achieve individually at the level required for the program, their behavior varied in a team environment. He identified a range of key 'team roles' and found that a team needs a range of people with different behaviors to be successful. In the Henley College program, the unsuccessful teams were either over-represented with members who had a particular team behavioral style or lacking members who had other complementary styles.

In business, dysfunctional teams may not achieve business outcomes, meaning (as at Henley College) reputations are also at stake. It makes sense that when everyone wants to lead the team the best outcome probably won't be achieved. It's the same if no one is prepared to lead, evaluate the options available or do any work. Imagine a TV show with four directors and no scriptwriter. It's unlikely the show would begin production let alone make it to the screen. It's the same for teams at work. Too many 'ideas people' and the work never gets started … too many leaders and everyone wants to be in charge … too many cooks spoil the broth, as they say!

Dr Belbin broke down the different team roles into three categories: cerebral (thinking), action (doing) and people-oriented. In his model, the cerebral roles are known as the Plant, the Monitor-Evaluator and the Specialist. Plants are the ideas people in the team who come up with the new ways of looking at things. The Monitor-Evaluator is the person who is always considering what's going on. You'll recognize them, as they're the ones who say, *"Hang on, have we looked at ...?"* The Specialist is the expert with the knowledge or skills required to achieve the team's objective.

The action-oriented roles are the Shaper, the Implementer and the Completer Finisher. As the descriptions suggest, these people make sure things get done. The Shaper steers the team in the right direction. The Implementer works out how to do what needs to be done. And the Completer Finisher is the perfectionist, who is never happy with the quality (they're the ones that think there is always time for one more revision).

The third team-roles category focuses on people: the Coordinator, the Resource Investigator and the Team Worker. The Coordinator organizes the work to utilize the team's resources; the Resource Investigator runs around, makes contacts and sources information and help from people outside the team; and last, but not least, the invaluable Team Worker happily does whatever the team requires.

According to the Belbin model, all these team behaviors have their pluses and minuses, with none being right or wrong, good or bad. Teams come down to people, and people have different approaches. The art of teamwork is to ensure you have a mix of styles. Seeing a team of Shapers fight it out over what needs to be done may be more entertaining to watch than be a part of. On the other hand, a team of Monitor-Evaluators, Implementers and Team Workers may not get anything done, but they'll have a lovely time working out how to do it! To ensure the team's success and a quality experience for its participants, you need all team roles and all types of people represented in a team for it to operate effectively.

Belbin's model is only one of many that look at teams, but it provides a helpful framework and insight into how teams work. At the very least, this can make you more tolerant of other people's behavior. If someone is annoying you because they keep talking about the project's deadline or they want to start allocating work while you're still evaluating the options, they may just be playing their team role, which brings value to the team and, ultimately, you.

Ultimately, if you have the ability to influence the composition of a team, you can ensure you have all the expertise you need and that the various team behaviors are represented. It follows that if all team roles are required to make a team effective, then what you contribute is always of value. Don't be afraid to contribute; you are an important part of any team.

Career Chick Hot Tip: Understand your role and appreciate the roles of others.

Chicks In Teams

Many team theories don't differentiate between the behaviors of men and women, but there's a trend to use attitudes to teamwork to explain differences between the sexes. Analogies are made that men bring their experience of playing team sports and translate it into 'the rules' of business. Experiences like keeping score, learning how to lose and knowing that 'what happens on the field stays on the field' have become part of the business culture, particularly in the team environment.

Whether this is true or not, the reality is that teams are an important part of the business environment. It's crucial that women understand the importance of teams in the workplace and the necessity of working with, not in spite of, them.

In teams, differences between male and female behavior can surface and create tension and frustration based on preferred *Operating Styles*. For the sake of your career, don't let these differences in style negatively impact on business results or your relationships.

One difference you will notice is that men assert themselves in a team to ensure their opinions are at least prevalent, if not dominant. A large part of teamwork occurs in meetings, and men are often more decisive and forceful in these situations so their views prevail. Their behavior isn't necessarily domineering or aggressive, but it can discourage others in the team, particularly women, from having their say.

In teamwork situations and meetings, make sure your *Operating Style* allows you to:

- cut in when you have an important point
- continue to speak if you are interrupted
- ensure that you get a say, and
- be respectful and assertive.

Chapter 8 covered how to operate in meetings, so you can review those techniques and apply these in team situations. Most importantly, make sure that your contribution is heard, so that your role is acknowledged in the success of the team.

Career Chick Hot Tip: Be respectful and assertive.

Be Aware Of Hierarchies

Another difference in teams is that men are often more aware of the hierarchy than women. That is, they are more conscious of who holds what position outside the team. This is especially true if the senior people in the team are men. They won't necessarily see themselves as equal team members; rather they'll expect to be respected for their position, expertise or skills (or all three). Men, in particular, can feel threatened if their position and abilities aren't understood and acknowledged.

If you show respect to all team members, you won't offend anyone – male or female. You may just need to be more overt in your appreciation with the men on the team. Practise the Career Chick *Communication* tips: acknowledge their position and credentials, don't talk over them and give them the most important information upfront.

Men who are aware of their position in a hierarchy may use the 'security' of their position as their credibility. They're often comfortable delegating tasks to the rest of the team. Women regardless of their seniority often think they should be part of the team and take on menial tasks. There's nothing wrong with pitching in – every task has value – but be prepared to be a leader, to delegate and to voice your opinions. This is a time to shine, not hide and be lumped with the role of the team's lowest common denominator.

Career Chick Hot Tip: Recognize the status, position and past contributions of your team members and yourself.

Relationships Are Assets

Another difference between chicks and guys in teams is that men see themselves as solution- and outcome-focused. On the other hand, women often make relationships in a team, rather than the business issues, a priority. Women think if you can get a team to work effectively through productive relationships, the business results will follow, but men can see this as a lack of focus on the business. Women may see this as uncaring and callous: *"How can we focus on an issue when we don't understand the people involved?"* they think. Neither approach is right nor wrong; they're just very different.

Men may think that women focus too much on relationships, but it is, in fact, one of a Career Chick's greatest strengths. Teams come and go and teams change, but relationships are a long-term investment. A relationship that develops as part of a team may be a huge asset in the future. Leverage your relationship skills, focus on the business issues, be aware of your role and you'll find teamwork an effective and rewarding way to achieve success.

Again, as in all of areas of your *Operating Style*, you need to be aware of how men may perceive your approach. You don't need to abandon the skills that make women effective. The ability to listen, be empathetic and build relationships is a competitive advantage in business. At the same time, if you can get down to business, men appreciate your focus on the issues.

Another thing to be aware of is that egos come out to play in a team environment. The way people position themselves in a team (and it's not just the men) can be a key distraction and cause of conflict. You don't want to unwittingly threaten someone's position. There's nothing to gain by making someone else look bad. Be mindful of who people are and what they do or have done. If you are working on a new process and the person who developed the last version is part of the team, they won't take well to hearing comments about how *"hopeless"* the last version was, or *"What planet were these people on when they came up with this?"* Situations where you look clever and someone else looks like an idiot can turn around pretty quickly if they decide to retaliate. Instead, look out for ways to give other people a win. For example, acknowledge their contributions. Recognize publicly that the needs and circumstances of the past were different. People are less likely to resist change if you acknowledge what went before.

Career Chick Hot Tip: Give others a win.

Take Credit

One of the most valuable things you can do is make sure the team's glory for their achievements is shared. Women are usually generous with their acknowledgments, but if you are a member of a successful team, rather than the leader, there are still opportunities to acknowledge your fellow team members both publicly and privately. This is a good habit to build into your *Operating Style*. An email to the team, a public mention in a meeting or a personal acknowledgment (*"Thanks for working with me on this"*) are all effective techniques.

On the other hand, if the team doesn't perform and you were the leader, you should take responsibility. The willingness to take responsibility, rather than expecting others to 'share the blame' can enhance your reputation. Women are exceptional at this, too. Sometimes too good, in fact, taking the blame for small things that go wrong even when the overall result is successful. This is not a good thing!

The results of the team are … the results of the whole team, and everyone should be acknowledged for their work. However, if you are the leader of or a key contributor to a team, your leadership and contributions also deserve to be recognized. Sharing the glory is something that women do well, but don't be so modest that others don't know what you did. Be generous in your praise of others and, if you deserve it, take the credit, too.

Career Chick Hot Tip: Share the glory and take the credit, too.

Team Milestones

Acknowledging milestones is an effective technique for teamwork to progress. Women are often very talented at doing this. This can have a major impact on team results. In some ways, it's easier to do this with a project team, because there's a beginning, a middle and an end, with defined accountabilities. Recognizing the transition between a project's phases helps a team move on to the next phase or even beyond the project. Formally recognizing the end of a project gives the team a chance to reflect on what has been achieved, understand their value to the team and then move on to their next challenge.

Permanent teams such as departments or work groups often don't have such defined milestones. Delivering of business objectives is ongoing, week in and week out. Each month, quarter or year brings new targets with more challenges than the last one, often with less people or fewer resources, making it even more challenging to maintain momentum. However, the factors motivating team members are the same: the desire to achieve business objectives, do their job well and have their contribution acknowledged. When you celebrate milestones, such as team anniversaries, significant business outcomes or even company reporting periods, it can invigorate the team, help them move from one stage to the next and provide recognition for their contributions. Whatever your role, there are ways to influence the team dynamics. And it doesn't have to be all business. Sometimes one of the biggest influences on team spirit is the team worker who organizes the casual get-togethers.

Career Chick Hot Tip: Celebrate and acknowledge team milestones.

Bring It All Together

Your main reason for being in any team is likely to be determined by your technical skills or your area of expertise, perhaps in finance, sales, administration or any other of the many fields where Career Chicks excel. Be generous with your expertise and the contributions you make to a team. Take the time and make the effort to listen, question, persuade, negotiate and share to the best of your ability. If you can incorporate these skills into your *Operating Style*, everyone will want you on their team and your reputation will soar. Stay focused, however, so you don't get asked to join teams that are not aligned with your business or career objectives. Remember, *"no"* is not a four-letter word; it only has two letters. You just need to say it nicely.

To be effective in a team you need to utilize a vast range of skills and this is where many areas of the Career Chick CODE come together. You need to utilize all your *Communication* skills, draw from every area of your established *Operating Style*, be mindful of the impact on your *Career Development* and juggle '*Everything Else*' on your plate. Ultimately, if you act for the good of the business, the team and the people in it, it's hard to go wrong.

Career Chick Hot Tip: Leverage your ability to build relationships and work in teams.

Career Chick Hot Tips to work in teams:

- Work in teams to be successful.

- Trust the team and concentrate on your area of expertise.

- Focus on your contribution to a team.

- Understand your role and appreciate the roles of others.

- Be respectful and assertive.

- Recognize the status, position and past contributions of your team members and yourself.

- Give others a win.

- Share the glory and take the credit, too.

- Celebrate and acknowledge team milestones.

- Leverage your ability to build relationships and work in teams.

Chapter 10

Negotiate

"If you want a puppy, ask your parents for a pony ..."
Katie McDonnell, at 11 years of age[1]

Katie McDonnell's mum couldn't believe it when she heard that gem while driving her daughter and her friend home from school several years ago. Although not an original idea, at eleven years of age Katie had already learnt an effective negotiating technique: ask for more than you expect, then negotiate back to what you actually want. In fact, there are many negotiating techniques that you can learn and apply to be successful in business.

The "pony principle" became part of the McDonnell family's folklore and entrenched in their household's everyday negotiations. However, now that she's a teenager, Katie's more likely to say, *"Mum, it's not like I'm asking for a pony"* or *"This is not the pony/puppy thing ... I really do need to go to this concert!"* Not surprisingly, Katie has had to learn a few more techniques to get by.

By learning a few negotiating techniques yourself, you can achieve better results for both you and your career. Negotiating is an essential business skill, and there are numerous training programs, books and coaching programs on the subject. There's a popular perception that women aren't strong negotiators, so it's an area that deserves special attention. Whether you want a puppy, a car or resources for the project you're working on, good negotiation skills are key to your success. So be willing to negotiate for both personal and business outcomes – it's fundamental to your *Operating Style* and your potential for success.

The thought of negotiating can be intimidating, conjuring up images of corporate mergers, industrial disputes and United Nations' peace treaties, but don't worry: it doesn't have to be scary. A negotiation is simply the process of coming to an agreement. That's something you do every day, several times a day, although you may not be aware of it.

Every day in your work and personal life, you negotiate with the people around you. On a personal level, you make agreements on many issues, from what you'll have for dinner to what you'll do on the weekend – even who gets to hold the remote control. At work, you also negotiate all the time; every time you come to an agreement about when something is due, what you'll work on next or what time you'll start or finish work, you have negotiated.

Career Chick Hot Tip: Recognize that negotiation is just the process by which you reach an agreement.

Be Willing To Negotiate

Negotiation skills are essential if you want to be successful. You must be able to work with other people and sometimes you'll need to negotiate to do your job effectively. Women are just as capable, competent and successful at negotiations as men – as long as they're prepared to do it. And don't forget to negotiate for personal outcomes, too. For the sake of your career, be willing to negotiate on everything from your salary and your position, to your accountabilities, resources, budget allocations and the time frames to get work done.

Unfortunately, there's a general perception that women aren't as capable at negotiating as men. Clearly they have never met Katie McDonnell. It's frequently claimed that women have lower expectations when it comes to negotiation outcomes and that they are reluctant to engage in the first place, whether the negotiations are for themselves or within the scope of their job. Women often fail to negotiate for sufficient time, budget or resources to deliver what is required, yet male colleagues manage to obtain all the support they want. Why? Men are more likely to ask for what they need.

Women often don't ask. They may think that if they are entitled to extra help, they'll get it. As if! You're just as entitled to whatever it is that you need, or want, as men are. If you need resources, budget or time, think about the implications for your customer, company, team or yourself if you *don't* get what you need. You won't get it if you don't ask for it. You have a responsibility to do the best that you can and that means being prepared to negotiate for the support you need. In the business world, it's expected that you'll ask for what you need to do your job.

Avoiding negotiations is not an option, whether it's for your company or for your own working conditions. When you're negotiating for yourself, the trick is to treat the negotiations as dispassionately as you would negotiate a business issue. Easier said than done, but here's a tip: pretend you're negotiating for someone that you work with, or consider the impact on other people in your life. For example, negotiate your salary on behalf of your partner because it will affect where you live, or negotiate for your vacation time on behalf of your family, who want to spend time with you.

When negotiating for yourself, consider the implications for the business if you don't get what you're asking for. If you are not as well rested or resourced as you need to be to do your job, your work will suffer. You wouldn't give away your company's profit by offering ridiculously low prices to a customer, or spend recklessly on office products without knowing the cost. Neither should you give away your salary, time or vacations. These kinds of negotiations are just as important as those you conduct on behalf of your company.

Career Chick Hot Tip: Negotiate for yourself as you would for someone else.

Ask For What You Need

Just as an aside, many women often do themselves a disservice, which no one ever knows about: paying for petty cash or other expenses out of their own pockets to avoid asking for reimbursement. Can you imagine your male colleagues doing that? No? That's because they don't.

Don't be afraid to ask for what you need. The people that you negotiate with are used to negotiating with others for what they want. This is normal behavior, so don't be timid or embarrassed. Others believe that you are entitled to negotiate; you should, too.

Career Chick Hot Tip: You are entitled to negotiate, so do it.

The Importance For Your Career

Your skill as a negotiator impacts not only on your business and personal outcomes, but also on your reputation and perceived value within the company. That's particularly important if negotiation skills are essential for the job you have or want.

If you are seen as a fair, reasonable and credible negotiator, people will want to work with you. If you always look for win–win outcomes and treat others with integrity, they'll respect you. Even if you are a tough negotiator, you'll attract goodwill if people know that you'll take the time to listen to what they have to say and be fair. Keep in mind the outcome that the other party is hoping for and the fact that a successful outcome will reflect positively on you.

There's no need for your approach to be apologetic, timid or uncertain. Be clear, firm and true to your personal style. Once you commence negotiations be confident, assert yourself and claim your right to be at the negotiating table.

The fact that you're involved in a negotiation means that you have something the other party wants. It could be your knowledge, time or expertise. What you have and what you know is your bargaining power. For instance, if you understand the complexity of a product installation, you can realistically negotiate a schedule with a customer. If you know who is available to work on a project, you'll have more chance of success when you ask them to work with you. If you know your numbers inside out, you'll be in a much more powerful position to ask for additional budget or salary. Knowledge truly is power and it can give you the confidence to negotiate to the best of your ability.

Career Chick Hot Tip: Be confident, assert yourself and claim your right to be at the negotiating table.

Do Your Groundwork

When it comes to negotiation, prepare thoroughly. This will give you the knowledge and confidence to ensure the best possible outcome. To prepare, you need to do some research, formulate your negotiation strategy and practise what you want to say.

Your research may include sourcing background information, finding out about any alternatives that have been considered and the current options. You should also try to find out who is involved, including their history, motivations and hoped-for outcomes. One of the most powerful ways to do this is to talk to people: your colleagues, your manager, your mentor (for some guidance) or people in your network. Track down and read any relevant materials, such as reports, support materials, external research and any other information you can find.

Make sure the data you collect includes accurate and up-to-date information and numbers. If facts talk in a negotiation, then numbers sing. When you know your facts *and* your numbers, you'll be in a better place to support your position. Nothing destroys your credibility faster than quoting incorrect information when you're trying to make a point. Do your research well, so you don't fall into this trap. If you have the facts, it's difficult for others to argue with you. For example, a budget negotiation will be much more successful if you can demonstrate exactly what you need to spend, rather than making an ambit claim. Excellent preparation helps you gain the respect of others.

Career Chick Hot Tip: Do your research – include background information, the alternatives and options, and find out about the people involved.

What You Need To Know

Before you decide how you will negotiate, you must know exactly what you want or are prepared to accept. What exactly do you want to achieve? How important is it to you? Do you have a fall-back position, and what are you prepared to offer? What are you prepared or able to concede or accept? What commitments can you deliver? At what point will you walk away from a negotiation and not do the deal? When you negotiate for yourself you need to know exactly what you want or need and what you can live with. Understanding this helps you take a much stronger position and stand up for yourself.

You also need to be aware of *why* you are negotiating. If you're asking for a pony because you want to enter a horse race, you would be pretty silly to accept a puppy. It's exactly the same if you are negotiating for yourself or on a work issue. If you are negotiating for extra time to complete a project, understanding the consequences if you don't get what you need will help you determine the potential strategies to use in the negotiation. You will also feel more comfortable that, whatever the outcome, you've done the right thing by asking.

If you're negotiating on behalf of your organization, you should be very clear about how much authority you have. There is no point reaching an agreement if your company won't honor the commitments you make. Going beyond your authority and having to backtrack won't enhance your personal credibility. Deferring a negotiation because you need approvals is a standard business practice and reflects that you are being honest. You need people to trust you.

Career Chick Hot Tip: Know what you want and are prepared to accept.

Your Strategy

When you know what you want and what you'll accept, it's time to develop a strategy to get it. Do you ask for more than you want then be prepared to negotiate down? Or do you lay all your cards on the table and make it clear that you've been 100% honest so no further negotiation is possible? There are many different techniques and styles for various negotiating situations. It's easier to decide on the appropriate style when you've completed your research, collected all the information about the issue and the people involved, and know exactly what you want and why you want it.

Your strategy needs to take into account what you are asking for, how you'll ask for it and what you are prepared to accept. There are many techniques for negotiating, so you need to identify the most appropriate ones for the situation and for you personally. Do your research: there are numerous books on the topic or your company may have training materials you can refer to and trusted advisors whose opinion you could seek. If you have a mentor or there is someone whose negotiating skills you admire, don't be afraid to ask for their advice. Most people will be more than happy to share their expertise with you. This will improve your understanding of your options and how to proceed.

The more you know about the issue the easier it is for you to consider which direction the negotiations may take. If you anticipate some alternative scenarios of how things could play out, you can prepare some possible responses. That way you won't be flustered or thrown if something happens that you hadn't planned on. This could still occur, but the more you've thought about it the better you'll react.

The better your preparation and the clearer your strategy, the more in control and confident you will be.

Career Chick Hot Tip: Decide on the most appropriate negotiation strategy.

If Agreement Can't Be Reached

Walking away from a negotiation is a legitimate negotiation technique, but it should only be used carefully when you are *actually* prepared to walk away. Sometimes it may be the only option you have. For instance, if you don't have the authority to offer a certain price to a customer and there are no other areas in which you can negotiate, you may have no choice but to say, *"I'm sorry, we can't do this business."* Women are not confident about saying *"no"*. They're not sure how to do it without causing offence. But it shouldn't stop you from engaging in negotiations. Just because you start a negotiation doesn't mean you have to reach an agreement – as long as you started it in good faith. If you prepare well and understand in what circumstances you'll say no or walk away, you'll be much more confident about your position. Realize that sometimes not being able to reach agreement is part of the territory when it comes to negotiating in business.

Career Chick Hot Tip: Be willing to walk away.

Practise Your Approach

You'll increase your confidence and control if you practise what you want to say and how you want to say it. Practise what you want to say in the appropriate tone so that it sounds natural. You don't want to sound too aggressive or whiny. Practising helps you find the right balance. If you can hear or visualize yourself doing or saying something, it will feel more natural and you'll be more confident when you do it for real.

Career Chick Hot Tip: Practise what you want to say and how you want to say it.

Relationships Matter

Traditionally, competitive, tough negotiations have been seen as the forte of men. As the political leaders and captains of industry throughout history, men have held the positions responsible for negotiations, which has led to them being seen as the superior, tough negotiators of the social, political and business world. But women in the same positions have proved they are just as determined and capable. Baroness Margaret Thatcher did not get the nickname the 'Iron Lady' by being soft and backing down during negotiations.

Women are seen as being softer, people-oriented and more focused on relationships. But this is a positive thing and can provide a real advantage. In negotiations, women are seen as more cooperative than competitive. This can be a distinct benefit.

Women are also known for using these skills to build strong relationships. This, too, can be a definite advantage in the negotiation process. The better your relationship with someone, the harder it is for them to say *"no"* to you, and the more likely you will find a compromise. Your request for an extra three people for your department may be cut back to one, or the one-month extension you requested cut back to one week, but you'll be better off than if you hadn't negotiated at all. Building relationships is often an innate skill for women and it can provide a real advantage in negotiations. People with solid business relationships try harder to find a compromise.

When high-quality relationships exist they influence the negotiation process itself. The relationships you develop and your credibility both help when it comes to sitting down and reaching an agreement. When people like and respect each other, they are more willing to find a mutually beneficial outcome. People don't like to say *"no"* to people they know. If they have to, they are much more likely to make the effort to explore alternatives. The time that you invest in developing relationships pays off big time when it comes to negotiations. On the other hand, the process of negotiating where you demonstrate listening, display your business acumen and behave with integrity is an excellent way to build relationships fast with new contacts.

Career Chick Hot Tip: Build and leverage relationships.

Timing Is Everything

Timing, as they say, is everything, and this also applies to negotiations. You need to pick *when* you negotiate. For example, when should you negotiate your salary for a new job? While you should know the salary range before you make a serious application, you wouldn't usually get into detailed negotiations at the first interview – they need to know that you're worth it first! (Salary is a particularly important issue for Career Chicks, so there's a whole Hot Tips chapter devoted to how to "Earn What You're Worth".)

Likewise, a customer will be less disappointed with a long installation time if the topic is raised as part of the sale negotiation, rather than after the fact. Although, in that case, you'd need to consider your timing and raise the matter after they decide they want your product but before they think you have left it too late and misled them. Similarly, your manager will be much more understanding if he or she is given notice that you need time off or that a project needs more resources or budget.

If you don't raise issues or start negotiations at the appropriate point you may not get the chance again. Later may be too late and put your entire agreement at risk. If there is a deal-breaker, it's better to know early on. Regardless, at least if everyone knows what's going on, they can explore alternatives.

Career Chick Hot Tip: Pick the right time to negotiate.

Honesty Is The Only Policy

Realistic alternatives are also more likely if everyone understands the real situation. Don't be afraid to be honest and to raise difficult issues. The issues are more likely to be resolved and your integrity enhanced. It may not seem so at first, but when others get over the bad news and go into solution mode, they'll appreciate your honesty. If there is a little bit of ranting and raving in the meantime, just realize it's the situation that they're upset with, not you. Okay, they may *seem* upset with you for a little while, but they'll get over it. When you have information that is important, even if it is unpalatable, assemble your facts, pick your timing and be honest. Think through the situation from the other person's perspective and try and move the discussion into solution mode as quickly as you can. Having a reputation for honesty and 'telling it like it is' builds trust and credibility with the people who negotiate and work with you.

Career Chick Hot Tip: Raise and be honest about difficult issues.

Do The Deal

Negotiating is an enormous subject and a vital skill for your career. In this chapter, we've skated over the surface of some of the issues and there is so much more that is important for you to know. However, you will have realized that not only are negotiating skills important for your *Operating Style*, but also that you need to be willing to engage in this process.

When you become known as a first-rate negotiator, you can achieve positive business outcomes, build your reputation and make your negotiating consistent with your overall *Operating Style*. If you act differently in a negotiation, you'll be labeled as inconsistent and unpredictable. Believe in your entitlement to negotiate, develop your skills, apply your communication skills, prepare well and you'll develop a negotiation style that you're comfortable with.

You can bring valuable assets to the negotiation process: your expertise, your skills and the relationships you've developed. Forget competitive men versus cooperative women stereotypes. Remember the purpose of the negotiation, act with honesty and integrity, look for a win–win situation and don't think that the end justifies the means. Be confident to do the deal and you never know … you may actually get what you want. And asking won't do you any harm.

Career Chick Hot Tip: Ask for the pony!

**Career Chick Hot Tips
to negotiate:**

- Recognize that negotiation is just the process by which you reach an agreement.

- Negotiate for yourself as you would for someone else.

- You are entitled to negotiate, so do it.

- Be confident, assert yourself and claim your right to be at the negotiating table.

- Do your research – include background information, the alternatives and options, and find out about the people involved.

- Know what you want and are prepared to accept.

- Decide on the most appropriate negotiation strategy.

- Be willing to walk away.

- Practise what you want to say and how you want to say it.

- Build and leverage relationships.

- Pick the right time to negotiate.

- Raise and be honest about difficult issues.

- Ask for the pony!

Chapter 11

Resolve Conflict

"The Chinese use two brush strokes to write the word 'crisis'. One brush stroke stands for danger; the other for opportunity. In a crisis, be aware of the danger – but recognize the opportunity"

John F Kennedy, 35th US President

Conflicts are not only crisis points, but also opportunities for you to shine in challenging circumstances. Back in ancient history (way back in 1962), John F. Kennedy successfully resolved the Cuban Missile Crisis – a defining event in his presidency. While he showed he appreciated the seriousness of the situation (a nuclear war may have occurred if the crisis had not been peacefully resolved) and his leadership style was considered consultative yet strong, it was his *approach* to conflict resolution that significantly affected how he was judged. Likewise, how you approach, manage and resolve conflict will influence your business reputation.

The way you resolve conflict in the workplace is a defining characteristic of your personal *Operating Style* and requires you to draw on every communication and negotiation skill that you have. Conflict resolution is the ultimate form of negotiation, and one that you simply can't shy away from.

How you manage your role in a conflict is important to the way that you are seen to manage yourself and your relationships with others. Your role may be as an arbitrator in someone else's conflict, for example, between staff members, colleagues or even senior managers. Conflict can occur within your organization, or between your organization and its customers or suppliers. Alternatively you may need to resolve a situation between yourself and another person or group. Regardless of the type of conflict or the parties involved, handling these situations well can impact positively on how others judge your performance and skills.

How you *handle* conflict can impact your reputation more than how you resolve it. Women are often seen as being too emotional and/ or too soft to deal with conflict. Being emotional at work can create a negative impression about your ability to operate in the rough-and-tumble world of business. Developing your skills will address any negative perceptions others have about your ability to negotiate (based solely on your gender).

Career Chick Hot Tip: Develop your communication and negotiation skills to resolve conflict.

Conflict Happens

Some conflict is healthy. It can stimulate ideas, creativity and healthy debate for problem-solving. But when you hear people explain their conflicts as *"creative differences"* through gritted teeth or pursed lips, then it has, perhaps, gone too far. Conflict is not healthy when it prevents business from progressing or damages relationships between the people involved.

From a work perspective, conflict can be frustrating because it can delay a project, cause rework and even stop what you are working on from moving ahead. The impact on relationships can be even worse. The time you invest to build relationships with your colleagues, managers, customers or suppliers can all be undone if a disagreement gets out of hand. None of these outcomes helps you achieve success in your business life.

Yet conflict is inevitable. As the famous French general Napoleon Bonaparte once said, *"The people to fear are not those who disagree with you, but those who disagree with you and are too cowardly to let you know."* Conflict provides the opportunity for everyone to negotiate and reach an agreement, rather than having relationships deteriorate due to unspoken issues.

So, think about how you deal with conflict, and how you are seen by others to deal with it. Do you want to be seen as someone who uses humor to gently diffuse situations? Or would you rather take a factual, solution-based approach to get business back on track, so everybody is comfortable with what's going on? Either approach is fine. Alternatively, would you pull a face to show your displeasure and have everyone around you second-guess what you think? Or yell at people until they do what you want? This last one is a real winner; everybody loves to be yelled at. Not. The choice is yours, so consciously develop your style until it becomes a habit and be confident that your skills in this area complement your business reputation.

Career Chick Hot Tip: Enhance your business reputation with a positive approach to conflict resolution.

A Fact Of Life

Conflict is a fact of life. It can occur when people are working towards totally different goals or outcomes. This incompatibility can put them at odds with each other. Other times, people have a history of not having worked well together in the past to the point where their relationship has broken down. Usually this relates to some past conflict that was not resolved. This can make it incredibly difficult for people to work together on a new venture. Simple misunderstandings can also cause conflict. For instance, someone may have been inadvertently left off an email trail and unaware of the progress that has been made on an issue. The next meeting they may come in 'guns blazing' because they think it is still unresolved.

Conflict can be positive. It can occur when the environment is very creative or when the parties share goals and are extremely passionate about an issue. But it can also be negative and destructive. It can have serious implications for the business if it causes non-delivery to customers, deadlines to be missed or costs to blow out. These can, and will, tarnish your personal reputation and business relationships. Customers, other staff, suppliers and you will all suffer the consequences. Don't let conflict stop you from delivering your objectives. Imagine the impact on your career if people think you can't negotiate to resolve conflict and meet your accountabilities. Don't be seen as someone who avoids difficult issues.

There are many types of roles you can play when conflict occurs, and your style needs to adapt to these differing circumstances. You may be the cause of the conflict, or the recipient, or the person with the responsibility to resolve the conflict situation. Where you have the power, information or role accountability it's up to you to sort it out.

Career Chick Hot Tip: Be prepared to deal with conflict.

Approach Conflict Strategically

The best approach to conflict is to be strategic. It is unlikely that all aspects of a conflict are equally important. Decide early on what must be resolved and which battles you really need to win. Pick what is most important to you and the business. You may win the battle but lose the war, so to speak, if you try and focus equally on every small issue. There may be areas where you are prepared to concede for the sake of a relationship or expediency in reaching agreement on your important issue.

Career Chick Hot Tip: Approach conflict strategically and focus on what is important.

The Earlier The Better

If possible, the best approach is to resolve important issues early. The longer it's unresolved, the bigger a significant area of conflict gets, even if only in people's minds. The saying about 'making a mountain out of a molehill' describes how little things can be exaggerated. A small misunderstanding left unresolved, can grow out of all proportion the longer people think about it, leading to more issues, as others ask, *"Why wasn't this solved earlier?"* The earlier the resolution, the less potential damage. Relationships stay intact, negative business impacts are minimized and people are more willing to compromise. Plus you are seen as more resolute and a stronger leader.

Career Chick Hot Tip: Resolve issues as early as possible.

Know Your Facts

Like any negotiation, the first step is to prepare: make sure you know your facts. You'll look like a goose (long neck, small brain) if you try and resolve conflict with incorrect information or insufficient research. You may even damage your credibility if you haven't spoken to all the stakeholders. Speaking to the relevant people and asking questions reflects favorably on you. When you know your facts you can be confident that you have the information you need, and that there won't be any surprises later on. You'll also have the support of those who think they need to be consulted.

Career Chick Hot Tip: Know your facts and consult stakeholders.

Develop Alternatives

As you would for any negotiation, it's vital to identify the key issues and develop some potential alternatives to resolve the situation. For the best chance of success your potential resolution should look for a win for all parties, be expressed in the language that the people involved are comfortable with and allow others to save face. Men are action-oriented and appreciate solutions that present what needs to be done. If you can develop alternatives that allow the other people involved to have a choice, or at least be involved in the decision-making process, they'll appreciate it; this will also assist with any big egos involved.

Career Chick Hot Tip: Develop solution-focused alternatives where everyone wins.

Be Generous

Often, whether someone is right or wrong about a business issue ceases to be the key matter to resolve the conflict. Anyone can be embarrassed if they are shown to be wrong. This can lead to stubborn behavior and unwillingness to concede even when they know they are wrong or there is a better alternative. Men, in particular, are extremely conscious of how they are seen. Be aware of the egos involved and explore the options to help others save face. Be generous – just don't come across as subservient.

One tactic is to have the conversations you need to have discreetly, one-on-one. This removes the potential to embarrass someone in front of other people. Think about where and how you have the meeting. There's no point having a confidential and private conversation to resolve an issue if everyone in the office knows where, when and what is being discussed behind closed doors.

Approaching issues from the other person's perspective is a highly effective way to resolve conflict. They may be adamant that they are right for many reasons. They may have data that supports their position or information about the people involved. Others may have different alliances, experiences and history that influence their perspective. The right way to resolve a conflict with one person can be different for another. Whether you think the other person is right or wrong, try to appreciate the issue from their perspective.

Change can be particularly challenging for men, especially those who have significant experience in their field and have successfully operated in a certain way. All of a sudden, along comes a generation of Career Chicks who don't seem to have the experience and skills that they do. When you think of it is this way, it's understandable, although not satisfactory, that there are resentments and conflict in the workplace. Showing you have respect for the experience and success of others shows them you are focused on the issue, not making a personal judgment.

Asking questions can be a positive way to convey your appreciation of their position. *"I understand you have experience with these issues. Can you tell me how you approached this previously?"* or *"How have you approached this situation in the past?"* is respectful of past experience and you may learn something, too. Acknowledging past successes, experience, expertise and skills is appreciated by everyone. It allows you to recognize the past, accept the other person's contribution, then deal with the issue at hand.

> *Career Chick Hot Tip:* Be generous in your acknowledgment of past successes, experience, expertise and skills.

Tough Conversations

If you are in conflict with someone else try to think about what's going on from their perspective. Put yourself in their shoes. Why are they approaching the situation in this way? What are they concerned about? What are their motivations? How does it impact them if they don't get it resolved to their satisfaction? Whether you think you understand the issue or not, talk to the other person, ask them and you're on your way to a resolution.

Some conversations will not be comfortable for you or the other person. But if you don't have them, you risk the problem getting worse and having a greater impact. It takes courage to initiate a difficult conversation, but if you make sure you have the facts and approach it in a business-like and respectful manner, the potential benefits of a resolution can outweigh the initial discomfort.

If this is a bit daunting, set up the conversation in advance. One way to do this is a short, well-worded email to say that you are concerned about the business issue and would like five minutes (or however long you need; the shorter the amount of time, the more likely you are to get it) to understand their position on the issue. A short email can work if you are concerned about what type of reaction you'll get if you call.

The best technique though is to pick up the phone, take a deep breath, and ask for their time. Practise what you are going to say if you are really nervous. For example, *"Hi, it's <<whoever you are>>. This is just a quick call about the <<XYZ issue>>. Would you have five minutes today to catch up as I would really like to understand the issue from your perspective?"* However they respond, it's unlikely to be as terrible as you imagined. If you do ask for time to understand the other person's issue, make sure you ask appropriate questions and listen to the answers.

Alternatively you may have information that the other person needs to know. This can provide a subtle change to your approach: *"Hi, I have some new information on the <<XYZ issue>>. Would you have ten minutes today so I can give you a quick run-through?"* If they say, *"No"*, ask if you can provide it to them on email? Or send something in the mail.

Depending on your relationship with the person, you may choose different locations to have these, sometimes, tough meetings. If it is someone more senior and very busy, his or her office is likely to be the best place. If it's a colleague, a meeting room may be a neutral venue. If it's someone that you have an existing relationship with, offering to buy them a coffee and stepping out of the office may take the heat out of the situation. And it's a lot easier to extend five minutes to 20 if you talk over a latte!

Career Chick Hot Tip: Don't put off the tough conversations.

It's Business

Whatever your role, and whatever the issue, keep in mind that it's only business. It's not about you, personally. It may have a personal impact on you, but whatever happens it's not a reflection of you as a human being, your worth or your value. If you can avoid taking an issue to heart, even if you really want to, you can approach a situation more calmly and focus on the facts rather than the emotions.

Men often see conflict as a necessary part of the game and the process to reach agreements. Men are comfortable that conflict is part of the process of negotiation and problem-solving. Conflict, for them, is all about the issue, and when the issue is resolved the conflict is forgotten. They do not, usually, take the conflict personally. As long as you don't make the mistake of hurting their ego or pride, men won't resent that they had a conflict with you. They expect conflict to occur and be resolved as part of what happens in business.

Career Chick Hot Tip: Don't take it personally.

Email War Games

There are many positive things you can do to resolve conflict, such as being proactive, dealing with situations quickly, having the tough conversations and considering the situation from the other person's point of view. However, there are some things you want to avoid so they don't creep into your *Operating Style*.

The first one is dealing with conflict by email. Don't get into an email war with anyone. The opportunities for misunderstanding and misinterpretation by email are many. What may sound one way in person, can be taken quite another way by email. Don't write anything that can be misinterpreted. Proof-read any potentially contentious email or, even better, get someone else to check it and ensure the meaning is clear. And don't reply to an email when you are angry or emotional. Go for a walk, do something else and, if possible, leave it until the next day before you respond. Angry exchanges back and forth will ignite, not resolve, a situation.

Also be aware of who has been copied on an email. Sometimes an email discussion escalates into a bigger issue if people who were cc'd get involved. Emailing people and copying their manager is a heavy-handed approach: they'll not only need to resolve the issue with you, but also explain themselves to their boss. They won't thank you for that. The best option is to get on the phone to the person involved. If this is not possible and you have to respond by email, do it without an audience: delete the cc'd email addresses and try to resolve the issue with the other party directly. You can then tell the others who were originally cc'd the resolution. This can only reflect well on you, as you demonstrate your ability to develop solutions and resolve issues.

Often public email battles are part of an organization's culture and are defended on the basis that they keep everyone in the loop or save duplicated communications. The truth is, issue management by email can literally take on a life of its own, waste valuable time (both yours and the company's) and blow issues out of proportion. Even if it's the culture where you work, you are responsible for your personal *Operating Style* and you don't have to play their game. Email war is not a respectful way to negotiate or resolve a conflict.

Career Chick Hot Tip: Don't play email wars.

Best To Avoid

Don't bring unrelated issues into a conflict-resolution discussion. Men will think that you're not focused on the topic at hand. You, like many women, may be good at multi-tasking, but you don't need to draw attention to the fact when you're in the middle of resolving a conflict. Men will think you're not focused on the topic at hand. Focus on the issue, not crossing things off your to-do list or solving other issues at the same time. All that does is complicate the situation.

And no matter what people around you might be doing, don't get involved in office gossip about the issue or the person involved in a conflict. At best you are wasting your time, at worst you may damage someone's reputation, including your own. Loose lips can disclose information that shouldn't be publicly known, embarrass someone or even put a commercial negotiation at risk.

Finally, don't be tempted to brag about how successful you were or how you outwitted, outsmarted or out-negotiated the other guy. The short-term benefit of having the admiration of your colleagues is overshadowed if you do this at the expense of another person. Worse still, they may find out what you have been saying (and you can bet they will).

Career Chick Hot Tip: Avoid unrelated issues, gossip or bragging at the expense of others.

When The Dust Settles

After a conflict has been resolved it's a great opportunity to check on the status of a relationship. This allows you to determine if there are any unresolved issues and demonstrate that your approach was all business and that you value your relationship with the individual. A simple question like, *"That got a bit heated for a while there, are we okay?"* or *"I'm glad we got through that issue, are you happy to continue to work as we planned on the next stage?"* can open up the communication. Otherwise, a simple *"Yeah, yeah, we're good"* response lets you know that your relationship is intact. If you get a negative response, at least you have uncovered another issue and have the opportunity to clear the air and get back to having a good business relationship. You don't have to be friends with the people you work with, but healthy relationships allow you to be productive. Building and maintaining relationships is the natural forte of Career Chicks.

When a conflict has been resolved, it's essential that you honor any agreements and commitments that you have made. Once you have a solution, a plan and agreed milestones allow you to demonstrate your progress and cement your credibility. Always thank people for their part in resolving a conflict. This follow-through signals that the issue has been resolved and the conflict is over. It reinforces that there is a mutual, beneficial agreement and that you appreciate and value their contribution.

Career Chick Hot Tip: Check on relationships, follow through on commitments and say thank you when a conflict has been resolved.

Don't Hold Grudges

When conflict occurs some women assign blame for the problem to the person they believe caused the problem or made it difficult to resolve. After the issue is resolved, they may hang on to those resentful feelings. To be honest, women are often good at holding a grudge long after an issue has been resolved.

When tempers flare in the heat of the moment it can be all too easy to lay blame or make personal accusations. You need to be aware that 'business is business', not a judgment on you, and instinctively apply this to your reactions to other people and difficult situations. Men see the issues as the issues, not as a reflection of you or them. Once a conflict is over they get on with business and ask, *"What's next?"* There's no need to personalize issues. You don't need to feel awful about yourself or other people.

If you do this you hurt no one but yourself. Holding a grudge is a negative, tiring activity, and causes the holder to feel anxiety, self-doubt and resentment. It damages relationships and causes problems when you have to work with the other person again. This is negative for the business and for you. It also just looks petty and gives women in the workplace a poor reputation. Men can be wary about women working together when they are concerned about this kind of behavior. This is one lesson to take from men at the end of a conflict; put it behind you and ask, *"What's next?"*

Career Chick Hot Tip: Don't hold grudges, put conflict behind you and ask, *"What's next?"*

Career Chick Hot Tips to resolve conflict:

- Develop your communication and negotiation skills to resolve conflict.

- Enhance your business reputation with a positive approach to conflict resolution.

- Be prepared to deal with conflict.

- Approach conflict strategically and focus on what is important.

- Resolve issues as early as possible.

- Know your facts and consult stakeholders.

- Develop solution-focused alternatives where everyone wins.

- Be generous in your acknowledgment of past successes, experience, expertise and skills.

- Don't put off the tough conversations.

- Don't take it personally.

- Don't play email wars.

- Avoid unrelated issues, gossip or bragging at the expense of others.

- Check on relationships, follow through on commitments and say thank you when a conflict has been resolved.

- Don't hold grudges, put conflict behind you and ask, *"What's next?"*

Chapter 12

Lead

"People think that at the top there isn't much room. They tend to think of it as an Everest. My message is that there is tons of room at the top"

Margaret Thatcher, former British Prime Minister

As the first, and so far only, female British Prime Minister, Margaret Thatcher wielded tremendous influence. Known as the 'Iron Lady' for her stand against the Soviet Union, she played a significant role in international politics, finding an ally in US President Ronald Reagan, as well as defeating Argentina in the battle for the Falkland Islands. She also broke new ground by driving an extensive program to privatize British industry, which reduced the Government's role and broke the power of the trade unions.

Some people credit Thatcher's political skills for her rise to power and others to her 'luck' of being in the right place at the right time. Either way she made the most of opportunities as they presented themselves because she was skilled, she networked and she placed no limitations on what she could achieve. Like her or not, she certainly had an impact. You, too, can have an impact in your chosen field when you develop your ability to lead.

Leadership is not about the big office, the perks of the job, and the number of people who report to you or your title. True leadership is about how you positively influence others to achieve outcomes. No matter what job you have, you can incorporate leadership skills into your *Operating Style*. This chapter is designed to provide Career Chicks like you with practical Hot Tips to develop your leadership skills and also to highlight some areas that should be on your radar – some particularly relevant to women.

Prepare For Base Camp

The comparison Thatcher makes between reaching the top and climbing a mountain like Everest is an appropriate one. Regardless of whether it's in politics or business the analogy is the same. There's only one way to achieve either of those goals: preparation. Before climbers set out to make their final ascent on a summit, they will have spent months, maybe even years, preparing to ensure they have the best chance of success. Fitness training, equipment tests and assembling an appropriately skilled team are just some of the things that climbers do before they leave home. Once they get to the mountain they establish their base camp before they start their slow but steady climb, which may involve potential avalanches, bad weather and the challenges of altitude. How they deal with these challenges depends on their skills and the depth and breadth of preparation they have made.

Similarly, the development of your skills to lead and influence others begins well before you take on senior positions and management accountabilities. You may or may not be in a formal leadership, management or supervisory position right now, but if you are ... Congratulations! You will already have come across some of the complexities of authority that have nothing to do with your field of expertise and everything to do with the variables of working with other people. For instance, that people just won't do what you want them to do, and there are many personalities and personal circumstances that impact what happens in the workplace. If you're not in a formal management position, you'll probably be aware that you can influence the actions of others and day-to-day decisions through what you do and say. The ability to impact or influence others is called leadership.

Career Chick Hot Tip: Recognize your ability to lead no matter what position you're in.

Girl Germs

To be a respected leader as your career progresses, don't let gender be an issue. However, other people may have their own ideas about how women should behave. Often, the advice is contradictory. On one hand men may say, *"Women shouldn't try to act like men."* Do they mean women shouldn't make lots of money and have a successful career? Another man will tell you, *"Women should try to be more like men."* Do they mean they should be less emotional and play more golf? The only thing that's clear is that men don't have the magic answer or even a consistent view about how they want female leaders to act and behave. Usually their response is a reaction to seeing a particular woman manage a situation or team in a way they didn't like. Their judgments are formed on the performance of individuals they have known.

However, the confused expectations of others and the stereotypes about the role of women are partly to blame for why women may not progress. Women are often seen as not being strategic or tough enough to 'make it' at the top, a reputation not supported by the performance of senior women – yet still the view persists.

It's also argued that the career breaks women take to have children or care for elderly relatives interrupt their careers and that they lose valuable experience during this time. It may seem hard to believe, but not so long ago, some managers wouldn't promote women on the basis that they were of child-bearing age. Fortunately, EEO laws have gone a long way to stamp out this kind of discrimination, but some managers still think those reasons justify excluding women from senior positions – although you won't hear them admitting it.

Like everyone, men may fear change. Seeing many women in senior positions would be a big change (unfortunately) for business at this time. Like keeping away from 'girl germs' in the schoolyard it may be easier for them to either run away or just try to maintain the status quo. But don't despair; you can do something about this by developing your own leadership skills. Change can happen, one Career Chick at a time.

The opportunity is for you to determine what kind of leader you want to be, to develop your skills and be judged on your own merits. Regardless of how much you still have to learn, you must assert your right to lead. Be confident and sure of yourself, at least in public, and show others that you have faith in your ability to do the job. Others won't have confidence in your leadership if you don't.

One slip-up that women make (often to avoid seeming arrogant or conceited) is to be apologetic or self-deprecating, making jokes or light-hearted comments at their own expense. Don't do it! You may have doubts about your ability but you don't have to share them! Instead of undermining your leadership, draw on the knowledge that you deserve to be in the role or position of influence and just get on with the job. Doing the job well sends the message that you have the right to be in it. If you're having a little crisis of self-confidence take comfort in the fact that someone else has demonstrated faith in your ability by putting you in that position. The more you get on with what you need to do, and the more successful you are, the more your confidence will increase and you won't need to waste time doubting yourself.

Career Chick Hot Tip: Be confident in your ability and assert your right to lead.

Your Style

Knowing how to act, react and be perceived as a good leader does not happen on the day you are promoted to your first management position. You don't wake up that morning and suddenly know what to do. Actually, you're more likely to convince yourself that you have no idea what you're doing! A management position does not automatically come with a manual telling you how to lead and influence other people. Rather, as you gain experience working with others, you tend to subconsciously realize what you do that influences others to work towards the same outcomes. Repeating those successful behaviors contributes to your leadership style.

No matter where you are on the leadership journey right now, start developing your leadership *Operating Style*. There are millions, probably billions of words, written about leadership, so read, learn and observe as much as you possibly can about this critical topic.

If you are working in an administrative position you have the ability to influence others who work with you. How? By the attitude you take to what happens in your area or department. Are you positive about supporting your department to achieve its goals? Or are you critical about senior management when you talk to your colleagues? They may seem like little things in your current role, but people will remember your attitude when you move up in your career or have to persuade them to do what you need. The colleagues that gossip with you now may well be leaders in the future or in a position to make decisions about your career prospects.

If you're not in management, there are a number of things you can do to develop and demonstrate your ability to lead. Whatever your current job you can start by:

- showing less experienced people how something is done

- talking through alternative options when a colleague is undecided
- helping someone resolve an issue by providing a different perspective
- building relationships with people in other departments
- talking positively about what your team or department is doing, and
- learning how to handle budgets and develop management skills.

All of these behaviors are relatively easy to incorporate into your daily activities. Make them part of your *Operating Style* and you'll have a solid set of leadership behaviors that you can use and point to as proof of your ability to lead. Most importantly, you can put these into practice no matter what role you are in now.

Career Chick Hot Tip: Develop your leadership style now.

Lead As A Manager

When you're not in management and your colleagues aren't pulling their weight it's tempting to think, *"If only I were their manager, I would just tell them what to do."* But when you make it to that position, the real fun begins. People don't like being told what to do. It's an ongoing challenge to lead people who have different personalities, skills and experiences. You'll need to keep developing and refining your leadership skills and style to adapt to new situations. Just when you think you've got the leadership thing sorted someone new will come along or circumstances will change again and you'll need a whole new set of strategies.

As a manager, you need to combine your skills to influence, communicate and negotiate. The earlier you focus on how to combine these skills and develop your own style of leadership, the more naturally it will come to you and the better you'll be at applying your skills to new situations. Although you'll keep developing these skills throughout your career, you may never feel that you have it right!

Career Chick Hot Tip: Combine your skills to influence, communicate and negotiate.

The Environment

One of the greatest assets you can have as a leader is to be perceptive. Be aware of both the environment and the people around you. Use your intuition to notice when things are going well to keep projects moving, or pick up the signs when things have stalled or people have issues that need to be resolved. One way to develop this ability is to apply your communication skills. Ask questions, listen to the answers, watch the body language of others and recognize when and how you need to intervene. People appreciate when you listen and understand the situation from their perspective. You may not always be able to give people what they want, but if you listen, they'll be much more receptive to your decisions. If you practise these skills all the time, your leadership skills will be second nature by the time you get to a management position.

Career Chick Hot Tip: Tune into your environment and the people around you.

Self-Management

How you manage yourself and your relationships with others can significantly impact your leadership style. The way you manage your own affairs can set expectations for potential staff about your management skills. If you're disorganized, always losing things, stressed and work ridiculous hours, others will be concerned that this is how you would manage them. If you are disorganized, can they rely on you to prioritize the work? Will they always feel under pressure and not be able to plan anything after work? Anyone considering your promotion into a management position may think, *"If she always seems stressed how is she going to handle the extra responsibility?"*

On the other hand if you appear cool, calm and collected, others will feel confident that you can capably lead a team. It doesn't matter whether you actually feel cool, calm and collected, you just need to act as if you are! The more you behave that way, the more comfortable you'll be and, hey presto, eventually that'll become your leadership style.

How you allocate and prioritize your time is also important. If you have a superwoman complex (and who doesn't?) you can try the 'do everything' approach. Unfortunately, there's a high chance that this won't work. You simply can't do everything. Work is too complex for you to have the skills and capacity to do everything yourself. Part of your job as a leader is to delegate work and secure resources. There are some key management skills and activities you'll need to develop: assessing employees' workloads, skill sets and experience levels, then assigning the work and supporting your team. Your success will be judged on how you lead your team to achieve their goals. To do this you must be prepared to manage yourself well, too.

Career Chick Hot Tip: Be cool, calm and collected to promote confidence in your ability.

Listen Up

Leadership is not some Machiavellian dark art where you manipulate people to do what you want. But as a manager, you do need to influence your staff, and rightly so. Hopefully you work with people who have the skills and knowledge to do their jobs. They, like you, want those assets to be valued. They have opinions based on their experience and it's appropriate that they share them. Your opinions, as a leader, may be 100% right today, but that won't always be the case.

It's amazing what you can learn when you take the time to ask questions and listen to the answers. You may learn something new or, at least, learn what's top of mind for them. You'll also hear the kind of language they use to express themselves, helping you to use a similar communication style when you talk to them. Your credibility will go sky-high if you modify a proposal or decision on the basis of what you have learnt from your team or colleagues. They will feel valued because you listened to them.

Career Chick Hot Tip: Listen and learn.

Clear Instructions

Sometimes though you will have to deliver instructions or make decisions. If you need something done, you don't want your requests to be taken as suggestions. The best approach, particularly with men, is to be very clear and give specific instructions. All adults resent being told what to do. Men like it even less when it's a woman doing the telling. Clarity is the key. There should be no ambiguity or wriggle-room. When you check on something you need urgently, you don't want a response like, *"Oh, I thought that was just a suggestion."*

Instructions should be specific and action-oriented, just be courteous and check that there aren't more urgent issues that mean you should reassign the task or review the timeline. As tasks get more complex and the skill level of the people required for the job increases, the level of detail that you need to give will decrease. But the premise is the same: be action-oriented and specific in your requests.

It's the same when you set performance expectations. Make it clear what accountabilities you are assigning, the deliverables or outcomes you expect and the dates they are required by. Put them in writing, so there's no ambiguity or chance of *"I thought you meant ..."* excuses in the future. This is just one of many good management practices. It's particularly relevant when you have males who work for you, some of whom may be tempted to 'test' just how strong you are as a manager by seeing how much they can get away with. This is more likely to happen when you're new to management and haven't yet established the boundaries of your *Operating Style*. Telling a member of your team, *"You need to achieve a 10% improvement on costs this year"* is clearer than, *"You need to reduce costs"*, which could be open to huge debate later down the track. Set clear accountabilities to treat each person as an individual within the context of the goals that the individual, team or department is striving to achieve.

Be fair in performance negotiations, but be reasonable within the context of your deliverables and the entire team. A reputation for being fair and reasonable is preferable to being seen as a 'softie' – which may also be attributed to you being a woman. On the other hand, a tough stance may earn you an 'Iron Lady' reputation, like Margaret Thatcher, where your style is again linked to being a woman. Chances are your style will be scrutinized no matter what you do, so the more comfortable you are with yourself the easier it is to be clear when setting performance expectations.

Career Chick Hot Tip: Be crystal clear when you set accountabilities and assign tasks.

Coaching And Feedback

When you give your team clear goals and defined milestones, they'll be more receptive to being coached or guided towards achieving what is required. Essentially you won't be able to teach anyone anything they're not prepared to learn. But the right approach can influence how receptive they'll be to learning from you.

When men work for women they may feel the need to defend their ego. Unenlightened maybe, but many men are concerned about what others will think of them if they willingly take orders from a woman. Plenty of positive, public feedback helps to alleviate those ego issues because people will feel they are being recognized as successful. It also helps if any advice, suggestions or negative feedback are given in private. Catherine the Great, who reigned over Russia in the late 18th century, is credited with saying, *"I praise loudly, I blame softly."* And that is still good advice today. The same is true when you need to deliver feedback. Be clear, direct and unambiguous.

Career Chick Hot Tip: Praise loudly, blame softly.

Tough Stuff

Your leadership style also includes how you approach and respond to difficult situations. As a leader you need to apply your negotiation and conflict resolution skills to handle challenges. Despite the discomfort you may feel or your reluctance to be critical, it's the leader's job to manage the hard stuff. This can range from performance issues, conduct issues or even personal problems that impact work. The best approach is to deal with these situations as early as possible and discuss them in private. Issues don't disappear by themselves. Unresolved issues and poor performing staff can also leave you vulnerable to being seen as a weak leader, who can't take the appropriate action for the situation. For your own sake and that of your organization make sure you deal with tough situations.

This raises a question about another aspect of your leadership style: how 'tough' do you want to be seen to be? It's likely that you want to be tough enough to be able to defend your position and decisions, yet flexible enough to listen to feedback and take on suggestions. You don't need to be tough just for the sake of it.

Then again, you don't want to be manipulated by others to make soft decisions so that people like you. As our pal for this chapter, Margaret (as in Thatcher, former British Prime Minister), once said, *"If you set out to be liked, you would be prepared to compromise on anything at any time, and you would achieve nothing."* You don't become a leader to make friends or be popular. But you do need to strike the right balance between having a single-minded focus on the business goals and still treating people as individuals.

Career Chick Hot Tip: Deal with difficult issues, early.

Manage Up

Success as a leader depends not only on how you influence colleagues or those who report to you, but also those more senior to you, whose support you require. This is often referred to as 'managing up'. Most women prefer to just do what needs to be done not talk about what they've done. But the reality is that you need to use your success to develop a positive profile. Otherwise, your good deeds will go unnoticed and you'll lose the opportunity to enhance your reputation. It's also likely that your team or project's work will also go unnoticed. This can have a negative impact not only on you and the team, but also on the business if future requests for similar projects, budget or resources are denied because no one knows about your past success. Everyone has someone above them to demonstrate their success to. Your manager has a manager, and even Chief Executive Officers (CEOs) must satisfy a board of directors.

The ability to 'manage up' involves more than just making sure the next tier knows how successful you, your department or your project are for the business. It also involves educating more senior people about what is happening to support the decisions they make. It all comes down to good communication. Use your listening and questioning skills to understand the issues, but be able to articulate your position, too. The time and effort you devote to educating your manager and securing the resources or support you need can be the difference between the success or failure of an initiative – and your reputation and credibility. The way that you do that (and the fact that you do it at all) will show you are a leader.

Career Chick Hot Tip: Educate and communicate to influence and support senior stakeholders.

Thoughtful Deeds

As a leader or manager, it pays to be thoughtful. Successful leaders are often very skilful in recognizing events and milestones that are important to the people around them. You can send birthday cards, acknowledge significant anniversaries (such as joining the company or department) and remember to say thank you. These thoughtful gestures are really appreciated by the recipients. A birthday or thank you card sent to a team member or colleague will often be proudly displayed on their desk for many months. Ok, maybe they aren't fastidious about tidying up, but it's still a constant reminder about how thoughtful you were. Don't shy away from making these thoughtful acknowledgements for fear it'll be seen as a 'chick-like' thing to do. If you are clear and consistent in managing performance and people issues, you can afford to be thoughtful when it comes to acknowledging what is important to others. If a girl can't do girlie things who on earth will?

You can even develop a process so that you remember to be thoughtful. Diarize the birthdays or anniversaries of your team members or colleagues, write all your cards at the beginning of the month or set up emails to be sent on the required dates. This doesn't have to be time-consuming or an onerous task but it will pay off in the goodwill it earns you.

Career Chick Hot Tip: Be thoughtful and recognize events and milestones that are important to the people around you.

Share Success

Being known as someone who shares successes and recognition with your team, or those you have worked with, reflects positively on your leadership style. Once you have led or been part of a team that achieved results, ensure the success is visible in the business. Quantify the success, acknowledge those who contributed, reward high performers and celebrate with those involved. These are all essential tasks for leaders.

Career Chick Hot Tip: Acknowledge, reward and share success.

No Room For Modesty

Recognize your own role as a leader and don't be too modest to take accolades for your leadership skills. If you've done a good job, be proud of it. Your male colleagues would be. Don't diminish your achievements by being modest. Take the praise you deserve. At the same time be receptive to feedback and continuously work to develop your leadership skills and style. This really is a never-ending story ... the more you work at it the more you'll find that you want to improve. It's just like the climbers who make it to the top of Everest, then set new goals to climb a certain number of peaks or a mountain on every continent. The satisfaction you gain from all that hard work makes you want to keep getting better and better. And remember to keep the challenge in perspective, like mountain climber David Breashears. He climbed Everest, not once, but twice. No mean feat, but Breashears' view of the mountain was: *"Don't forget it's really just a big pile of rocks."*[1]

Career Chick Hot Tip: Go after your Everest!

Career Chick Hot Tips to lead:

- Recognize your ability to lead no matter what position you're in.

- Be confident in your ability and assert your right to lead.

- Develop your leadership style now.

- Combine your skills to influence, communicate and negotiate.

- Tune into your environment and the people around you.

- Be cool, calm and collected to promote confidence in your ability.

- Listen and learn.

- Be crystal clear when you set accountabilities and assign tasks.

- Praise loudly, blame softly.

- Deal with difficult issues, early.

- Educate and communicate to influence and support senior stakeholders.

- Be thoughtful and recognize events and milestones that are important to the people around you.

- Acknowledge, reward and share success.

- Go after your Everest!

Chapter 13

Get Back Up

"It is not enough to know how to ride.
You must also know how to fall"

Mexican proverb

Picture a cowboy from the old Western movies (think John Wayne), his face hidden by his Stetson hat, ambling across the desert on a horse. Suddenly, without warning, the horse stumbles on a rock hidden in the sand. The cowboy, realizing he's falling off the horse, manages to position himself so that he lands as safely as possible. Once on the ground he checks that he has no broken bones, then slowly stands up, dusts himself off and climbs back on the horse to continue his journey. He may be a little bruised, but he's still able to keep going. Not only did he manage the situation so that the consequences were minimized, but he also learnt from the experience.

You may not be working in a desert and hopefully you're not wearing a Stetson hat to work, but the analogy of this story is relevant to the workplace. The skills and approach implicit in both the Mexican proverb and the cowboy story are the same ones you need to manage career disappointments and keep going on your journey.

No matter how prepared you are, how hard you work and how much you know, there comes a time when things don't go exactly as planned. Disappointments are part of business life, but you can incorporate your ability to manage these disappointments – and how you are seen to manage them – as part of your *Operating Style*.

No matter how hard you try, you can't control every variable that influences your work life. In any organization there are politics, personalities and conflicting priorities to deal with, so not every outcome can be positive for you as an individual. Often decisions are made that have absolutely nothing to do with you, so there's nothing you could have done to change the situation. Other times you may not have made the best choices or decisions to achieve what you wanted. Regardless of the cause, disappointments happen. The important thing is to know how to manage them and how to get back up on your feet again.

The impact of challenges and disappointments, your attitude to them and the skills and techniques required to overcome them are the same for everyone, male or female. Everyone needs to develop their skills so that they can deal with bad stuff when it happens. Like the Mexican proverb says, you must know how to fall so that you can ride as safely as possible. That way you can minimize the damage and get back up again.

You need the skills to help you get back up (whether there's a horse involved or not) to be able to:

- recognize hazardous situations
- manage the situation with minimal impact
- check you're okay
- dust yourself off, and
- get back on your way.

Learning and applying these techniques will ensure there's minimal harm to both yourself and your career prospects, plus dealing with disappointments in this way can positively impact your reputation. Being able to manage yourself in hard times is a skill that's often very much admired. Not only will you be older and wiser, but also your positive management of the situation will reflect well on you, and you'll be able to share your experience with those less experienced than yourself.

Career Chick Hot Tip: Learn how to fall.

Hazardous Situations

Disappointments may include missing out on a promotion, a bonus or a salary increase that you were certain you deserved. They can also include receiving negative feedback about your performance to having your ideas or proposals rejected, right through to subtler forms of rejection, like not having your contribution recognized.

When they happen, give yourself permission to be sad, disappointed or angry. Just not in front of work colleagues. Retreat to your family and friends. People who support you, regardless of what's happened or why. Take some time to talk, cry or have a whine. Or all three at once if you need to! Maybe you just need some time to be on your own to reflect on the situation. Give yourself some time but not so long that you blow the situation out of proportion or let it prevent you from focusing on what you need to do next.

As soon as you can, step back from the situation and evaluate what happened. Sometimes you'll have to console yourself that there was nothing you could have done to avoid the situation. You can't anticipate everything that may be in your path. You just need the ability to deal with the consequences. If you recognize things you could have done differently, then consider it as an excellent learning experience that you can use in the future.

Whether you could or couldn't have done something differently, don't beat yourself up over it. Women often spend too much time reliving a situation and berating themselves over something they could or should have done differently. They replay the disaster over and over in their minds, cringing as they hear the words they wish they had or hadn't said again and again. Sometimes to the point where the remembered experience is much worse than what actually happened! Analyze the situation, learn from it and move on. Others usually forget as soon as something is over; you need to, too.

Career Chick Hot Tip: Give yourself permission to be disappointed, then move on.

Check For Broken Bones

Keep in mind that whatever happened, it's not about who you are as a human being. You need to separate what happens to you from who you are. More than likely the situation has come about because of where you are in the organization at a particular time or other circumstances, priorities or pressures. Decisions are influenced by multiple factors, many of which you can't control or even know about.

Sometimes bad stuff just happens and you need to be able to get on with things. But first check that you have no broken bones. You need to know that you are okay. Take the time to review what has happened. Assess whether all your relationships are intact. Ask yourself, *"Is there anyone I need to clear the air with or talk to about what happened? Is there anything I need to do differently? Are there any behaviors I want to change? Is there something I can learn from what happened?"* If there is anything you need to do, put together an action plan and do what you need to do as soon as you can.

Don't put off conversations you need to have or contacts you need to make. It'll only get more difficult the longer you put them off. And if you decide that you need to do things differently or learn something new, work out your action plan and implement it straightaway. If you want to change your behavior, start today. If you need to learn something new, buy a book, enroll in a course or identify and approach a mentor. Don't put it off. Your resolve is never stronger than when you first make a decision to do something, so get in and do it. Otherwise, you risk suffering more disappointments in the future for the same reasons (which just seems dumb).

Once you've had an honest review of the situation you need to put what's happened in the past. You could try this exercise. Mentally picture a gorgeous decorated box (lipstick pink with diamantes, or mermaid green covered with sparkles are a couple of decorating suggestions). In your mind, open the lid, put your disappointing situation into the box and slam the lid shut. Then move the box to the back of your mind, close enough that the lessons won't be forgotten but far enough away that the feeling of disappointment won't dominate your thoughts or erode your energy and self-confidence.

Career Chick Hot Tip: Honestly review the situation and lessons learnt, identify actions and implement them.

Get Back On The Horse

How you get back on the horse, so to speak, is something that other people will notice. How you handle setbacks (often referred to in business as how you 'get back up again') can have a positive or negative impact on your reputation – sometimes more than how proficient you are at your job. Being openly emotional or disappointed doesn't help the stereotype that women are too sensitive for the business environment. If you cry, get angry or sulk, people will think you're more interested in yourself than the bigger picture. Get on with the job at hand and you will be seen as focused and mature.

To regain your focus think back to your original goal or objective. Remember what you were working towards and why, then focus on what you need to do to get back on track. Your action plan is much easier and clearer when you know what it is that you want to achieve.

Many decisions are made about people's careers on the basis of how they handle difficult situations. Every time you overcome difficulties in a professional and mature manner (interpretation: no emotion) and remain focused, it shows you're capable of dealing with future difficulties and, potentially, more challenging roles.

Career Chick Hot Tip: Refocus on your goals and how to achieve them.

Develop Strategies

Your best defense mechanism, both on a personal and business level, is to develop a range of strategies to use when things go wrong. You need different strategies for the different types of setbacks or letdowns. The more prepared you are, the more options you have and the easier it is to deal with challenging situations. There are tactics you can develop in advance so that you are prepared for those hidden 'rocks'. One overall strategy to help you build a robust *Operating Style* is to develop skills to manage stress.

Generally, you will be better equipped to deal with whatever is thrown at you if you are calm (well, relatively anyway), and not stressed to the eyeballs. If you work in a pressure-cooker environment where you're doing too much and not looking after yourself, one disappointment or minor incident can turn into a huge blow-up because you are stressed. This can give the impression that you are overly emotional or can't cope with the demands of your job. Career success is often associated with those who are calm, measured and take adversity in their stride. The ability to manage your personal stress level is a key strategy to managing setbacks or disappointment.

There are many ways to manage stress and what works for you may not work for someone else. Some techniques include managing the hours you work, doing physical exercise, spending time with family and friends (sometimes stress inducing!) and on hobbies or interests that you are passionate about. These things are not just 'nice to have' or a luxury but an important investment in improving your disposition and therefore central to your *Operating Style*.

Career Chick Hot Tip: Manage stress to help you take disappointments in your stride.

Know Yourself

Apart from managing stress levels, another key strategy to prepare for future falls is to develop your level of self-awareness. Understanding how you like to work, how you see the world and how you are likely to react to different situations is valuable preparation for developing coping strategies. Self-awareness is potentially the single most important skill to support the development of your *Operating Style*. If you understand who you are, your strengths, weaknesses and preferences, then you can apply this understanding to everything you do.

There are numerous tools around to help you understand your likely reactions to stress and pressure. For instance, the Myers-Briggs Type Indicator (MBTI) is a psychometric questionnaire used to indicate how you ideally prefer to work and operate. It also suggests how you are likely to react under stress. If you have this insight you will be able to develop strategies to help you. For example, if you know that under stress you are likely to react emotionally, withdraw or become introspective, you can recognize it and learn to manage your reactions. Likewise, if you become emotional in stressful situations you can make sure you remove yourself from the situation to avoid being seen. Or if you know you always need to talk through what has happened, you can make sure you have trusted advisors, outside of work, who will listen. Bear in mind that the way you deal with stress may be different to someone else in your team. If you tend to withdraw and become quiet, perhaps go to a different coffee shop from the people who need to talk about what happened!

Whether it's MBTI or any of the many other tools available (such as the Belbin, DISC, Benziger or Keirsey models) there's no time like the present to start building your self-awareness. Don't wait for disappointments before you start to learn about yourself.

Career Chick Hot Tip: Develop your level of self-awareness.

External Factors

As well as understanding yourself, you need to be honest with yourself about the situation or circumstances, which may include your performance, the realities of the business environment, or other people's motivations and agendas. Sometimes disappointments can be avoided if expectations are realistic. There is no point building yourself up for a large salary increase when you know your business is facing cost pressures. Or, having your heart set on being rewarded for an achievement that no one knows about. While you don't need to limit your aspirations, knowing the issues and the environment helps you to be realistic and, if necessary, develop plans to change the circumstances so that you achieve your goals.

Career Chick Hot Tip: Understand the issues and external factors that impact you.

Negative Feedback

There are a number of disappointments in business that you may need to deal with, and one common one is receiving negative or unexpected feedback about your performance. Ideally, Career Chicks don't receive any nasty surprises because they continually monitor and evaluate their performance, and are aware of their strengths and weaknesses and able to take remedial action. Be realistic and honest with yourself, but be positive. There's no need to be modest either. And when you do well, be kind and acknowledge it to yourself.

If you do receive negative feedback, one approach is to:

- acknowledge what has been said
- thank the person for their comments
- ask for time – if you need to think about what they said
- ask questions and clarify your understanding
- go into solution mode and take action – this could be anything from resolving an issue to enrolling in a course to develop your skills
- evaluate what you have learnt
- mentally file away the experience, and
- move on!

When you get negative feedback others will watch to see how you react. Remember, no tears. Don't be emotional, and find ways to give yourself some space. Don't cry; bite your lip if you have to, even excuse yourself from the meeting as soon as you can if need be. There are several ways to manage the initial receipt of negative feedback. If you are in a meeting with a number of people you may be able to excuse yourself or just take the issue off the agenda and ask for it to be discussed later, in private. For instance, saying, *"OK, can we discuss this after this meeting?"* buys you time to think through your reaction to a situation. Whatever you do, don't get into a debate about your performance in public. If you receive critical feedback in a one-on-one meeting with your manager, you don't need to react or resolve the situation there and then. If you need time, say you want to think about what has been said and make an appointment for further discussion. Be calm, logical and self-confident, whether you feel that way or not!

Career Chick Hot Tip: Be action-oriented and solution-focused.

The Opportunity To Learn

Fortunately, receiving feedback, whether positive or negative, is a good opportunity to learn. You'll know how to go about things next time, and what you could do more or less of. Then again, you may realize that you are working for someone who has no idea about how to help you develop, or that the environment is not right for you. Whether feedback is positive or negative there is always something you can learn.

Whatever the feedback, don't beat yourself up for not being or not being seen to be perfect. Don't replay and relive the situation, as only women seem to do. Accept it has happened, learn what you can and move on.

Career Chick Hot Tip: Learn from feedback.

Invisible You

Some disappointments can make you feel as if you're invisible in your organization, such as being overlooked for a promotion, a salary increase or bonus or even just not being recognized for your contributions. Don't jump to assumptions about why it happened that way, instead identify the appropriate people and ask questions to find out. Once you have the information you need, develop a solution and take action.

If you missed out on a promotion it may be that your achievements weren't visible enough for you to be considered, so you may need to work on 'being seen'. Or you may find out that your manager considered you for the position but thinks you are more suited to something else. This is a great opportunity for you to discuss development or training options for the future or even just to share your goals with them. Whatever you find out about why you missed out, following it up means you can create the opportunity to do something about it. Be seen to put your plan into action. Involve the people you proactively asked for feedback, evaluate what you have learnt, file away the disappointment and move on.

Career Chick Hot Tip: Find out why you missed out and develop a plan.

Don't Doubt Yourself

When bad stuff happens, women often judge themselves more harshly than a man would in the same situation. Women doubt and blame themselves. Even worse, they do it publicly. It's hard enough to ensure that your contributions and talents are seen and recognized, without you casting doubt on your abilities or skills, too. When things do go wrong, which they do, women ask themselves, *"Did I do enough? Did I say the wrong thing? Did I forget something?"* And on and on and on … They relive a minor incident until they are mortified about what they did or said. A man, on the other hand, is much more likely to shrug his shoulders and move on.

When something goes wrong, women often believe that it was their fault. Don't make this your default position. Be honest with yourself, but don't assume it is your fault. Take a lesson from the men: look at the big picture and all of the influencing factors.

Career Chick Hot Tip: Don't judge yourself too harshly or assume it's your fault.

Know How To Fall

Whatever happens you can find a way to deal with it. It may be as simple as clarifying a point of information or it could be as serious as a complete breakdown in communications. Whatever it is, it can be resolved. It may take anything from a short conversation to ... a new job with a new company. Whatever it is, there is always a solution. You do need to give yourself time to fall and heal, but if you get back up and get on with things, others will notice and be impressed rather than focusing on the fact that you fell in the first place.

If you do find you have some scars after a disappointment, you'll be stronger (and wiser) for them. In the business world your scars shouldn't leave an ugly mark, although they may need a BAND-AID®, but you will be more experienced for them. They are also the greatest chance to learn about yourself.

The more prepared you are for disappointments (even if it's just being aware that they happen) the better you can respond. This helps to reinforce your chosen *Operating Style*. Like knowing how to work well in meetings and teams, how to negotiate and resolve conflict, and how to lead others, knowing how to 'get back up' becomes identified with your work persona and identity. It sets expectations about how you will act and react, and is a powerful asset for your career. If you know how to get back up, you will not only survive but actually thrive in your chosen profession.

Career Chick Hot Tip: Fall with style and get back up!

Career Chick Hot Tips to get back up:

- Learn how to fall.

- Give yourself permission to be disappointed, then move on.

- Honestly review the situation and lessons learnt, identify actions and implement them.

- Refocus on your goals and how to achieve them.

- Manage stress to help you take disappointments in your stride.

- Develop your level of self-awareness.

- Understand the issues and external factors that impact you.

- Be action-oriented and solution-focused.

- Learn from feedback.

- Find out why you missed out and develop a plan.

- Don't judge yourself too harshly or assume it's your fault.

- Fall with style and get back up!

Career Chick Hot Tips
for creating your successful
Operating Style:

- **Be seen**

- **Meet successfully** to demonstrate your skills

- **Work in teams** to deliver superior results through productive relationships

- **Negotiate** to do business

- **Resolve conflict** that gets in the way

- **Lead** to influence business outcomes

- **Get back up** when bad stuff happens

Unlock the **CODE**
for career success...

career
development

Chapter 14

Plan Your Career

"Even if you're on the right track, you'll get run over
if you just sit there"
Will Rogers, cowboy, actor, humorist and columnist (1879–1935)

Will Rogers made that observation some time ago, but it's just as relevant today. During his career, Rogers appeared in 71 movies and wrote six books and more than 4000 syndicated newspaper columns – he even made it into the Guinness Book of Records for his achievement of throwing three lassos at the same time. You can only assume that he must have practised what he preached. Being overtaken by others, even when you think you are where you should be, is exactly what can happen to you if you don't have a career plan.

Regardless of how well you communicate and develop your *Operating Style*, you also need to focus on the third essential component of the CODE for career success: *Career Development*. This is a necessary and legitimate part of your work life that requires focus and proactive management. Developing your career involves some key activities, such as building and implementing a career plan, networking and working with mentors. You also need to develop the ability to know when it's time to move on, the skills to get the job you want and be willing and have the skill to negotiate for your salary and conditions.

These are all areas that women tend to neglect (usually for genuine and justifiable reasons). Most women focus on doing their jobs well and balancing work with the rest of their lives. But there are factors that women fail to take into account, such as the importance of career-development activities and the commitment needed to prioritize and allocate time to them. Women may also be unsure exactly what they need to do or how best to do it.

If you're not quite sure how to go about something, even if you do understand its importance, you can waste a lot of time trying to figure out what to do – time you could well spend doing something else. That's what often happens with career-development activities. Women focus on what they need to do then just get in and do it. They put the business first, often at the expense of their career. Their male colleagues, however, whether they are as capable or not, often take-off up the career ladder. The real difference is that many men spend time and effort on *Career Development* and management. They don't think about it or question whether they should do it, it's just a part of how they expect to work.

What's more, companies expect you to spend time on these activities. The days of having a job for life when companies looked after their employees are long gone. The general view is that most people only stay in a job for two to three years, so it's not economical for a company to make a huge investment in each employee's *Career Development*. Companies do invest heavily in those they identify as high-performers or high-potentials, but you can't rely on this as your career-development strategy. No matter how talented you are there are many reasons why your organization may not focus on your *Career Development*. And even if they do, their focus will be aligned with the company's vision of what you need, not necessarily your personal plan or goals. The only person who is responsible, passionate, and really, really interested and committed to your career, is you.

Career Chick Hot Tip: Take responsibility for your career plan.

It's Your Choice

What you offer to an organization is the sum of your knowledge, skills, experience and attitude. When you are interviewed for a new job or role you will often be asked, *"Where do you see yourself in one/five/10 years?"* or *"What do you see as the next role after this?"* These questions not only test your attitude but also your approach to your own career management. Like the skills that you develop as part of your *Operating Style*, the skills to manage and develop your career are essential to achieving success.

You can choose to put time and effort solely into your job or focus on your career as well. The choice is entirely yours. It's not unlike the decisions you may have made about your approach to study. Did you work around the clock to achieve the highest marks possible? Or achieve the best results you could and devote some time to other activities? Often the people who found a balance between these approaches have the contacts and opportunities after completing their formal education. For some people the results are all that count to ensure they get into a higher-level course or are employed by a big-name firm. But for many, it's the additional skills and the people they met as part of the broader educational experience that they enjoy and benefit from in the future.

Generally, guys choose to do what they need to do for their job *and* spend time on their *Career Development*. The result is that guys are promoted while the chicks are applauded for their work ethic. Great. It's important to be valued for your work ethic. It's something you should be proud of – but not at the expense of your career progression. Being excellent at your job is only one part of what is required to achieve career success.

Career Chick Hot Tip: Allocate time to your *Career Development*. It's an investment.

You Need A Plan

To make the most of the time you invest in your *Career Development*, you need a plan. This involves some common-sense activities that you would use to approach any important project that you are responsible for as part of your job. You simply need to set goals, identify the actions required to achieve them, then conduct regular progress reviews. This is nothing more than the standard approach you would use to achieve business goals. Successful Career Chicks use these skills every day. The secret is to apply them to your own *Career Development*.

The process for creating a career plan is the same for men and women. The challenge for women is to actually do it. When you know what you want to achieve, what work you'd like to do, which companies you want to work for and even the level of seniority you want to reach, you've created the foundation for a plan. A career plan is your guide to what you want to achieve and the steps you need to take to get there. It will provide you with a mechanism to ensure that you are on the path to set your objectives and realize them.

Career Chick Hot Tip: Build a plan.

Set Your Goals

If you aren't really sure yet what you want to achieve, then set yourself some goals. As Lewis Carroll wrote in *Alice's Adventures in Wonderland*:[1]

> Alice came to the fork in the road.
>
> "Which road do I take?" she asked
>
> "Where do you want to go?" responded the Cheshire Cat.
>
> "I don't know," Alice answered.
>
> "Then," said the cat, "it doesn't matter."

Goal setting enables you to understand your priorities and work out whether your aspirations are compatible. Once you know what your goals are you can develop a plan to turn them into reality.

Of course, not all your goals will be work-related; they may cover different aspects of your life over various time frames. As part of your life plan you may have goals for your health, wellbeing, finances, family and friends, as well as for your career. The focus here is on your career goals: what type of work you want to do, how much you want to earn and/or what position you want to achieve, or any number of other objectives you might set yourself. Preferably, your goals should be specific and aspirational but, most importantly, they should come from the heart and be based on what you really want.

Sometimes the knowledge of what you really, really want isn't quite as simple as sitting down for half an hour to write a list. It can be confusing and even confronting to think through all the options and decide what is really important to you. Hopefully, your efforts to build your self-awareness will assist with the process. By gaining a better understanding of who you are and what you like, you can improve your decision-making. It can also help you understand how you think and make decisions. If you know that you think best out loud, then discuss your goals with family, friends or a mentor. If you need space to think, then make sure that you create it for yourself.

If you need help to set goals, start by analyzing:

- where you are now – your skills, knowledge and experience
- what you are good at

- what you like to do
- how you like to work – with people or on your own; in large or small teams; or when you have lots of autonomy or specific direction
- how you make decisions – or how you've made them in the past, and
- what steps you currently have in place to develop your career.

You don't need to be limited by the past or your current skills, but they can help you decide what you want or need to do to realize and set your goals. For instance, if you don't have the skills right now to read a P&L (Profit and Loss) statement it doesn't mean that you can't aspire to a job that requires this skill, but it does mean that you need a plan to learn how. Similarly, if you've always excelled in jobs where you get to work with lots of different people, you may find it challenging to set a goal that involves spending huge amounts of time on your own. (Author's note: like writing a book but that's another story …)

When you set your goals, focus on the work you want to do rather than the job title. Things change overnight in many organizations and a specific job may be gone before you're halfway there, which can be disheartening and distracting. On the other hand, if you understand that your goal is to manage people or to have a certain level of responsibility, changes to a company's structure won't throw you off track.

You may have perfect clarity about what your goals are, which is excellent. But if you don't, narrow down the things you like to do and know you do well. You don't have to map out your entire career, but deciding on a few specific things you want to achieve means you'll have some goals to work towards.

If you don't know what you want to achieve you may need to do some research. Read, contact people who have the knowledge or get some exposure to the environment where you want to work. Most managers are quite willing to spend time with people who are researching and developing their career plan. For instance, if you are interested in becoming a manager in a certain area you could approach someone who is already in the role, or talk to your current manager or even your Human Resources department. You may need to work in with their schedule or demonstrate your seriousness by emailing your questions in advance. But most people are generous to those who want to learn and they'll usually find time to spend with you or, at the very least, refer you to someone else who can help.

By taking this approach, you can achieve a couple of objectives. Not only will you learn what skills, knowledge and experiences are needed for the job (and if it's as good as you thought), but you also send an important signal about your interest and your professional approach to your career. The people who you approach now may be key decision makers or influencers in the future.

Career Chick Hot Tip: Decide what you want and set your career goals.

Write Them Down

It's crucial to write down your goals. It's so easy to think, *"This is important. I won't have any problem remembering what I want to achieve,"* but it is incredibly powerful when you see what you want written down. When you see your goals written down it helps you validate if they are what you really want. 'Become a manager', 'Double my salary' or 'Work for XYZ Company' can be confronting when you see it in black and white. Writing it down may make you feel confident that your goals are achievable. On the other hand, you may feel overwhelmed or even embarrassed by how high you have set your sights.

The good news is that you don't have to share your goals with anyone, if you don't want to. What's the worst thing that can happen? If you write down something that you want to achieve and don't achieve it, the only person you'll disappoint is yourself. Then again, if you can go back and tick off all the goals that you have achieved you'll feel sensational.

If you write your goals down and they don't seem quite right then you may need to do some more thinking or research. Sometimes you think you know exactly what you are working towards but writing it down makes you start to question if that's what you really want. This is a positive result, too. It's much better to find out early that you need to reset your goals, rather than wasting a whole lot of time and effort on the wrong objectives. It provides you with the opportunity to decide what you really, really want and work out how you are going to achieve those goals.

Career Chick Hot Tip: Write down your goals.

Develop An Action Plan

When you identify what you want, where you are now and the difference between the two, you can develop a plan to bridge that gap. Not surprisingly, this is known as a gap analysis, which provides clear guidelines for the development of your action plan.

Your action plan should include:

- specific actions – what you will do
- time frames – when you will do them
- measures – how you will know that you're on track.

Your specific actions could include how you will gain the skills and knowledge you need to learn. For instance, who you need to make contact with, what you want to learn from them or who you need to promote yourself to. Other actions can include making contacts with or expanding your network, obtaining a mentor and appointing a board of advisors. These will be discussed in more detail later.

Measures may include the number of people you will contact within a specific time frame, the completion of a course or the achievement of a business objective. The key is that once you set these measures, you need to go back and review your progress against them. When you write them down you have a specific, measurable and implementable career action plan.

How you document your plan can be as complex or as simple as you want. It should be recorded in a way that you find easy to manage. A spreadsheet, a Word document or a notebook kept in your handbag or bottom drawer, whatever works for you. Have a look at the Sample Career Plan at the end of this chapter for some ideas. To make it more interesting than your usual work projects, perhaps you could use a slightly more glamorous notebook!

Career Chick Hot Tip: Set actions, time frames and measures to address gaps in your skills, knowledge and experience.

Career Plan Solutions

Two of the potential solutions to address the gaps you have identified are to use mentors and your network. Mentors, for instance, are crucial to gain knowledge, get insightful career advice and understand the politics of your organization. For some development opportunities, finding a mentor who can guide you is a viable and attractive solution. Your plan is the perfect place to identify who you need to work with, track your contact and progress with them and assess your future requirements.

Likewise, your plan is also ideal for tracking your networking activities. Your network, which is simply who you know, is an excellent resource for your *Career Development*. The people in your network will be a rich source of information. They may be role models, able to teach you new skills and an exceptional source of information about future job possibilities. They are your conduits to the hidden job market, that is, the positions that are never advertised.

If networking is a foreign concept to you or you don't have a terribly high opinion of it, be assured that there are ways to network with integrity that you can adapt to your own *Operating Style*. It's the depth of relationships that you make, rather than how many people you know, that's important. People do need to know you (rather than just have a vague recollection of having met you at a function) to be prepared to actually help you. But you do need to strike a balance between the two and make sure that you know enough people in enough areas to have a variety of people to call on when you need them. Your career plan is the perfect place to keep track of this and make sure that you do enough. Contacting someone in your network, or adding some new people to it, may just be the solution to address some of your knowledge, skill or experience gaps.

Career Chick Hot Tip: Include mentors and people in your network, as actions to achieve your plan.

More Ideas

Another method you can use to support your *Career Development* is to appoint yourself a Board of Advisors. Now this group doesn't have to sit around a boardroom table or even get together over cocktails or coffee (although that would be fun). In fact, your advisors don't even need to be aware that they are part of your board. But what they will be is very clearly identified in your mind, and hopefully in your plan, as key members of your network that you can develop, or seek to develop, deep relationships with. These relationships allow you to have a high level of trust when you seek their advice.

Your personal board may include a range of people with different skill sets. This allows you to draw on their different areas of expertise when you need help in their specialty area. They may be very politically astute and have a strong understanding of the whys and wherefores of what is happening in your organization, or they may just be really clear thinkers who can help you look at various issues and situations from different perspectives. Don't make the mistake of appointing a board who all think exactly like you, approach situations in the same way and agree with everything you say. You will have a lovely time when you get together, but they won't necessarily give you a whole lot of new ideas or challenge or stretch you. That's why you need a strong level of trust in these people. That way, when they do challenge you or suggest a completely different course of action you'll be receptive to what they say.

Career Chick Hot Tip: Appoint a board of advisors.

Cultivate Sponsors

There are others who influence your career that you may not even know about: your sponsors. They can sing your praises or recommend you for a position, project or other opportunities. Sometimes you may never know who spoke up for you because your *Operating Style* and achievements impressed them. If you can identify the people that are potential sponsors, or influencers, put them in your career plan and keep them informed about the progress of your career. For instance, you could identify a previous manager who was impressed with your work and let them know of your ongoing achievements. A quick call, a couple of lines on an email or an occasional coffee may be all you need to do to keep the lines of communication open. If the people who can influence outcomes for you know of your current skills and success, they'll probably speak well of you to others. You never know, they may even have an opportunity for you in the future.

Career Chick Hot Tip: Positively influence potential sponsors.

Review Your Plan

Regardless of what's in your plan or how you keep it, it's important to review it regularly. The frequency will probably depend on the time frame for your goals, but every three months is about right. The review allows you to measure your progress against your actions and make any adjustments that are required to your plan. You may be really happy with your progress or realize that although you achieved what you set out to do in the time frame you're not moving towards your goals as fast as you'd like. You may need to renegotiate your time frames and measures. You may even want to delete actions, if they are no longer necessary. Just don't do it because you are too busy doing something else that is not an investment in your career.

Make an appointment with yourself to conduct your reviews and schedule time in your diary. Approach this as you would for anything important you do at work. Because this is just as important as the work you do.

Career Chick Hot Tip: Review your plan and update it regularly.

Stay On Track

Ultimately, you do actually need to have the skills, knowledge, and attitude to progress your career. You need to be first-rate at your job. As a talented and capable Career Chick, your career plan will help you leverage your results and ability to achieve your goals. It will provide you with actionable steps to measure your progress. The knowledge that you have a plan and are progressing towards your goals will give you confidence that you are on track. Even if you decide to make changes to your plan in the future at least you are on the way. And as an added bonus you'll also develop skills to plan your career, not wait for it to happen to you. Like Will Rogers said, if you don't keep moving you'll get run over.

Career Chick Hot Tip: Plan your career and achieve!

Career Chick Hot Tips to plan your career:

- Take responsibility for your career plan.

- Allocate time to your *Career Development*. It's an investment.

- Build a plan.

- Decide what you want and set your career goals.

- Write down your goals.

- Set actions, time frames and measures to address gaps in your skills, knowledge and experience.

- Include mentors and people in your network, as actions to achieve your plan.

- Appoint a board of advisors.

- Positively influence potential sponsors.

- Review your plan and update it regularly.

- Plan your career and achieve!

SAMPLE CAREER PLAN

GOALS			GAP ANALYSIS		ACTION PLAN			
Objectives	Time Frame	Goal Requirements	Current Status	Gap	Actions	Time Frame	Measures	Review/Further Actions
Example 1								
Decide on career goals	3 mths	Know what I want to do	Unsure	Need to evaluate options and decide	Talk to current and past managers to gather feedback	1 mth	Completed and reviewed	
		Understand my strengths and weaknesses	Understand from my perspective but not from the point of view of others	Need to increase my self-awareness	Complete MBTI, Belbin or similar process to gain a greater understanding of my working style (Increase self-awareness)	2 mths	Completed and reviewed	
		Research options	Some ideas	Need more information	Talk to colleagues in areas of interest (Network)	6 weeks	Contact 6 people	
Example 2								
Be in the top 10% of performers in current job	6 mths	Outstanding performance	Currently exceeding some accountabilities but have missed a couple of deadlines and budgets	Need to develop financial and time-management skills	Identify current top performers and talk to them about their knowledge and processes (Network)	1 mth	Completed	
					Read business publications on these topics Book/Internet (Research)	2-3 mths	Read 3	
					Identify appropriate courses (Learning)	1 mth	Identify 3 potential courses	

GOALS			GAP ANALYSIS			ACTION PLAN		
Objectives	Time Frame	Goal Requirements	Current Status	Gap	Actions	Time Frame	Measures	Review/Further Actions
Example 3								
Increase confidence to make presentations	6 mths	High level presentation skills	OK at presentations but very nervous	Skills to present with complete confidence	Ask Manager for coaching and to attend a presentation skills program (*Research & Learning*)	1 mth	Set meeting and agree next steps	
					Attend Presentation Skills Course (*Learning*)	3 mths	Course feedback & confidence	
					Practise skills through making presentations (*Learning*)	3-6 mths	Completed 4 presentations	
Example 4								
Become a People Manager	12 mths	Achieve results	Currently exceeding all objectives	Nil – but need to maintain	Need to maintain current performance levels	On-going	Review results quarterly	
		Understand how current department works within the broader organization	Basic Knowledge	Knowledge of relationships between departments	Make contact and meet with one person in each key department (*Networking*)	2 mths	Meet with 5 key areas	
		Future opportunities	Unsure of future opportunities	Need to understand	Meet with current manager and mentors to understand future opportunities and role requirements	1 mth	Meetings held	
		Knowledge of company human resources processes	Limited knowledge	Learn	Complete appropriate online courses (Company Intranet)	6 mths	Complete online courses	

Chapter 15

Network

"It's not what you know but who you know"

Anonymous

There's a reason why people repeat maxims like the one above: they're generally true. This one, however, is often used as an excuse to explain why someone else has done well. Many times it's an implied criticism, insinuating that the other person hasn't really earned their good fortune or achievement, but rather relied on knowing someone else to get ahead. What these critics don't acknowledge is that establishing a group of contacts – a network – that can help you when you need it, is an achievement in itself.

A network of people that you can rely on is vital to your *Career Development*. There are times when you need to call on people, such as when things get tough, when you don't know how to handle a situation or even when you're looking for your next opportunity. Generally speaking, women don't put the same amount of time or effort into building their network as men do. Somehow they think that building relationships on the basis of what they can get out of them is a bit selfish, self-serving and even a bit dishonest. Women often think that leveraging relationships for things like promotions, jobs, more money or prestige is underhanded, and they prefer to earn these rewards through hard work. The truth is that if you don't have a network to draw on you'll only make things difficult for yourself and, more than likely undermine your own hard work.

On the other hand, guys actively work their network – and get ahead as a result. Some women resent the amount of time that men devote to networking and the way they use their contacts to get ahead. But Career Chicks should see networking as an essential activity; others must know who you are before you can achieve career success.

The challenge for Career Chicks is to find a way to network in a professional manner – and one that you feel comfortable with. You don't need to stalk strangers at functions and give them your business card. Neither should you treat networking like speed-dating where you meet someone then quickly move on to see if you can find someone better.

Networking is simply the process of getting to know people who have similar or common interests, then building and maintaining mutually beneficial business relationships with them. It's also about having conversations; if the rumors are true, that's something Career Chicks are very comfortable doing!

> *Career Chick Hot Tip:* Have conversations to meet new people, get to know them and develop mutually beneficial business relationships.

Depth Vs Breadth

Some people measure their networking success by the number of business cards they collect at functions. But when push comes to shove and you need advice or help in the future, can you rely on people you met once to help you out? Alternatively, if you build solid, mutually beneficial relationships with the people you meet, they are much more likely to support you when you need it. Choosing a network with depth rather than breadth pays off.

Your network should include people you trust and respect. It's even better if they're people you like! And, ideally, they'll be people who trust, respect and like you, too. Deep networks are made from strong, long-term relationships.

Putting time and energy into building and maintaining a network can have a variety of benefits for your *Career Development* and help you be more successful in your current job, which is ultimately beneficial for your career. A strong network can help you:

- learn new information or skills
- discover ideas – and enjoy some stimulating discussions
- find out how to do things better in your organization
- know who to go to in an organization, and
- identify future job opportunities and promotions.

For example, the recruitment industry tells us that a significant number of job vacancies are never advertised and that there is a hidden employment market that people access through their networks. So if you don't have a network to provide you with information, referrals or to let other people know who you are, it limits your career options. Deep relationships, built on trust and respect, are necessary to access information, ideas and to learn new skills.

Career Chick Hot Tip: Focus on depth rather than breadth in your networking relationships.

It's Your Job

You may think that networking takes up time that you should be spending on doing your job. There's no doubt that you need to juggle many aspects of life: work, home, family, friends, study, exercise and time for yourself. All of these put considerable pressure on your time and when you start to question how to manage everything you want to do, another one of those oft-repeated maxims turns up: 'Work smarter not harder'. But what does that mean? Women strive to work efficiently and effectively and focus on what needs to be done, so when they're pressed for time, having a coffee with a colleague to find out what's happening in his or her department is usually considered an extracurricular activity. The fact is, networking is actually an important part of your job, not a discretionary activity.

When you talk to the men you work with you'll find they've woven networking into the everyday fabric of their job. Contrary to what you may expect, guys ring each other, catch up for coffee and make time for lunch to keep their networks going. For men, networking is integral to how they work.

The way that men use and develop their social connections for role and *Career Development* often seems to exclude women, and their networks are labeled 'boys' clubs' or 'old boys' networks'. Unfortunately, these do exist, but in the male-dominated business arena, it's understandable that many of their contacts are 'boys'. However, it's more likely that they have maintained contacts from school, sport and other social activities, as well as people they met throughout their career. Typically, men develop these contacts into business relationships by going through various stages. They start with *'I have something in common with you'* and progress to *'I know you'* to *'I like and respect you'* to *'I will help you/do business with you.'*

Women, on the other hand, often need the justification of a professional relationship before they'll allocate time to develop it. Women go through these stages in their business relationships: *'I work with you'* to *'I respect you'* to *'I like you'* and, later, *'I'll help you.'* The relationships that women make in business in this way are often incredibly deep and can become life-long friendships. The downside though is that women are often so busy doing their jobs that they don't take the time to progress to the *'I'll help you'* stage. It's wonderful to make some deep friendships during your career but the purpose of networking isn't about finding your next bestie. It's about mutually beneficial *business* relationships.

Men understand that the time they spend building and maintaining these relationships is an investment, not a waste of time. It can be invaluable to spend thirty minutes having a coffee or even 10 minutes catching up on the phone learning about something new or innovative, hearing about how someone else achieved success in their role or discussing ideas. The benefits of these opportunities can far outweigh the time spent. The worst-case scenario is that you waste your time or the other person's, but if these are long-term, mutually beneficial relationships you'll both see this time as an investment.

> *Career Chick Hot Tip:* Invest time in your network. It's not a discretionary activity for your job or your career.

Recruit The Best People

There are many different types of networks and different sorts of relationships within networks. They can be formal or informal. Formal networks can include the people you meet through organizations set up specifically for networking, industry associations and company-sponsored programs. Informal networks are made up of people that you meet, often through your everyday activities.

Networks can include short-term associations and/or friendships that last a lifetime. What is most important is that you have the right people in your network. Consider including people who:

- you respect and trust
- have been recommended to you by someone you trust

- are recognized as strong performers – they are good at what they do
- demonstrate genuine interest in you, your work or your role, and
- have strong networks of their own.

These are just a few criteria you may want to consider. It doesn't matter if they are older or younger, male or female, more experienced or have a specific title. They just need to be people who have the knowledge, skills or an approach that you respect. For example, if your current career ambition is to improve your sales skills and you work in an extremely male-oriented business, it makes sense that the experienced and competent salespeople to learn from are men. Or there may be a younger graduate who has up-to-the-minute knowledge in your field or is a whiz with technology. There are no rules about who you should learn from. Don't be trapped into thinking that it's only other women or people like you who should be in your network.

Career Chick Hot Tip: Identify people who you trust, respect and are good at what they do. Recruit the best people.

Have A Plan

Building and maintaining a network is a legitimate business activity and one that should be built into your working life. You need to approach it like any other business activity that you undertake: develop a plan, implement it, review it at regular intervals, then update and refine it as required.

Your plan can be as simple as a spreadsheet, an online document or even written down in your glamorous notebook. It just needs to include enough information to keep you on track (although you could make it as detailed, as you like). Some basic details to include in your plan for each contact are obvious, such as name, position and contact details. It's also helpful if you keep a record of:

- your networking objective with the person
- how often you want to keep in touch with them
- how you'll catch up with them – for example, a coffee every couple of months and an email in-between

- when you last caught up with them, and
- when you'll contact them again.

Down the track you may want to include other personal or business information about their families, interests or other activities. Particularly if you have trouble remembering these kinds of details! Keep whatever notes you need to make this a valuable document that you actually use.

Writing down your networking plan means that you have something tangible to follow (like your career plan) but it also helps you make a commitment to yourself to follow through. The process of thinking through who you want to maintain contact with and why also helps you prioritize what you want to achieve.

You also need to establish some criteria on how you'll measure your success and review your achievements. You may measure success on inputs like the number of meetings, emails or catch-ups you commit to in the plan, or by the achievement of some other objective, like learning one new thing or generating one new idea a month. Whatever your measure of success you'll need to implement your plan to make it happen.

Career Chick Hot Tip: Have a plan for your network and write down your objectives and relevant details about the people and your contact with them.

Building Your Network

A common attribute that people who are successful in organizations share is that they have strong internal networks. This helps them achieve success because not only do they have a wide appreciation of the business but they also know who to ask to get things done. A great place for you to start building your network is within the company where you work or with the people you already know.

People who are highly successful, not just in one organization but throughout their careers, have far-reaching networks. Your contacts can be drawn from people you meet socially through friends, sporting activities or hobbies, as well as people you meet in business. Another source of contacts for your network is people you have worked with in the past, as they move onwards and upwards in their careers. Ex-colleagues are a valuable source of contacts for your external network, as they know you, how you work, the types of experience you have and your achievements and abilities. These relationships already exist, so it's often just a matter of taking the time to stay in touch with them.

You can also participate in formal networking and industry events and seek out people who you admire or impress you at the event or even the people you're seated near. Be careful not to pre-judge others in this environment because you don't think they work for a big enough company, have a sexy enough title or other superficial criteria. You need to spend time to get to know people to understand who they are.

Identify people who you respect and admire and include them in your network. You could draw your network from those you:

- work with on a daily basis
- have previously worked with on projects
- met on a course or training program
- can find a genuine reason to meet, for instance they work in a role or on a project similar to yours (you can compare notes).

One of the most powerful ways to make contacts is to be introduced by someone else in your network. By being introduced, you immediately gain credibility. It's the way business works; people help people who they know and trust. An introduction, or even the use of a contact's name as a way of introducing yourself to someone new, implies that you are known and trusted.

Career Chick Hot Tip: Build your network from people you know, both inside and outside your organization.

How To Meet People

One question Career Chicks often ask is how do you make quality contacts at events? One way is to identify someone who you respect on the basis of their presentation or role in the event. Make a quick introduction: *"Hi, I'm really interested in the trends you mentioned your company is seeing. Would you mind if I gave you a call to discuss this further?"* Look for a positive response and then swap business cards. The door is now open for a follow-up call or email and you're on your way to expanding your network.

Similarly, if you participate in training or events with people from outside your company, make sure you take some business cards and use this as an opportunity to add to your network. Watch and listen, then introduce yourself to anyone who impresses you during the program. Offer to swap contact details and once you do, the ball is in your court to make contact with them or even invite them for a coffee.

Coffee is the great equalizer between the sexes. Once upon a time, networking happened over boozy lunches, on the golf course or in pubs and bars. These days a catch-up for coffee is very much the done thing and allows for much quicker meetings. It's also a comfortable and safe environment for women to meet up and spend time with men. When you invite someone for coffee it sets a casual tone, takes people out of the workplace and makes it easier to spend a bit more time with them than in a formal meeting. If you don't like coffee, drink tea, hot chocolate or mineral water! It's not about what you drink but the relaxed environment, which is conducive to building relationships.

Before you go out to meet new people, prepare something to say. If you proactively approach people, you need your elevator pitch, your 30-second summary, about who you are, what you do, and why you're interested in talking with them. If someone you know will introduce you to new people, have some 'one-liners' prepared so that you can answer questions. Not only can this help you make the most of the opportunity, but it can also help you hide any nerves. Most people are not at their most impressive when they are tongue-tied! Your prepared answers may be as simple as what you do or why you're at the event.

One of the most effective techniques you can use when you meet new people is to ask them lots of questions. Everyone (well, almost everyone) likes to talk about themselves, their work or their company, and they will start talking with a few questions to prompt them. So have some prepared. Use the basic how, what, why and when questions as your starting point. And listen to the answers so that you can ask follow-up questions. Spend time when you meet someone for the first time, enough to have a conversation, but not so long they feel they can't get away from you to talk to other people.

Career Chick Hot Tip: Introduce yourself to people you want to meet, and prepare questions and answers to help conversations.

Reasons To Keep In Touch

Once you've met people it's reasonably straightforward to create opportunities to stay in touch. Your regular contact can be as simple as forwarding some information that would be useful to them or dropping them an email to stay in touch. However, if this person is someone you want to develop a deep business relationship with over time, make sure that you don't rely just on technology and casual contact. You need to call or meet with them to build a relationship.

Worthwhile reasons for them (and you) to have contact may include providing them with information that would be of interest, for example, keeping them abreast of developments in your area, or asking for their help or a referral to someone else who can help you in your job or with your career planning. Everybody likes their opinion to be valued, so sharing what they think or know can be rewarding for them, too.

Successful business people are interested in learning new information and helping out colleagues with information. They may not always have time for you when you ask but they will respect that staying in contact with you is worthwhile if you have had quality contacts. As your relationship develops and you identify a wider number of common interests the approach down the track may be as simple as, *"It's a long time since we caught up, how about a coffee/sandwich/ drink?"*

Career Chick Hot Tip: Create worthwhile reasons to maintain contact.

Stay In Contact

To ensure you stay on track, regularly refer to your networking plan. If you fall behind in sticking to your plan (and you will at times), then prioritize. You could change the frequency of contact (you could defer someone for a month) or the method of contact (drop them an email rather than meet for coffee).

Making time to contact your network should be built into your daily life. Send your emails first thing in the morning or when you get back from lunch. You're probably thinking, *'Humph! I don't have lunch.'* If that's the case, send them an email while you eat at your desk. Set up your coffee, lunch, or whatever in your diary a month ahead so that you feel obliged to keep to them. Don't prioritize something else and reschedule them when they come around. They are a priority.

If you find that you slack off your networking activities (and this will happen to everyone at some stage with big projects at work or priorities in your personal life) just be aware that this happens from time to time. Focus your efforts on re-establishing or increasing contact as soon as you can. Don't use deadline after deadline as an excuse not to network at all. The world of work allows you to give as much as you can and there is no shortage of deadlines. Don't fall into the trap of spending so much time 'doing' that you don't spend enough time developing yourself to take advantage of how talented you are.

It's easy to stay on track when you genuinely like and respect the people in your network. Why? Because you enjoy spending your time with them! To be honest, it's pretty hard to build and maintain a relationship, even on a business level, if you don't like the people. On the other hand, it's exciting to look at your diary for the next day and see that you have time booked with someone you look forward to seeing or talking to. Networking should be fun and enjoyable, don't let your work be too serious.

Career Chick Hot Tip: Keep in touch with people in your network.

Adds, Moves And Changes

What you should be serious about is taking advantage of opportunities to expand your network. Some regular occurrences in business can provide these opportunities. When you change roles or jobs, think about if there is anyone you have been working with that you should, or want to, stay in contact with. If there is, add them to your plan. Or when someone else in your company or team moves on, add them to the plan, if you want to stay in touch. Think about who you have met or developed a deeper relationship with and whether they should be added to your plan.

Your plan is dynamic. It should change as circumstances change. It should be what you want it to be. If you find that staying in touch with someone really isn't working for you, for whatever reason, use the 'Delete' key on your keyboard. It's very conveniently placed. They don't need to know they have been erased.

Additions, moves and changes will result from reviewing your plan. You can get away with a formal review every three months, but ideally you should think about your progress on a monthly basis, at least. When you review your plan, you need to:

- update the plan with contacts you have made
- plan your next scheduled contacts
- add these into your diary
- evaluate the level of contact – too often/not enough?, and
- review your progress towards your objectives.

Regularly evaluating your networking objectives and progress ensures that you invest your time wisely.

Career Chick Hot Tip: Regularly review your networking plan and add, move or change it accordingly.

Give Back To Your Network

The relationships in your network may help you now, but many are an investment in your future. Developing a relationship is not only about what they can do to help you, but also what you can do to help them. People that you help now are more likely to be there for you in the future. This may be as little as a positive mention about them in a conversation with others, help on a project, or even listening when they are trying to resolve an issue. Never underestimate how much people appreciate the time you spend with them.

If you live by the adage (or even have a sneaking suspicion that it may be true) that 'What goes around comes around', then introduce people in your network to each other. A simple introduction between two people you trust and respect that's helpful to both of them can be incredibly powerful in building goodwill for you. Just think about the strength and depth of the bond you build with these people when you help them make other quality contacts.

Career Chick Hot Tip: Give back to your network by introducing them to other contacts.

It's All Yours

When you meet people who stimulate your strategic thinking or creativity, provide you with the opportunity to learn new information, give you ideas, listen and critique your thinking, or even introduce you to others who can do any of these things, you'll do your job better and be more successful as a result. Networking is the ultimate form of 'working smarter not harder.'

Your network, like your career, is yours and yours alone. You may meet people through other people, you may introduce people to each other, but the network of people you know, value and choose to spend time with is uniquely yours. Enjoy networking, don't feel guilty about the time you invest and remember the purpose of your network: your *Career Development*.

Career Chick Hot Tip: Enjoy the conversations with people in your network.

Career Chick Hot Tips to network:

- Have conversations to meet new people, get to know them and develop mutually beneficial business relationships.

- Focus on depth rather than breadth in your networking relationships.

- Invest time in your network. It's not a discretionary activity for your job or your career.

- Identify people who you trust, respect and are good at what they do. Recruit the best people.

- Have a plan for your network and write down your objectives and relevant details about the people and your contact with them.

- Build your network from people you know, both inside and outside your organization.

- Introduce yourself to people you want to meet, and prepare questions and answers to help conversations.

- Create worthwhile reasons to maintain contact.

- Keep in touch with people in your network.

- Regularly review your networking plan and add, move or change it accordingly.

- Give back to your network by introducing them to other contacts.

- Enjoy the conversations with people in your network.

Chapter 16

Consult With Mentors

"People seldom improve when they have no other
model but themselves to copy"
Oliver Goldsmith, 18th-century Irish writer (1728–1774)

You've probably never heard of Oliver Goldsmith, but do you recognize the term 'goody two-shoes'? This was made popular by the 18th-century children's story *The History of Little Goody Two-Shoes*, which was published anonymously but is believed to have been written by Goldsmith. In the story, orphan Margery Meanwell is a good, happy little girl who only owns one shoe. When she is finally given a pair she is so excited that she tells everyone about her 'two-shoes' and acquires the nickname 'Goody Two-Shoes'. The moral of the story is that when little Margery grows up, she marries well and becomes a wealthy woman – evidence that her virtuous behavior has been rewarded.

Over time, the meaning of 'Goody Two-Shoes' has taken on a negative connotation, referring to someone who is, perhaps, a bit too nice or a bit too virtuous. But Goldsmith's observation still rings true: *"People seldom improve when they have no other model but themselves to copy."* In other words, if you want to improve yourself, look for a role model or a mentor. The term mentor, which originally meant to look after someone younger, originates from Greek mythology. The story goes that when the Greek king Odysseus left for the Trojan Wars, he asked his friend, Mentor, to look after his son. In modern times, the term 'mentor' has evolved to represent an expert in a particular field who guides and assists others.

You'll hear the term used today in various situations, including business, sport, education, and social programs. Whatever the context, a mentor describes someone more senior, knowledgeable, skilled or experienced who can provide guidance to someone who wants to develop in the mentor's field of expertise. A mentor isn't necessarily an older or more senior member in an organization's hierarchy. For instance, if you ever change careers it's very likely that people younger than yourself will have more expertise or be more skilled than you – at first. Or if you are looking to master some new piece of technology, your best bet may be a nine-year-old mentor who can quickly figure it out.

A mentoring relationship can provide you with feedback, fresh ideas and approaches, knowledge, expertise and advice. It can be a formal relationship, a lifelong friendship, or something in-between. It can provide you with:

- knowledge

- guidance – your career/an organization's politics/your communication style

- a sounding board – to discuss how you handled a situation or how you should tackle something in the future

- access to your mentor's network, and

- honest, valuable feedback.

The benefits are numerous and invaluable in helping you reach your potential, whatever your field or current level of achievement. Business tycoon Donald Trump acknowledges his father as his mentor. Oprah mentored 'Dr. Phil'. Michael Jordan, Roger Federer and David Beckham have all acknowledged their mentors as being important to their success. Any top achiever you can think of will have had a mentor or coach – someone to guide, counsel and provide advice. Someone who can look at their performance, provide a different perspective and advise strategies. It's the same in business. Leaders from all types of backgrounds credit one or several mentors for their guidance along the way. Entrepreneur Sir Richard Branson of Virgin brand fame acknowledges Sir Frederick Laker, a British airline entrepreneur, as his mentor, and the late Dave Thomas, the founder of Wendy's hamburger chain, was mentored for many years by KFC's Harland "Colonel" Sanders.

The fact that these famous, talented and successful people made use of the skills and expertise of others illustrates that having a mentor is a legitimate, not to mention successful, strategy to develop your career. Many women often don't appreciate the potential benefits of having a mentor, don't know how to go about getting one or don't make the time for *Career Development* and miss this tremendous opportunity. Having one or more mentors is a crucial area of focus for your *Career Development*.

Career Chick Hot Tip: Appreciate that mentors are crucial to your *Career Development*.

Why Mentors Mentor

You may be thinking, *"Why would someone be willing to help and mentor me?"* There are a number of reasons. They might do it as part of a formal mentoring program, or because they are your manager and see it as part of their job, or because they recognize your potential. Whatever the reason, the fact is that people, generally, like to share their knowledge and have their expertise recognized.

There are also some significant business and personal benefits for mentors, too, particularly those who help younger or less experienced people. Often mentors can get closer to what is actually happening in the business and learn new things that aren't otherwise obvious. At the same time, mentors can extend their own network down and through an organization. And in this technological age, there's also the potential to learn about new gizmos or new applications that they can utilize.

For these reasons, and many others, organizations are usually extremely supportive of mentoring relationships, both through formal programs and informal relationships. Formal mentoring programs can help organizations attract, retain and develop high-performing talent. Often, there are other, more subtle benefits for organizations, such as promoting common values and reinforcing the organization's culture. For instance, developing mentoring relationships and trust between individuals can support co-operation and confidence on a broader scale.

Career Chick Hot Tip: Recognize that mentors and organizations benefit, too.

The Roles Of Mentors

There are many different types of mentor relationships. Some may be more appropriate than others at different times in your career. When you are new to a role, your manager may be your mentor. In fact a lot of managers and first-line supervisors see their role as a mentor, providing technical expertise on how to do a job. This relationship does not need to be formalized with a *"Will you be my mentor?"* proposal on bended knee with accompanying soft music! Fortunately, your reporting line already provides you with a formal relationship.

A mentor may also be someone who performs the same role as you and is a top performer. They may work in your team, in another part of the organization or even at another company. The opportunity is to learn from these people, not only what they *know*, but also what they *do* that makes them so successful. You don't need to mimic them. Just take the best of what they do, or what a number of top performers do, and incorporate it into your *Operating Style*.

A mentor may have expertise in one particular skill set that you know you need to develop. For instance, it may be someone who has in-depth knowledge about a particular process or someone who has a reputation for being an excellent communicator. You may just want to learn one thing from a particular mentor, or 'pick their brain' on a wide range of topics if they have broad business experience.

At different times in your career there'll be various things you need to learn, so it's likely that you'll need a number of mentors, at various times. You may not want to have more than one or two at the same time. Like your network, it's the depth of relationship you have with your mentors rather than how many you have, that is most important. If you have identified a number of activities to work on in your career plan, you may need to be selective and prioritize those that a mentor could help you with.

Not all mentoring relationships last a lifetime. They may only be appropriate, for one or both of you, for a short time. Or they may continue throughout your career. These long-term relationships are like gold. They are rare, valuable and can have a huge influence on your *Career Development*. As your career progresses you might build a board of advisors with whom you consult. There may be some that you have a deep relationship and history with and newer additions who have expertise specific to your current role or ambitions.

It doesn't matter if your mentors are men or women. Just that they are the people who have the skills, knowledge or expertise you want to learn. If you work in a field that is male-dominated, or where most of the senior or influential people are male, chances are you need male mentors. Alternatively, if your want to learn how a particular woman has been successful in a male-oriented environment, she's the one.

Career Chick Hot Tip: Have different mentors to learn different things.

Know What You Want To Know

It all boils down to being very clear about what you want to learn from a mentor. A mentor will take you, and your request to work with them, seriously if you specify where you are in your career, what you want to learn and why, and what specifically you would like to learn from them. If you have done your career plan (as discussed in Chapter 14), you should have a very clear idea of what you need to learn and why. This makes it much easier to explain your motivations and what you hope to achieve.

No matter how much potential mentors are prepared to help they don't want to waste their time. You'll need to assure them that you are serious and seeking their help for the right reasons. Some people, who don't understand the true value of a mentor, try to use a relationship with a more senior person as a free ride to a promotion. A mentor is an aid to your career, not a shortcut to avoid developing the necessary skills, knowledge and experience. Having a mentor doesn't replace taking responsibility for your career.

Career Chick Hot Tip: Know what you want to learn from a mentor.

You're Responsible

It's your responsibility to identify your mentors. However, many companies do have formal mentoring programs where more junior and senior workers are paired up for development. If you get that opportunity, grab it! Sometimes the person you are paired with under these circumstances is not the person you would have picked for yourself. Still, someone has chosen your mentor for a reason, maybe for a purpose you can't see, and this can be a great opportunity to learn something new. Sometimes it won't work out though, and that's okay, too. At the very least you will have learnt what type of person you find it hard to learn from or what circumstances aren't conducive for learning.

But don't sit back and wait for your organization to provide you with a mentor. It's fantastic if they do, but it's not their responsibility. The only person who is going to be disadvantaged if you don't do everything you can to develop your career is … yep, that's right, you. By taking responsibility for yourself and identifying your own mentors you can create your own future. Sounds a whole lot better than waiting around for your company to notice what development you need.

As the responsibility to identify mentors is yours so, too, is the way you manage your relationship with them. It's not your mentor's responsibility, it's yours. The successful people you select as mentors are likely to be very busy or, at the very least, efficient with their time. It's highly unlikely that they need to think of things to do to fill up their day. They won't want to chase you to see how you are. It's up to you to be proactive, take responsibility for making contact and keep the commitments you make. Mentoring relationships often break down through lack of contact. Perhaps, the mentor has some pressing issues and cancels a meeting, and then the mentoree gets cold feet and decides that their mentor must be too busy or too important to spend time with them. And that's the end of it. If someone has agreed to take you on they won't think like that. But if they are busy they'll think that it's your responsibility to get back in their diary. You need to follow them up.

If you and your mentor agree that you should do something, say investigate potential training courses for you to evaluate together, you need to do it. It's a complete waste of their time (not to mention yours) if you haven't made any progress by the next time you meet. Worse still, you'll disappoint your mentor, which could lead them to question your commitment and the time they're investing in your development. Of course, things happen and you may have to renegotiate timeframes or expectations with your mentor. Just do this as professionally as you would any other part of your job.

Career Chick Hot Tip: Take responsibility to appoint mentors and manage your relationships.

Who To Appoint

You can find mentors in many different places. Consider people who:

- work in your organization that you work with every day – for example, an experienced colleague
- are in your organization but removed from your day-to-day activities – a previous manager or someone in another department, and
- you meet through your work or networking activities but are external to your current organization.

Career Chick Hot Tip: Find mentors in your organization and through your networking activities.

How To Approach Potential Mentors

Once you have identified what you want to learn and from whom, the next step is to establish the relationship with your proposed mentor. This is the bit that women often cringe at because they either don't know how to ask or they are nervous about being rejected. There are a number of different strategies that you can use, depending on who your intended victim (that is, your prospective mentor) is and how well you know them. The worst that can happen is that they'll turn you down. As long as you ask professionally, there is no reason not to give it a go.

If you approach someone you have an established relationship with you may refer to their knowledge of you or leverage your existing credibility. You don't even have to use the 'M' word (mentor, that is!). Here are a couple of approaches: *"I'm currently working on improving my presentation skills, and I was wondering if you would be able to spend some time with me so that I can discuss your approach"* or *"It's really helped in the past when we've talked through issues. I wonder if you would have time to discuss some of the career options I'm considering at the moment?"*

These approaches cover both why you have identified them as someone to work with and what you want to learn from them. Even if they say *"no"*, it will be for a genuine reason, such as time or work pressures, not because they don't want to help you. At the very least you will have represented yourself as a professional who is serious about your career. But if they say *"yes"* it could be the beginning of a potentially rewarding and beneficial business relationship. Alternatively, you may want to give a relationship time to develop before you formally ask the person if they will mentor you. This can take some of the angst out of the formality of this kind of relationship until you get to know them better.

One opportunity to find a mentor is when a current manager moves on to a new position, whether it's within your current company or elsewhere. This assumes, of course, that this manager has skills that you want to learn. (There are some managers you are more than happy to see walk out the door!) Who could resist this kind of approach: *"I am so pleased that you have this new opportunity, but I'll miss learning more about your approach to working with senior managers. Do you think you may be able to continue working with me on this as my mentor?"* Formalizing your relationship at this stage makes it legitimate for you to make contact even if they are up to their necks in alligators in their new role. They will remember the commitment that they made and make time for you.

> *Career Chick Hot Tip:* Be specific when you approach a mentor about what you want to learn and why.

Establish Expectations

Once you have appointed a mentor, you need to set some clear expectations. You'll find the experience more successful if you both understand the objectives and the framework for how you will progress. Initially, these expectations should include:

- the mechanics of how and when you will meet
- who is responsible to set meetings, and
- what outcomes you want to achieve.

Your mentor, particularly if they have formally mentored others before, may tell you how they would like your relationship to work. Others may be open to your suggestions. The responsibility though is on you to raise the topic in your first meeting and ask how they would like to approach it. If you are undertaking a formal program, you and your mentor may have been given very clear guidelines. It's appropriate to confirm these arrangements. For example, *"I understand that we are meant to meet every other week. Is that okay with you? What time of day would you like to regularly schedule this for?"* On the other hand, if your mentor is someone you have proactively contacted, even if you work on the sneaky, *'I'll get them to know and like me first and then I'll formalize that they are my mentor'* approach, you still need to establish an ongoing framework if you don't want your first meeting to be a one-off event. After the initial meeting you could try, *"It's been really helpful to hear about your approach. Do you think it might be possible for us to meet again next month? I would really love to discuss my progress and development in this area with you."* Who could resist? They'll be your mentor before they even know what happened!

Setting formal expectations about outcomes can be more involved than establishing meetings. How will you measure that you have learnt a particular skill? Or that you increased your capability to make better decisions in the future? These are quite subjective areas, but if you discuss up front that this is what you want to achieve, you'll both be able to judge if you are developing in this area as your relationship progresses.

Career Chick Hot Tip: Set objectives and establish expectations early in the relationship.

Ask For Feedback

The better you know someone, the more likely you are to respect and pay attention to any feedback they give you. And the better they know you, the more insightful and helpful this feedback is likely to be. To make this a really valuable development exercise you need to be able to handle criticism and suggestions openly and honestly. Unless you are perfect, which is possible but somewhat unlikely, some of the things you do or say could be improved. Be aware that you may hear some things you aren't thrilled about. It goes with the territory when you ask for feedback.

Hopefully, you'll only get negative feedback on development opportunities that you already know about and are working on. However, if you hear about things you could do better that you weren't aware of and it comes from a trusted source, such as your mentor, consider it valuable. It gives you the opportunity to ask questions, and find out exactly what you could be doing better or differently. If you react defensively to negative feedback or suggestions, you will have lost a valuable opportunity to learn how to make improvements. Remember, that's why you are working with a mentor in the first place.

So as you deepen your trust in your mentor, take advantage of the situation and ask for feedback. The more detailed and specific your questions, the more targeted feedback you'll receive. Then you'll understand exactly what behaviors or actions to repeat, or do differently, in the future.

Career Chick Hot Tip: Ask for and be open to feedback.

Review Your Progress

If your mentor has been formally allocated to work with you, the program will probably have a definitive end date. You may want to say thank you for your time and commitment over the course of the program, shake hands and walk away. But if you want your mentoring relationship to continue, it's up to you to ask your mentor. You may want to say, *"I have learnt so much from you while we have been working together, would it be possible for us to continue to meet?"*

While a formal program has obvious times to review progress and ongoing commitments and actions, a relationship that you have initiated will not have the same structure, but still needs to be reviewed regularly. It is beneficial to evaluate the ongoing benefits of the relationship so that both you and your mentor know that your *Career Development* is on track. For instance, it is much more professional to acknowledge that things have changed or that you are moving into a new area of development and formally acknowledge the end of the mentoring relationship, rather than just let it meander on. In this situation, you could say, *"Thank you so much for your time and the expertise you have given me during the last six months. I've learnt a lot from you and it's made such a difference, putting your ideas into practice. I'm going to keep working on the things we've discussed and I'm now going to move to the next stage of my career plan. I'd really appreciate keeping in touch and letting you know how I progress in the future, if that's okay with you?"* Obviously you would tailor this to the particular circumstances. Acknowledge what you have learnt, how you are going to apply it, say thank you and keep the door open for future communication. Even if a mentoring relationship has run its course, maintain the lines of communication. You never know when they may act as a sponsor for you. When someone is no longer your formal mentor, move them straight into your networking plan or onto your board of advisors to ensure that you proactively maintain contact with them.

Sometimes a mentoring relationship develops into a long-term association. Your connection deepens, you continue to learn and your mentor is supportive but you end up meeting less frequently. When this happens consider whether to include another mentor in your career plan. If you have other skill or knowledge gaps, appoint a new mentor so that you can continue to learn.

Career Chick Hot Tip: Review the ongoing relevance of the relationship.

Be A Mentor

As you develop your career you have another opportunity to learn by being a mentor to others. You may not even be aware that you have knowledge that can help others. It may be what you know, who you know, your ability to look at a situation from a different perspective or even your positive approach. If your skills or knowledge can help others, sharing them can be a valuable experience. Not just for up-and-coming Career Chicks but anyone who's interested in learning from you. Often requests like, *"Have you got five minutes?"* or *"Would you have time for a quick coffee?"* are calls for help. Alternatively, if you see someone struggling with a particular area, rather than telling them what to do (which most people resent), subtly inquire if you can help them.

When you do invest the time to mentor someone else, you'll most likely get a lot out of the experience. The benefits can include an increased awareness of what you know, the opportunity to take time out to think about what it is that you do, and the chance to learn from and expand your network with the mentoree. Mentoring someone else is a cross between an investment and a gift: you get a return on your investment and enjoy the experience as well. As you learn and develop your skills, smart Career Chicks will realize they have the responsibility to help others in return. As Madeleine Albright is known for often saying, *"There is a special place in hell for women who refuse to help each other."* Ouch! Of course, you don't only have to mentor women. What you know is universal and men are people, too. Well, that's the rumor anyway!

Career Chick Hot Tip: Share what you know and be a mentor to others.

Career Chick Hot Tips to consult with mentors:

- Appreciate that mentors are crucial to your *Career Development*.

- Recognize that mentors and organizations benefit, too.

- Have different mentors to learn different things.

- Know what you want to learn from a mentor.

- Take responsibility to appoint mentors and manage your relationships.

- Find mentors in your organization and through your networking activities.

- Be specific when you approach a mentor about what you want to learn and why.

- Set objectives and establish expectations early in the relationship.

- Ask for and be open to feedback.

- Review the ongoing relevance of the relationship.

- Share what you know and be a mentor to others.

Chapter 17

Know When To Move On

"You always know when the relationship is over. Little things start grating on your nerves: 'Would you please stop that? That breathing in and out, it's so repetitious'"[1]

Ellen DeGeneres, comedian

Sometimes the effort required to do your job feels as productive as bashing your head against a brick wall. Over and over again. It's not very constructive; in fact it's tiring, frustrating and a complete waste of time. The problem is that often, even though your head hurts, you're still tempted to keep going. You think that if you just keep trying you'll eventually break through. Maybe you will. And maybe you won't. The trick is, knowing when to stop before you hurt yourself.

Career Chicks, like you, need to feel capable, confident and in control so that you can be the best that you can be. That's why you don't want to waste your time trying to demolish these 'walls'. Sometimes it's better to recognize that the wall is not going anywhere and that it's time *you* moved on before you get really frustrated and angry or waste any more of your time.

Whether you're trying to get ahead in a job or advance your career, the skill is in knowing when the time has come to move on. Different circumstances can initiate this kind of change, both negative and positive. Sometimes you need to move on to a new role or company because your current circumstances no longer work for you. Maybe your boss is hopeless, you're in a dead-end job or you realize your company offers few opportunities. However, career moves can also be initiated by positive circumstances, and there are good reasons to make a change. Perhaps you've been presented with an opportunity that's too good to miss, or one that you worked on as part of your career plan finally comes off. Being able to recognize when it's time to move on is a skill and another weapon in the Career Chick arsenal to help you get ahead and support your *Career Development*. There isn't much point being a brilliant communicator and a talented operator, with an inspired career plan, a deep network and knowledgeable mentors, if you don't make the moves you need, at the right time, to achieve career success.

Career Chick Hot Tip: Develop the skill to know when to move on.

Be Prepared

If you're prepared to act, you can take advantage of opportunities as they come up. For instance, you may hear about a start-up project in your company that needs talented people, or an unexpected vacancy that's in line with your career plan, or even an opportunity that you had never considered before. To take advantage of these opportunities you must be prepared to act when they present themselves. That way you can leverage your abilities to achieve career success. To be prepared, you'll need:

- your career plan – see Chapter 14
- to know the type of work you like and the environment you like to work in
- a mentor to call on for an emergency discussion, and
- a network to call on to find out more about the opportunity.

With these preparations at the ready you will be able to use them to help you make decisions when opportunities arise. You can be ready to move at a moment's notice. Of course, your moves don't always have to be reactive. In your career plan you may have scheduled a number of steps to get the skills or experience you need across a range of areas. These are moves you can make in a thought out, planned manner. Whether your moves are planned or reactive, be prepared so that you recognize opportunities when they appear.

Career Chick Hot Tip: Be prepared to move when opportunities present themselves.

Recognize The Signs

The ability to know when it is time to move on is a skill all of its own. Often, women are so focused on doing their job that they miss the signs that things are changing. Make sure your radar's on so that you notice when things are changing and opportunities come your way.

So what should you look out for? If someone calls you up to ask, *"Do you know anyone who may be interested in a new role/project/*

whatever?" don't treat it as an interruption. Maybe they're sounding you out to see if you're interested. If you just say, *"No, I'm sorry, I don't know anyone,"* that opportunity will be lost forever. Even if the opportunity isn't right for you, recognize that getting calls like these is a good thing. You are being asked for your opinion, which indicates that it is valued. At the very least, you'll have the opportunity to become someone else's sponsor by recommending them. However, you may also uncover a fabulous opportunity for yourself. Stop what you are doing and ask, *"Could you tell me a little bit more about what you are looking for?"* If you uncover enough information to indicate that they are sounding you out say, *"Actually, I would be quite interested in that myself, could we set up some time to discuss this a bit further?"* If you don't ask, you don't get! If they think enough of you to contact you in the first place, there's no harm in asking for more information.

Times of change can bring significant opportunities. If you know what is going on, you can recognize the signs when things are about to change. Look out for the clues, which can lead to career opportunities:

- organizational change
- restructures
- management changes
- major new customer contracts
- industry developments, or changes to government regulations or even changes at your competitor/s organizations.

Organizational changes, restructures and management changes all provide possibilities. New or project roles are often created and vacancies can appear when others get promoted or moved. New customer contracts or changes in the industry or your competitors' tactics may lead to the creation of more or new roles. Even rationalization in your industry or company can create change and opportunity. Whenever things change, new or different roles can emerge and these are openings to move forward in your career. But, you need to know that they are there.

As these changes play out, men, who traditionally devote more time to their network, are usually straight on the phone to their contacts to find out what is going on. This means that they are often the first to know about the opportunities that are coming up. If you are not across what is going on, the opportunity may have been and gone before you even hear about it.

To be aware of approaching change, watch out for what's happening in your company and your industry. If you hear about cutbacks in a competitor's company it may mean that they are struggling due to your company's success, but it could also mean that the industry is retracting and cutbacks are headed your way. Also watch the behavior of others in your organization, particularly senior managers, to gauge how much pressure they are under. Learn to tell the difference between normal business pressures and when managers look as if they are carrying the weight of the world on their shoulders. While you don't want to be second-guessing what everyone else says or does, if you do see a trend it may indicate that change is on its way. Another indicator of something going down is poor behavior within the organization. Being given unreasonable deadlines or people flying off the handle at little things can indicate a management team that's operating under an inordinate amount of pressure. Poor cultural norms, such as inadequate timeframes, inappropriately raised voices or personal attacks becoming commonplace, are also indicators that all is not well.

Have you ever heard about someone being appointed to a new role that you didn't even know existed? If so, you may have thought, *"I wouldn't have minded that. Oh well, next time ..."* Although you weren't aware of it, an opportunity presented itself and someone else was there to take it. It won't be any different next time unless you're the one ready to take advantage of the opportunity. That means you have to be on the lookout for them in the first place. Ramp up your networking, make some calls, meet a few people for coffee (decaf is okay!) and find out what's going on.

Career Chick Hot Tip: Actively keep across what is going on and recognize times of change.

Put Up Your Hand

You have a responsibility to yourself to leverage the opportunities that change presents. Once you find out about opportunities you must do something about them. Ask questions and find out more about what is going on. Ask about the changes, how the work will be done, what new jobs might come up, what skills are required and even if anyone is in line for these roles. Prepare for when these opportunities emerge, evaluate them against your career plan and talk with your network and mentors. Do some quick thinking and decide whether the new role is right for you. If it is, put your hand up (so to speak). Formally apply if that is an option, or tell someone who matters that you are interested. You must be in there to have a chance.

Organizations rely on this kind of proactive behavior to help them discover talent and also move with the pace of change. In an ideal world, managers have time to comprehensively review all the talent available to decide who is absolutely the best person for the job. But the world is not ideal and managers don't necessarily have the time, skills or knowledge to do this perfectly when change is imminent. They rely on proactive people to put up their hand for opportunities and make themselves known. This indicates that the person is across what is happening, that they're proactive and interested in the business. The people who proactively manage their career and recognize these opportunities are first in line. If you feel uncomfortable about when to put yourself out there and be seen, think of change as being a good excuse to step up your activities. The higher your profile and the more you're valued, the better you'll be able to take advantage of these opportunities when they happen.

Career Chick Hot Tip: Put up your hand when opportunities present themselves.

Learn Your Craft

While you don't want to stay in a role so long that it gets stale and frustrating, you also don't want to move around so often that you never actually learn anything. Spending time in one role, especially early in your career, allows you to learn your craft (whatever it is that you actually do – sales, finance, customer service, human resources, etc.).

What is important is that you don't move your focus up the career ladder before you have your feet firmly on the rung you are standing on. Manage your moves so that you learn and gain experience in the basics of your line of work. It's often said that those who move frequently, do so to avoid anyone finding out that they don't actually do, or know, anything. Not the image you want to have; a good reputation relies on having a certain level of stability. You really need to judge the dynamics of your organization and industry to determine how soon is too soon.

No matter what your area of expertise – selling, marketing, administration, finance, human resources or operations, for example – it can become your 'trade'. It may not have an apprenticeship like a traditional trade, but even if you have formal qualifications, you still need some practice on the job. You may not have to do the same thing day in and day out (thank goodness), but you do need to stay long enough to make sure you are proficient at the basics before you move on.

However, don't let this hold you back if an environment is wrong for you. Move to a similar job that lets you continue learning but in a setting that's more conducive for you.

Career Chick Hot Tip: Manage your moves so that you retain focus and learn your craft.

The Time Is Right

The ability to evaluate when the time is right to take on the next challenge is a skill all on its own. Women often see a new opportunity but don't go for it because they only have 80% of the job requirements and don't feel qualified. They want to be 110% ready and have all the criteria nailed so that there is no question of their suitability. And they want to have their current role under control and perfect, too. Men, on the other hand, say to themselves, *"I've got 5% of what that job needs, but I could do that. I'll throw my hat in the ring."* That may be a tiny exaggeration (maybe they only do that if they have 10% of a role's requirements), but they certainly don't wait around to be perfect before they put themselves forward. Is it any wonder Career Chicks get left behind in the stampede to move on and up?

Your career plan should include timeframes for when you plan to move to different roles to learn new skills. Use this as a guide, but don't let it prevent you from taking up new opportunities. If someone taps you on the shoulder and says, *"We have this fabulous promotion for you,"* or *"A new, highly visible project is about to start up and we want you to be part of it,"* don't say, *"I'm sorry but according to my career plan I need to do this job for another six months."* Unless it's something that's completely out of synch with your goals, you should grab the opportunity. On the other hand, if you score a really bad manager, don't stay just because your plan says you should. Your career plan is a prompt to make sure you go out and look for the next move when you are ready. Not wait until you are past your use-by date.

What you need to do is to establish some criteria and benchmarks to know when the time is right to move. Here are some questions to ask yourself to help you decide.

- Is the move in line with my career plan?
- What alternatives do I have?
- Who should I talk to for more information?
- Is this a unique opportunity?
- What are the potential benefits?
- Do others, whose opinion I value, support the move?
- What's the worst that can happen if it's the wrong move?
- What's the best thing that can happen if it's right?
- How can I make it happen?

To answer these questions you need to draw on your network and mentors and how well you know yourself. When you have the answers to these questions you will have the information to decide if you are ready and if this is the right move. It helps if you develop an understanding of how you make decisions. If you are faced with a choice and you don't know which way to go think about how you made successful decisions in the past. Consider how you made them, who you talked to and whether you followed your heart or your head. If they worked in the past, these can be a pretty reliable set of criteria to apply to your decision-making.

Career Chick Hot Tip: Evaluate if the time is right to move and understand how you make successful decisions.

If Things Go Bad

While a new opportunity can be the catalyst for moving on, you also need to recognize when things go bad and it's time to walk away. You may have followed all the Career Chick Hot Tips for handling difficult situations but the situation is beyond repair. Sometimes it takes a bad situation, a bad manager or a bad culture to make you realize it's time to go.

Nobody wants to give up or walk away the minute things aren't perfect, be seen as a quitter or feel that they have given up without giving something a genuine go. But you also don't want to stick with something for so long or try to make it work to the point that it has a negative impact on your work, self-worth, relationships or even health. The skill is being able to recognize when it's time to move on: when you have put in as much as you can to make the situation work, but before it has a negative impact on you.

Things don't always need to be a complete disaster to know that your current circumstances aren't working out. When you work in a job you love you are excited and energized. At best you get into a zone and really enjoy what you do. It may not be realistic to feel this way all the time. However, if you are never energized or excited and are always drained and tired, these also could be strong indicators that you should at least consider a change.

A poor manager can be a key trigger for a job move. It doesn't mean that they are a bad person but if working for them does not support your job satisfaction or career aspirations it may be time to move on. They may not be as skilled as they need to be, they may have poor communication skills or you may simply have a mismatch of personal values. Or it may be that they just aren't the right person for you to work with. Any of these circumstances could mean it's time to go. If you evaluate that this is a short-term issue with your manager (or there's a really good rumor that they are about to leave!) you may decide to ride it out, for a short time anyway. Either way the important thing is that you make the decision. Don't feel that you have no choice or other options.

Women, more than men, wait to be noticed and are disappointed when no one does. They get frustrated with the company, the management or the culture that they see as the blocker to their career progression. After beating their heads against the company career brick wall, women often mobilize and choose to leave the company or business life altogether. Although this is a huge win for all the small businesses, home businesses and other activities where women go on to spend their time, it isn't for the women who set out to pursue a career in the business world, nor for society or the economy, which miss out on the talents of these capable women.

There are many people and companies who will value you. You don't need to continue to work in a detrimental environment or for an ineffective manager. If things are difficult, do what is reasonable to fix or resolve the situation. But if it doesn't work for you – move on. A proactive move that puts you in charge of your destiny gives you the confidence that you had the courage to make the decision and others will see your decision positively. If things don't work for you and can't be fixed, you must make the right decision for you and move.

Career Chick Hot Tip: Move on if things go bad and can't be fixed. Do what is right for you.

You Are The Priority

It is not only what happens at work that motivates you to consider a move. There can be numerous personal considerations, too. Whatever the reason, don't leave it until it is too late or you have burnt out. The physical, personal and subsequent career repercussions can be severe and take a long time to get over. No job, repeat, no job is worth losing your health, peace of mind or family relationships over. No job. When you hop into a really crowded elevator most people glance up to make sure the warning light of a passenger overload isn't flashing. No one wants to be the passenger that triggers the warning. Don't wait to move on until your personal overloaded sign is not only flashing but the bulbs have exploded. Be aware of personal impacts and renegotiate your commitments before things get to that point. Alternatively, you may need to make some more substantial changes. You'll keep your credibility intact if you renegotiate your workload, ask for help or make other changes, rather than try to manage everything and fail. A step back to a more junior position or even part-time work is not the end of the world. These are viable options to balance your life, let you regroup and keep your reputation intact to take-off up the career ladder at another time.

Career Chick Hot Tip: Prioritize, step back and regroup if work takes too big a toll.

Develop Alternatives

Preparing yourself to deal with change requires you to develop alternatives and have options that are ready to implement. Your options provide you with confidence when changes are imminent. You can choose to either put your plan into action or ride out whatever is going on. It's so much easier to choose to stay if you have a Plan B and don't feel trapped.

Your options are in the pages of your career, networking and mentor plans. You have researched the career choices that are available to you and understand the options both internal and external to your current company. You have identified next steps and actions to pursue. You have a network to draw on and a mentor to discuss options with. Change, whether positive or negative, may simply mean that you bring these plans forward and step up your activity. It may be because you need to escape or because an opportunity has emerged sooner than you planned. Either way, if you are prepared you can act.

One way to prepare is to apply for an odd role that isn't your dream job but is on the right track. As long as you don't waste their time this can allow you to establish your credentials with a recruiter, learn what they're looking for and practise your interviewing skills. You never know you may even get the job! Even if you don't, the time you invested will be worthwhile if it gives you confidence, when the time comes, to apply for the one you really want. Better some time spent practising than sheer panic that you don't know how to find a new job when you need one. This is a proactive step to develop the skills to build alternatives when you need them.

Dedicating time to develop options, such as applying for new jobs or networking, is a genuine and necessary aspect of career management. As we've discussed, women tend to get the guilts about anything that distracts them from their immediate and short-term responsibilities. Don't. Ask your manager, or others who you respect, what they did or are doing to develop their career. Something like, *"I am working on my career plan at the moment, and trying to get a few ideas. I was wondering if you could give me some examples of what activities you have done to develop your career?"* Chances are they won't tell you about meeting with recruiters or jobs they are applying for, but they will, more than likely, reel off some of their current activities. It may be anything from doing some business reading, studying or 'keeping in the loop' by catching up with regular contacts. The important thing is not what they are doing (although this could give you some ideas), but they will be completely unfazed by your expectation that they are working on their career at the same time as working in their job. Ask several people you respect and see how common this understanding is among successful business people. Compare the reactions and answers you get from men and women. Hopefully, there won't be too much difference … and there may be some men who are not being proactive in this regard … but the sad truth is it's likely that women will struggle to answer this question more than men will.

If you do get some fresh ideas from these discussions – use them. Well, within reason anyway. You wouldn't run around and try and imitate anyone. You are you, and your value and career plan is uniquely your own. But if they have an idea, something you haven't thought of, someone to talk to, something to read or an organization to join, do it. There is nothing wrong with using an idea; as long as it's a good one, and you give credit for it.

Don't feel guilty about borrowing ideas or even about spending time on your career. And don't be shy about asking for help or indicating what you want. When substantial change comes along the only person who you can rely on to be looking out for you, is you. You may get some help from other quarters. In fact, the more effort you put into your *Career Development* the more likely others will be there for you. But you can't rely on them. You must back yourself, have faith in your ability and your ability to contribute, and trust yourself. That trust in yourself develops as you increase your skills at whatever it is that you do. Plus, when you have a plan that gives you choices, your confidence in yourself also increases and you can pat yourself on the back for being so clever. This confidence reflects in your decision-making and empowers you to take control of your career, rather than letting your job control you.

Career Chick Hot Tip: Develop options and alternatives before you need them.

Take Action

Whatever the trigger, the need to move on provides the perfect opportunity for you to fit all the pieces of the Career Chick CODE together for your career success. The options you have available are impacted by your communication skills, whether you allowed your good work to be seen, how you worked effectively with others in teams and meetings, the strength of your networks and the support of your mentors. When you combine these with the ability to know when to move, you're on your way to career success. What is important now is that you take action and move when you know it's time.

Career Chick Hot Tip: Act when it's the right time.

Career Chick Hot Tips to know when to move on:

- Develop the skill to know when to move on.

- Be prepared to move when opportunities present themselves.

- Actively keep across what is going on and recognize times of change.

- Put up your hand when opportunities present themselves.

- Manage your moves so that you retain focus and learn your craft.

- Evaluate if the time is right to move and understand how you make successful decisions.

- Move on if things go bad and can't be fixed. Do what is right for you.

- Prioritize, step back and regroup if work takes too big a toll.

- Develop options and alternatives before you need them.

- Act when it's the right time.

Chapter 18

Get The Job You Want

"Find a job you love and you'll never work a day in your life"
Confucius, Chinese philosopher (c.551–c.479 BCE)

Have you ever saved up for a car, or a new pair of shoes? As your cash grew you probably did some research? Perhaps you took a car for a test drive or tried on a gorgeous pair of shoes, even ones that were a half size too small? Sure the color of the car and the options you originally wanted weren't available, and the shoes weren't exactly the right size, but ... you had to have them. Your previous resolution to wait had disappeared and you needed whatever it was right then.

When rational thought gives way to your emotional needs, the result is that you may not negotiate to the best of your ability or you may accept something that isn't quite right. You settle for a car in a color that isn't your first preference or decide you don't really need a sunroof, if it means you have to wait. Or you convince yourself that those shoes will be absolutely fine even thought they are a half-size smaller than the shoes you've been wearing all your adult life. These are the decisions you often regret later as you gaze wistfully at other cars with sunroofs or hobble around with blisters on your feet.

A car without a sunroof or tight shoes may not be the end of the world, but when it comes to getting a job, you definitely don't want to settle for less. The ramifications of rushing in and not taking the time or exercising the patience to ensure that the job you get is the job you really want, can be far more serious. You may decide to start looking around because it's the right time for your career plan or events have indicated that it's time to move on. The danger is that once you make the decision to move, you start to feel desperate. This sense of urgency can lead to a feeling of discontent and, consequently, poor decision making. You can throw a pair of shoes to the back of the cupboard, but it's more of an issue if you don't make the right career decisions.

It's important to get the jobs you want throughout your career to keep moving in the right direction. That way you can leverage the opportunities that become available and ensure that you enjoy the work you do. As Confucius said, when you love what you do, work doesn't feel like work. By understanding how to get the jobs you want, chances are you'll find work that you love, rather than settling for less. To do this you need to develop the skills to get the job you want.

Career Chick Hot Tip: Develop your skills to be recruited to a job you love.

The Importance Of Being Successful

Apart from your own satisfaction, there are four important reasons why getting the job or promotion you want will help your career. Firstly, changing jobs often provides a major leap forward in your career (and salary!). Secondly, the process to be recruited or promoted requires preparation, time and effort, so you may as well be as successful as you can be. Sure there'll be disappointments along the way when you don't get a job, which is okay, too. As long as you learn from these experiences, they won't be wasted. Just check you're okay, dust yourself off, and get back on your way. Integrate what you learn into your next application. That way you'll significantly improve your chances of being successful next time.

Thirdly, applying for new jobs gives you the opportunity for exposure, whether it's with more senior people in your company or in a different organization. If you're successful in gaining an interview, or even if your resumé is just being evaluated, a job application is a wonderful opportunity to tell and sell your story. You'll be highly visible to people who are in the position to make decisions about your career, either now or in the future. Sometimes you may not get the job that you apply for (sad, but true), but managers often remember the people they have interviewed and consider them for future roles. This exposure is a valuable opportunity. For your credibility it's crucial that you do the very best you can when you apply for a job.

And finally, applications that are aligned with your career goals allow you to be a credible applicant. You don't want to apply for roles willy-nilly and be seen as a serial applicant who goes for whichever promotion or position is on offer. That's a sure way to lose credibility, fast. Make sure that what you apply for is what you want.

> *Career Chick Hot Tip:* Use the opportunities that job applications provide to tell and sell your value.

Decide To Apply

When you see or hear about a job you want, apply for it. Women often make the mistake of holding back and not applying for roles that they are qualified for. Not that they aren't ambitious or capable of doing the job, but women often work hard and wait for their contribution to be recognized and rewarded. As we know, this doesn't always happen. On the other hand, men ensure that what they have achieved is quantified, understood and recognized. Successful Career Chicks need to do this, too. You need to know and understand your contributions and be able to say, *"I am one of the people who creates value around here."*[1] Be able to articulate how you do that – and believe it yourself. Don't sit around waiting to be recognized. Help others see it. You need to 'Be Seen' (review Chapter 7 for more details) – this should greatly increase your chances to achieve the recognition and the opportunities you deserve.

Women also often hold themselves back from applying because they don't think they are sufficiently qualified or have enough experience to do a role. Some think they need to wait until they have the experience, credibility and can demonstrate success at every aspect of a job before they can apply for the next one. Men learn about an opportunity and think to themselves, *"Yep, I can do that,"* and apply for it, even when they haven't done the job before. It's generally not because they have over-inflated egos or they've lost their grip on reality. They just see something, think they can do it and apply. They have confidence in themselves and what they have done before, and they believe they'd be able to do the job.

When men evaluate the requirements of a position, they compare it to their existing skills, knowledge and experience. If they had to learn about a new part of a business in the past, they believe they can do it again. If they have been a successful first-line manager, they see no reason why they can't be successful as a more senior manager. They don't wait to say, *"I have done it."* They genuinely believe they can do it. They have tried new things in the past and been successful, so why wouldn't they be successful in the future? So they apply and often get the job.

When a man with less skill and experience gets a job (because he applied!) women can get annoyed. Don't limit yourself to apply for jobs that you could easily do. Evaluate your skills and experience in relation to a new opportunity and decide whether you can do the role. And if you think you can, you can. It may take a leap of faith; but do it anyway.

> *Career Chick Hot Tip:* If you have good reason to think you can do a job, apply for it.

Quantify Your Value

The confidence that men have in the culture of business (which is basically male culture anyway) means that they are in a powerful position to play the recruitment game. Men keep score. On everything. From their salary to their ranking in the hierarchy, from the size of their last deal to the value of their contribution to the company over time. They measure everything. Women tend to remember and discuss different things. Like the success of a team or how happy a customer was, rather than the specific numbers that demonstrate how they drove business outcomes. When it comes time to validate that they are the best candidate for a job, men will have the numbers to prove it. Women often won't.

Whether it's in your application or at an interview, numbers matter. Recruiters only want to put forward quality candidates. Also, the future success of a manager who is recruiting is linked to how capable the person is that they find for the job. Numbers that quantify and verify your success will assure them that you were successful in the past and will be in the future. You need to help the people that you want to recruit you to do just that.

Get into the habit of keeping a scorecard as evidence to support why you should be selected for a job. Make it a standard practice to track and record numbers. For example, the size of budgets or projects you manage, the revenue you brought into the company or even changes over time to revenue or costs. Know the numbers associated with the quality, quantity or ranking of anything you do: increased volumes over time; improved customer satisfaction; employee opinion results, for example. Whatever it is that you had an impact on, know your numbers. Not only will you be able to use these generally to cement your credibility, but you'll also have them on hand when you go for the job you want.

Career Chick Hot Tip: Know your numbers and quantify your value.

The Negotiables

It's vital to know what you want from a job. This includes the type of role you want, the style of manager you work best with and the kind of company and culture you prefer. These decisions require some thinking and even a little soul searching to understand what's really important to you. Your career plan is the place to do this thinking, but when a job opportunity presents itself, it's often a trigger to revisit your plan and see if you're still on the right track.

When you know what is important to you, you need to decide *how* important it is. You need to choose what is and what isn't negotiable.[2] A non-negotiable condition may be anything from the salary level to the type of work to the culture of the organization. Whatever it is, it needs to be so important that you would walk away from an opportunity if this condition isn't met. Recruiters and organizations like to work with people who are very clear about what they want. They don't have time to be your career counselor. You can use your list of non-negotiables as a framework for you to ask questions, either in the fact-finding stage or at interview. That way you won't waste anyone's time, pursuing jobs you don't want.

The issues you're prepared to negotiate on are a little different. They're important to you, but they're not show-stoppers. You may want to negotiate for a particular benefit, but you're not going to walk away from the job if your request can't be met. Again, these provide you with a framework for discussions and demonstrate that you have thought about what is important to you. If you do negotiate for them you're much more likely to get at least some of what you want. If not all!

Career Chick Hot Tip: Decide what is negotiable and non-negotiable when applying for a new role.

Your Resumé

Your resumé is often the first opportunity to state your case when you apply for a job. This document needs to be short and succinct. Chances are that whoever is reading your resumé is reading many others at the same time. They won't have time to read between the lines to understand who you are and what you're offering. Make it easy for them. Make yours concise. Look for the keywords in the job advertisement and use them in both your covering letter and your resumé. Recruiters often put applications through a keyword search as a shortcut to find the relevant ones before they even read them. Using keywords from the ad prevents you from being culled before anyone has even read yours. Once they read it, make it easy for them to put you forward to the next stage. The best ways to do this are to:

- make sure that your application addresses the requirements of the job
- include numbers to demonstrate your achievements, and
- use positive, action-oriented language.

It's also imperative that you are 100% honest in the claims that you make. There is no point inflating your resumé to get an interview, or even a job, then have it all come tumbling down because you didn't tell the truth or you exaggerated. It's a waste of time and effort for everyone involved and will severely damage your credibility.

Career Chick Hot Tip: Use your concise resumé to sell your value with appropriate keywords and numbers.

Sell Yourself To Recruiters

Your next chance to make a positive impact is at the first interview. If it's with a recruiter, you have to sell yourself to them before you get near the company. They want assurance that you meet all the job criteria, have demonstrated success and are a quality candidate to put forward to their client, the company you want to work for. No matter how good a rapport you develop with the recruiter, remember: the company is their client not you. Never exaggerate to a recruiter as they have very well-developed fib radars. They talk with people all day, every day and know the difference between a true story and a story that is just too good to be true.

Often your first contact with a recruiter is specific to a particular role you are interested in. Put all of your effort into presenting yourself in the best possible light for that opportunity. However, if the opportunity doesn't work out, and you have established some rapport with the recruiter, ask them if it's okay to keep in touch regarding future opportunities. Once they agree, add them to your networking plan and diarize them for a regular phone call or even an occasional coffee. This allows you to keep them abreast of your job-hunting efforts and enquire about new opportunities. Recruiters are interested in having a high quality pool of candidates to draw upon. When they get a new role to fill, it makes life easier if they have the perfect candidate on their books, which adds significantly to their credibility with their clients.

Career Chick Hot Tip: Sell yourself as hard to recruiters as you would to the company you want to work for.

Do Your Research

The research and preparation you do for interviews is, in many ways, just as important as the interview itself. Recruiting managers will often gauge how interested and enthusiastic you really are by how much research you have done.

You should also find out who will conduct the interview. If your first interview was with a recruiter it's perfectly legitimate to ask them who will be involved in the second interview, their position, how it relates to the job you're going for and any specific criteria that person will look for. If your initial interview is directly with the company rather than a recruiter, ask whoever sets up the interview time with you for this information. Once you know who you'll be meeting, draw on your network to see if there is someone who knows the person or has worked with them previously. An online search may help you with some background information, such as positions they have previously held. Although they shouldn't, interviewers often talk about themselves or things they have done. Asking a question like, *"Was* *that in your current role or when you were with <<XYZ Company>>?"* is an easy way to demonstrate your preparation and enthusiasm without showing off.

Prior to an interview you should ask what is expected of you. Are you required to make a formal presentation? Is there a job description or any other support materials that you can read in advance? If you are given any documents it's important that you read them and demonstrate your knowledge of them in the interview.

Career Chick Hot Tip: Research the role, company, industry, interviewers and requirements for the interview.

Prepare Examples

You also need to prepare by thinking about yourself in relation to the job. Many interviews are conducted as behavioral interviews where you will be asked for specific examples of how you have previously demonstrated the skills they want. Take some time and prepare your very best examples. If you know one of the criteria is teamwork, have at least two examples (three would be better) where you worked successfully with a team. Be prepared to talk about how you worked with the team, what you did and the result. If a job requires achievement of specific business targets, have examples of targets you achieved in the past, how you went about achieving them, the results you realized, and so on, for whatever criteria the job requires.

You may even be required to undertake tests as part of a recruitment process. These can include online psychometric tests, attendance at an assessment centre, fact-finding and role-play exercises, and panel interviews. These may be held before or after the initial interview stage. The results can form the basis of questions at a subsequent interview. Don't panic about what these tests may reveal about you. Ask questions and research the skills that have been tested and prepare examples that demonstrate these for the interview. There should be no surprises: clever Career Chicks understand themselves well enough to answer any tricky questions – as long as they have prepared.

Career Chick Hot Tip: Prepare examples of how you have successfully demonstrated the requirements of a job.

Attitude Matters

Your preparation should also include your appearance and your attitude. Unless it's part of the job description, an interview is probably not the place to display your creativity by what you wear. You can't go wrong with these two rules: look business-like, and aim to be the best-dressed person in the room. Wear that killer outfit that always feels fabulous to give yourself a magnificent confidence boost. (If you can't justify a shopping expedition to yourself on the basis of a job interview you just aren't trying!) And keep in mind that, no matter what the fashion industry tells you, black is the only black – it always looks appropriate!

Once you look fabulous, you can focus on how you'll communicate. Plan to make direct eye contact, be proactive with your handshake and conscious of your posture. Many recruiting managers, especially men, are not confident at reading the body language of women. Often they just don't have as much experience at doing so. As guys grow up they acquire intuition about whether other guys are lying, exaggerating, or embellishing the facts. This means they often base judgments and recruitment decisions on what they believe is the *real* story. If your body language is ambiguous and they are just not sure about you, it's easier for them to select a man (whose weaknesses they do understand) for the job.

Career Chick Hot Tip: Demonstrate your positive attitude with a killer business outfit and positive body language.

The Interview

You're likely to find that the interview is conducted as a behavioral interview, where you'll be asked questions about how you demonstrated the required skills of the position in previous jobs. (If you haven't had much work experience you may be able to draw on experiences at university, part-time work or even in clubs, sporting teams or social groups.) These interviews often include questions like,

"Tell me about a time ...", "Can you describe a situation where ..." or *"Please give me an example of ..."* The purpose of these questions is to look for specific knowledge, skills and abilities in your past to indicate the likelihood that you will demonstrate them again in a new position. If you think through your examples prior to the interview and get asked these kinds of questions, just describe the situation, what was required, what you did and the result you achieved. If you can do this succinctly and without prompts from the interviewer they will think you're a legend.

When assessing your suitability, interviewers are also influenced by the words you use. It makes sense to use positive 'can-do' words that indicate confidence, action and expectations of success. Words and phrases such as accomplish, success, will, move forward, progress, positive contribution, momentum, specific actions, results, achieved, managed, changed, verified and defined are just a few.

These positive words will assure the interviewer that you can be successful in the position. You should use as many relevant numbers as necessary to support your positive approach. They are your evidence. To optimize the potential of selecting the best candidate, a recruiting manager will select the person who appears the most likely to succeed.

Career Chick Hot Tip: In interviews use action-oriented, positive, solution-focused words and provide evidence of what you have achieved.

The 'Mommy Issue'

Hot Tips for Career Chicks aims to highlight some of the most important requirements for success in business life within the workplace. Not tackle the problems of life, the universe and everything. These include the very real challenges of work–life balance and managing family responsibilities, but the 'Mommy issue' and how you handle it at an interview does bear mentioning at this point.

As a result of Equal Opportunity legislation, interviewers and recruiting managers can't ask you details about your personal life. They can't ask your age, marital status or whether you have or are planning to have children. Yet lurking at the back of many interviewers' minds are the questions, *"Is she going to get pregnant and leave me with a vacancy?"* or *"Does she have children?"* And if so, *"How does she manage being a mother and working?"* These questions are not top of mind when they interview men. Harsh, not fair, unacceptable, and people know it's wrong to think this way but they still do.

The mere fact that you're a woman raises these issues in the mind of some managers. Because they can't alleviate their concerns by asking you outright, there's a chance these issues can work against you. One option to consider is putting the issue on the table so that you can remove this as an area of concern.

You don't even need to raise the issue directly but you can still address it. For instance, if you talk positively about your three-to-five year plan, an interviewer will be impressed that you are committed to your career. It doesn't mean that you won't be taking a career break in the next three years, and if you do, you'll have a chance to establish your credibility and value first.

If you have children you can also minimize potential concerns about your ability to manage by raising the issue in a positive way. For example, if there is an opportunity you could say something like, *"I'm very skilled at time management. I have two children and a lot of support (you could add partner, parent, childcare if you want to embellish), so I am quite experienced at managing all parts of my life."* Enough said. You don't need to labor the point. Whether you address these issues is a very personal decision and yours alone.

Career Chick Hot Tip: Consider whether to alleviate concerns about the unsaid 'Mommy issues' at an interview.

Referees

If an interview process is successful and a job offer is imminent you'll be asked to provide two to three referees to attest to your suitability for the role and support your claims for the position. Before you provide the names consider whether a particular referee:

- would support you as being suitable for the role
- has seen you perform the functions required, and

- can confirm your level of skills, experience and knowledge in the relevant areas.

Ideally you will have a pool of referees to draw upon. You can build up this group each time you move to a new role or company by asking appropriate people to be a referee for you in the future. As you are leaving an organization, let your chosen people know you're moving on and ask, *"I was just wondering, given we worked together on <<whatever it was>>, if I could call on you to be a positive referee for me in the future?"* It's always advisable to ask if they will be a 'positive' referee. Better to find out now if they don't want to say good things than when they talk to your now not-so-potential new manager. Once they agree, add them to your networking plan and keep an accurate record of their position and contact details. Check that these details are correct each time you provide them as a referee.

Before providing them as a referee, you need to call them to let them know they may be contacted. You need to brief them on each job including:

- the company
- who will contact them
- the position you have applied for and some brief details
- why you want this job and believe it's right for you, and
- how the requirements of this job relate to their knowledge of your abilities.

Ideally, you should call them, although in a worst-case scenario you could send an email – as long as you have left a voice-mail message first. This shows you made the effort to contact them, and at the very least, they will have all the details before they get the call.

Only supply your referees once you're past the interview stage and a very likely candidate for the role. Don't list them on your resumé. You don't want them to be contacted before you have time to brief them on the role. You want to be respectful of the time and effort you are asking them to make by being a referee. Also, holding back on giving referees until later in the selection process allows you to have more information to ensure that you provide the most appropriate referees for the job you want.

Career Chick Hot Tip: Identify the appropriate people as positive referees for a job and brief them on each position.

Believe In Yourself

Ultimately, your career success comes down to your knowledge, skills, experience and attitude and how you build your business reputation. Be the best that you can be; believe in yourself and you will have a distinct competitive advantage. Practise the tips and learn the skills and go for the job you want.

Career Chick Hot Tip: Go for it!

Career Chick Hot Tips to get the job you want:

- Develop your skills to be recruited to a job you love.

- Use the opportunities that job applications provide to tell and sell your value.

- If you have good reason to think you can do a job, apply for it.

- Know your numbers and quantify your value.

- Decide what is negotiable and non-negotiable when applying for a new job.

- Use your concise resumé to sell your value with appropriate keywords and numbers.

- Sell yourself as hard to recruiters as you would to the company you want to work for.

- Research the role, company, industry, interviewers and requirements for the interview.

- Prepare examples of how you have successfully demonstrated the requirements of a job.

- Demonstrate your positive attitude with a killer business outfit and positive body language.

- In interviews use action-oriented, positive, solution-focused words and provide evidence of what you have achieved.

- Consider whether to alleviate concerns about the unsaid 'Mommy issues' at an interview.

- Identify the appropriate people as positive referees for a job and brief them on each position.

- Go for it!

Chapter 19

Earn What You're Worth

"The minute you settle for less than you deserve,
you get even less than you settled for"[1]

Maureen Dowd, New York Times' columnist

"It's not just about the money," women all over the world say, inadvertently launching a Scud missile directly through their salary negotiations. *"Of course I want to be paid fairly,"* they continue, *"but I really want to do interesting work/use this job to advance my career/ make a difference/feel valued and so on."* Even if they don't make the mistake of voicing these sentiments out loud, this is often how their self-talk goes. Women often think that negotiating for themselves and their remuneration is somehow tasteless, and that being driven by such a selfish motive will lessen a decision-maker's interest in them for the job.

But, in fact, the opposite is true. By not negotiating hard for remuneration, women send the message that they don't have the confidence to stick up for themselves. The money discussion is a key opportunity to demonstrate confidence in your skills, knowledge and experience, and what you believe you are worth. This is a key area to focus on to ensure that you achieve the success and rewards you deserve as you develop your career.

Unless you are independently wealthy or an heiress with significant expectations, there is a pretty reasonable chance that money is one of the main reasons you work. Yes, there's that dirty little five-letter word. Money. It not only makes the world go round, it pays the bills, buys the food, dictates what type of house you live in, the vacations you can afford and, one day, what type of retirement you will enjoy. It is important for your lifestyle. Career Chicks are also driven by the desire to achieve and no doubt you want to make a difference, be valued and advance your career. But chances are that you do need to earn money to live. If you must work, you may as well optimize the amount of money you make to support the lifestyle that is important to you.

However, there is another much more subtle reason why the money you earn is important to your career. The business world tends to be incredibly hierarchical and the amount of remuneration that you are perceived to receive, establishes your importance on the career ladder. Your perceived relative importance in an organization can impact how seriously you are taken and, consequently, your potential capability to do more senior jobs. If a man perceives that he is of higher value than you because he earns more or is on a better bonus structure, even if he is more junior in rank, he may dismiss what you say. You may have to struggle to have your ideas or directions taken seriously. Salary and remuneration negotiations are critical not only to what you are paid, but also to your reputation and status.

Downplaying your monetary value diminishes you in the eyes of others, making it seem like you're not as serious, tough, skilled (at negotiations, at least) or confident. Men have significant experience at putting a dollar value on their worth and negotiating hard for themselves. Women are often concerned about looking pushy when they negotiate and may settle for less than their male counterparts. The success of men, and the relative failure of the *'notice how good I am and just pay me fairly'* approach of women, suggests that their strategy works better.

Career Chick Hot Tip: Appreciate that how much you're paid is important to your career.

The Salary Gap

Yes, there is a significant salary gap between men and women. Women are often paid less when they start as graduates, throughout their career and even drastically underpaid when they reach the highest positions in companies. In the United States a 2008 study found that the total compensation for female CEOs was only 85% of that of men.[2] The theme is widespread. A Catalyst study of MBA graduates in the U.S. Canada, Europe and Asia has found that women earn less than men from their first job and that this trend continues for remuneration and ranking throughout their careers.

A 2008 report in Australia by the Government's Equal Opportunity for Women in the Workplace Agency (EOWA)[3] based on their 2006 Census of Women in Leadership found that not only were there not as many women in what they defined as Top Earner positions as men (surprise, surprise), but also that there was a significant difference in remuneration based on gender. The report found that female Chief Executive Officers (CEOs) of ASX 200 companies earn only two-thirds the salary of their male counterparts. Take one step down and the female Chief Financial Officers (CFOs) and Chief Operating Officers (COOs) earn, on average, half of their male equivalents' salary. Some women have made it to the top but even they don't earn as much as the men.

The Australian report also found that lower remuneration for women isn't confined to the more senior positions. Across the census of all Top Earner positions, the EOWA study found that women's overall median pay was 58% of the overall median pay for men. It gets worse. In Human Resources, where women in senior positions are more common than in some other fields, the pay gap is still 43%. And these results are for women classified as top earners! In the United States the 2008 median weekly earnings data also showed a significant gap for women in management, professional and related occupations–earning only 70.1%[4] of men's earnings.

For Career Chicks who aren't in the top-earner category, it's no better. In the US in 2008 the median weekly earnings of full-time working women was 80% ($638 a week compared to $798) for men.[5] In the UK in 2009 the median weekly pay for full-time employees was also 80% of the male rate for women.[6] The gap between men and women's average weekly earnings was 35% for all employees earnings and 21% for full-time employees in Australia in 2009[7] and 26.7%[8] for all employees in Canada.

The numbers tell a convincing story. Nevertheless, it is not the whole story. This is to say the least, a complex issue. While there's no doubt that there is a significant gap, it doesn't necessarily mean that the guy at the next desk, doing exactly the same job as you, is taking home more dollars. (If you think he is, then it's time to negotiate with your manager ... keep reading!) There are issues of career-breaks, fields of study, occupation, employer selection and the number of hours worked. But when you look at like for like (such as CEO compensation) it does mean that there is a trend in the business world for men to earn more than women for the equivalent work, and that something, somewhere, is not right.

Many issues have contributed to this gap. It's not just down to discrimination by men or that women have failed to negotiate appropriately for themselves; it's a complex issue. Women are still seen as the prime caregivers in society and many, as discussed earlier in this book, take career breaks or work part-time. There is a lingering perception that women have a choice about whether they work or not (obviously these guys are fairly out of touch with the price of groceries) and think that money is not as high a priority for women. It doesn't help that women are often reluctant to negotiate for themselves. The salary gap is also often blamed on the fact that women may have discontinuous careers and lose traction with their *Career Development*. Rather than justifying the difference, it would be more beneficial to change the business culture to support people who, for all sorts of reasons, need a career break.

The issue has its roots in history and the role of women in society. Women have, by and large, been paid less since the beginnings of the Industrial Revolution. But the desire is there for equal work to be compensated with equal pay. In 1963 John F. Kennedy signed the Equal Pay Act in the United States, the U.K. followed a little later in 1970 and Canada introduced its first federal pay equity legislation in 1977. In Australia it took from 1969 when a ruling made by the Australian Conciliation and Arbitration Commission in 1969 established 'equal pay for equal work'. The ruling didn't cover all women in all occupations and the fight has continued in various forms since then to ensure that women get their fair share. In spite of the various there is still a gap. Whether the current gap is an improvement on the past is, in large part, irrelevant. It's still unacceptable. If you do the same work surely Career Chicks deserve to earn what the work is worth? The way to ensure you do is to ...

Career Chick Hot Tip: Be prepared to negotiate for what you deserve.

Have An Impact

The good news is there is a lot you can do to make sure you earn what you're worth. To positively impact what you earn, you can:

- choose jobs and professions that pay well
- be prepared to negotiate

- learn the unwritten rules of salary negotiations
- know when to negotiate
- ask for what you want, and
- don't settle for less than you are worth.

If you increase your knowledge of these areas you may not make it to the top of the rich list, but you will be much more confident and better equipped to have the discussions that you need to have.

Women impact their remuneration potential from the start of their careers through the types of roles they take on and the areas in which they choose to work. Women have gravitated towards what are described as 'soft skill' jobs – support roles like human resources and operations. You know, the easy ones (not!) that involve dealing with the most complex variable in an organization: people. Unfortunately, these are often the lowest paid roles. If you like this work you should feel free to pursue a career in these areas, but you may not make your fortune. The roles that are much more likely to pay are line-management positions, particularly those with profit and loss responsibilities, such as sales and finance. Also, some industries usually pay higher salaries, such as telecommunications, information technology, finance and pharmaceuticals. When you choose your career path consider the remuneration implications of the type of job and the industry.

Career Chick Hot Tip: Consider the remuneration implications of the job and industry you choose.

Negotiate For You

Regardless of what discipline or type of organization you select, the opportunity is there for you to negotiate the best deal you can. However, women are often reluctant to do this because they:

- are concerned about being seen as too aggressive
- think they'll be seen as self- rather than business-focused
- are uncomfortable with negotiating
- don't know what to ask for, and
- lack confidence.

The answer to all of these concerns is to learn how to negotiate for your remuneration. Men learn how and when to negotiate from each other. In pubs and coffee shops they discuss what others earn and benchmark their own relative position. They hear stories about how salary increases have been negotiated. They ask questions and learn. How women got the reputation for being over-the-back-fence gossips is a mystery. Men are the masters! They talk about everyone and everything; they probe and are far less embarrassed about discussing topics like money. Even if the stories they tell have a whiff of *"My dad caught a bigger fish than your dad,"* and the stories get taller each time they are told, the key principles are repeated and learning is passed on.

This knowledge provides men with the framework, principles and unwritten rules of how to negotiate for themselves. They approach this as they would any other important strategic negotiation. Because of this they get many of the personal outcomes they want and enhance their reputation by demonstrating their excellent negotiation skills. They also win because they have the satisfaction of knowing they are valued and positioned appropriately in the organizational hierarchy. They don't have to waste time or energy feeling they have been ripped off or treated unfairly. This is a serious win–win situation.

The effort that women often put into carrying around a chip on their shoulder when they find out that their male equivalents are paid more than them could be put to better use by focusing on their own *Career Development*. The solution is to find out what the guys know and learn from them. Talk to them and they will tell you what they know.

Career Chick Hot Tip: Talk to men and learn how they negotiate for their remuneration.

What's Negotiable?

The first thing to find out is what you can negotiate for. Numerous items and benefits can be part of remuneration negotiations, including:

- salary
- performance bonus
- flexibility – working hours or remote working arrangements

- club or association memberships
- study assistance
- tools of trade – like laptops, cell phones and personal organizers
- healthcare
- shares or stock options – although you may need to be a reasonably senior Career Chick for this to be an option, and
- parking space – ditto.

This list is not exhaustive and only some of these things may be relevant for your organization. Your company may offer other benefits like childcare or health cover. Find out which of these apply to your role and organization so you can decide what you should negotiate for.

Career Chick Hot Tip: Understand what is negotiable.

Background Research

Apart from knowing what you are able to negotiate you need to do some other background research before you start negotiating for your salary and benefits. You need to know the benchmarks of the average remuneration packages for people in your job, your industry and in your organization. There are lots of credible online recruitment sites where you can research your industry. Talk to some guys in your network: they'll know. Most companies have a range or guidelines on what they'll pay for a position based on an applicant's skills and experience, not to mention negotiating ability. This kind of research is factual and based on data that is generally verifiable.

But there is another kind of research that men do as well. They don't just find out about the published data and guidelines. They gather stories about what is really going on. They find out what others who do the same role are paid, as well as people who do a similar role in another division of the same company, and people in similar positions in other organizations.

Men aren't embarrassed about discussing numbers. They are not afraid to ask questions. They may not come straight out and ask, *"So, what are they paying you?"* except when their mate is telling them about his new job or promotion. Women see this kind of information as personal and private. Men don't think that way. For a man, being asked this question gives them the chance to brag and increase their status.

Men don't always ask direct questions, but they will probe to gather more information: *"That's great news about the new job! Did they throw in a parking space with that? They did? Excellent. How do they pay the long-term incentive? Oh, right you're not on the incentive. Sounds like you scored big, buddy!"* Without even asking the dollar question they can find out that their mate has managed to get a parking space but isn't on the long-term incentive. They already know which level of roles get which conditions and with this information they can make some pretty accurate educated guesses about where this person is positioned and the likely value of their remuneration. This gets filed away for when they or someone else needs the information. They won't necessarily tell each other exactly what salary someone else is on, or use it in an actual negotiation, but they will know where they fit in the scheme of things and where to pitch themselves.

The 'official' data you gather about remuneration ranges is of value, but the reality can often be quite different. It's not important what the company *says* it will pay, but rather what they are actually prepared to pay. If your coffee shop research shows that the company pays people in your area 20% more than the 'official' going rate, this is much more important to know. There is a chance that everyone is considered overpaid compared to the going rate. If that's the case … you want to be overpaid, too! In cases like this, there's a fair chance that you will be successful if you pitch strongly for an amount higher than the official figure suggested to you.

Your likelihood of success increases greatly with the amount of information you have and how confidently you use it. Once you understand how this works (and it does) you will be able to share it with your female colleagues.

Career Chick Hot Tip: Do your research and find out what companies say they will and actually do pay.

The Added Extras

Apart from your salary there may be other extras that you can negotiate for. Find out the value of the non-salary benefits so that you can quantify their value as part of your negotiation. If you are negotiating a position with a new organization make sure you ask exactly what is included in the package they offer. Companies often talk in terms of total remuneration packages that may or may not include all the benefits that are important to you. Some packages can be inflated by the inclusion of items such as a parking space and a value being placed on cell phones and laptops. The actual offer may not be nearly as attractive as it looks.

It is now commonplace for remuneration negotiations to extend beyond salary. For instance, negotiating for a higher bonus is one way of providing a manager with a guaranteed return on investment. You agree to meet certain performance criteria in return for a higher bonus. When you do this you demonstrate that you are backing yourself to achieve performance targets and will reap the rewards when you do. It also gives you the opportunity to maximize your potential earnings. When you have favorable results, the amount of your bonus to be paid is often easier to negotiate, as you have strong and relevant data as proof of your performance and contribution. But you still need to be ready, willing and able to negotiate.

You need to be clear about what is important to you. Have your wish list but decide on the relative order of importance, what is non-negotiable and what you are prepared to concede. Determine how important these are to you and what you are prepared to do if you lose. If you don't get the salary that other similarly qualified people are getting for the job, are you prepared to walk away? Or will you take the job for whatever you can get? If you get the money but lose out on some extra benefits will you be satisfied?

When you have this information you can start to decide what you will ask for (the correct answer: at least what the men get), what you are prepared to accept and how you will approach the negotiation.

Career Chick Hot Tip: Decide on your priorities, what is non-negotiable and what you're prepared to accept.

When To Negotiate

Opportunities to walk into the boss' office to negotiate for a raise don't happen every day. And this technique is unlikely to be the most successful negotiation tactic. Most organizations have quite strict protocols and restrict increases to the annual review process to help manage costs. But there are other openings when the time is right for you to negotiate for your remuneration, such as:

- at your performance appraisal/annual salary review
- when you get a new job or promotion, or
- when you have delivered something significant to the organization.

Annual reviews and performance discussions are obvious opportunities to talk about your salary, your bonus and other benefits. There is often a clearly articulated process that runs to the company's time line. Even if the monetary decisions get made behind closed doors and you are not given the opportunity to formally state your case, you can create it. Check with your Human Resources department or your manager about how the process works and the time line. Create the opportunity to negotiate by raising the topic with your manager two or three months out from the start of the formal process. Put the topic on the table by asking questions like, *"How is this year's salary review/bonus payment going to work?"* or *"Is there a way for my <<insert your most fabulous achievement in the last six months>> to be considered at bonus time?"* As you get closer to the review, put some numbers on your expectations: *"Do you think that a 5% increase is viable in light of my contribution during the year?"* Leave yourself some bargaining room so that you can create a win–win negotiation by appearing to compromise.

Other crucial times for serious salary negotiations are when you get a new job, a promotion, move to a new role or have a significant change in your accountabilities. Any change in your employment status is an opportunity to talk money.

If you have made a significant contribution, this also provides you with a bargaining opportunity. Strike while the iron is hot. If you have just delivered the coup of the century to your company you may want to table the issue when you are being congratulated by your manager with a tongue-in-cheek, *"Thanks, I hope you'll remember this when we sit down to do my salary review at the end of the year!"* This achieves a few outcomes. Firstly, you draw a very straight line between what you have delivered to your organization and your remuneration. And secondly, you have opened a door that you can follow up at the appropriate time with, *"As you would remember when that big deal came in during the year you agreed that this would be taken into consideration for this discussion."* Thirdly, if you say it with a smile in a questioning tone, this will ensure it's taken as a tongue-in-cheek comment. If you have made a significant contribution, there is a pretty good chance that your manager will be in high spirits and open to a positive discussion.

Career Chick Hot Tip: Know and use the appropriate opportunities to negotiate for your remuneration.

Have A Plan

A negotiation for your remuneration is exactly the same as any other business negotiation. It needs the same planning and strategies as discussed in the section on your *Operating Style*. The only difference is that it feels more nerve-wracking because the personal stakes are higher. The best way to mitigate this risk is to research and prepare even more thoroughly when it is on your own behalf.

Know your own value by keeping a scorecard of how you have contributed. This was discussed last chapter in relation to ensuring that you get the job you want. It's equally important when negotiating your remuneration. For example, knowing the value of what you have contributed means you can position this in relation to the requirements of the job and what you have delivered or will deliver.

Decide on your negotiation plan and tactics. It could be to bluff (a little) by asking for more than you want, then being prepared to back down (a little) or even to negotiate a future increase against business deliverables. Whatever technique you choose, just make sure it's appropriate to your *Operating Style* and that you are comfortable with it. Apply all of your negotiation and communications skills as you would for the business … only this time it's for you. Develop a plan for your negotiation and if you are still not confident talk it through with a mentor or a trusted advisor in your network. People who support you are usually incredibly helpful when it comes to preparing for this crucial negotiation – men, in particular, because they use exactly the same approach. Preparation gives you the confidence to represent yourself to the very best of your ability.

Career Chick Hot Tip: Prepare a robust plan for your negotiation.

Implement Your Strategy

No matter how much planning and research you do it all comes down to actually asking for what you want. You need to overcome any reluctance you have and just negotiate. One technique that can help is to think through the repercussions: what will happen if you are told no? How dreadful will it actually be? If you have raised the issue appropriately and demonstrated your knowledge of the market and your worth, will you really be any worse off? If you ask for what you want, will your manager, or prospective manager, look at you aghast or burst out laughing, and say, *"You have to be joking!"* and then proceed to tell everyone you have ever met that you dared to try and negotiate for more money? Would you become a laughing stock, lose your job and home, and have to move to a hippie commune or remote South American village? Possible, but highly unlikely.

There are many more likely scenarios. The answer could just be yes. Or it may be no, but for reasons your research would never have uncovered. Even if you are turned down for the most predictable reasons – cost pressures, the timing or company policy – you will not lose your reputation and you certainly won't have to go into hiding. The reality is that you will have at least opened a door for future negotiation. Or you may get part of what you ask. At the very least, you will have demonstrated confidence in yourself and affirmed your value.

The style of how you approach these negotiations is important. You don't want to plead or beg or come across as needy, desperate or dateless. The crucial thing is to be clear and firm about what you are asking. Don't dance around the subject. Ask for what you want, then go back and fill in the details as required. You can start with a simple comment, such as, *"I'd like to talk to you about my expectations for the annual salary review,"* or *"I know that you will be reviewing the performance bonuses over the next few weeks. I'd like to discuss mine with you."* Make it clear what you want to discuss.

Once you're into the discussion, it's important that you stick to your plan. Women, once they have plucked up the courage to raise the money issue, usually state their case well. But they often accept the response and settle for whatever is offered or, worse, being told no. Women, generally speaking, back off too soon. Men push the point.

Unless information about what others earn is publicly available, a man won't say they know what a particular individual is on, but they use that knowledge. Not only to determine their own pitch, but also to indicate that they know what these positions pay. They may not even be completely sure of all their facts, but if it seems credible they will often give it a go. They are also less likely to acquiesce easily to the reasons provided for a no. A man is more likely to meet an, *"I can't approve that; I would need to get approval,"* response with, *"Okay that's fine. Please ask for the approval."* Whereas a woman is more likely to say, *"I'm sorry, I didn't want to make work for you ..."*

Men feel more confident to push the point because of their experience at reading each other; they know when to back off. Indeed they are quite comfortable with this (maybe not happy, but comfortable) because they have gone into the negotiation knowing their exit position. They know if they are prepared to walk away from the job, negotiate for a future discussion or accept whatever they are given. It is vital that you know your exit position and how to get there before you even start – exactly as you would for any business negotiation.

Increase your confidence by role-playing the conversation with yourself (or someone you trust) beforehand. Anticipate some of the responses you may get and formulate some potential answers. Decide how far you are going to push, what you will accept and how you can bow out gracefully if you really need to!

> *Career Chick Hot Tip:* Negotiate, hold your ground in a discussion and know your exit position.

Develop Your Career

Prepare, research, plan and negotiate for yourself. Call on your mentor and those that you trust in your network for help. Enhance your reputation, and increase your own confidence and the confidence of others by negotiating to earn what you are worth. Using these methods, you may just start to even up that salary gap for all Career Chicks. And when you do, share what you learn with the rest of the gals. All Career Chicks deserve to be paid what they're worth.

Career Chick Hot Tip: Share what you learn with other Career Chicks.

Career Chick Hot Tips to earn what you're worth:

- Appreciate that how much you're paid is important to your career.

- Be prepared to negotiate for what you deserve.

- Consider the remuneration implications of the job and industry you choose.

- Talk to men and learn how they negotiate for their remuneration.

- Understand what is negotiable.

- Do your research and find out what companies say they will and actually do pay.

- Decide on your priorities, what is non-negotiable and what you're prepared to accept.

- Know and use the appropriate opportunities to negotiate for your remuneration.

- Prepare a robust plan for your negotiation.

- Negotiate, hold your ground in a discussion and know your exit position.

- Share what you learn with other Career Chicks.

Career Chick Hot Tips
for *Career Development*:

- **Plan your career** so that you achieve your goals (and know what they are).

- Have conversations with your **network** to expand your knowledge and identify opportunities.

- **Consult with mentors** to learn and develop.

- **Know when to move on** to the next opportunity.

- Develop the skills to be recruited so that you **get the job you want**.

- Negotiate so that you **earn what you're worth**.

everything else

Chapter 20

Prioritize What's Important

"Things which matter most must never be at the mercy of things which matter least"

Johann Wolfgang von Goethe, writer (1749–1832)

Now you know that focusing on how you *Communicate*, your *Operating Style* and your *Career Development* will make your achievements stand out, enable you to leverage your knowledge, skills and experience, and realize your potential in the business world. However, there's one more challenge to complete the CODE for Career Success: knowing how to manage '*Everything Else*' you need to do your job well and support your career.

For Career Chicks, '*Everything Else*' covers a wide variety of activities, tasks and sometimes competing objectives. It covers anything that's important to you, from your work commitments to family and social responsibilities, as well as your personal goals and ambitions. The focus of this chapter is on priorities within the work environment to achieve career success, but recognizes you may have other priorities outside work, such as developing a plan for financial independence, deciding where to go for relaxing vacations or even finding a partner who supports your career aspirations. In the future, you may need to consider other priorities, like taking a career break to have children or handling parenting and care responsibilities, all while keeping that work–life balance. What's important to you will change depending on your circumstances at different times throughout your career.

When your career is going well, you should feel challenged, valued and fulfilled, knowing that you are contributing and doing your best. If you are tired or stressed from trying to juggle too many things, you won't enjoy any of these benefits or be in the position to perform at your best. The final clue to unlocking the CODE is no secret: the only way to manage '*Everything Else*' is to decide what is important to you and prioritize.

Career Chick Hot Tip: Work out what's important to you.

Prioritize

Now you have the first three parts of the CODE (*Communication*, *Operating Style* and *Career Development*) to focus on. If career achievement is important to you these will be your priorities. But still there's '*Everything Else*' that you have to do.

Working out what is important to you will show you where to focus your time. Bear in mind that you may not be able to do everything that you want, and some things that you'd like to do just won't get done (because something else has priority). It's not about what you have the capability to do, but the capacity. Learning to live with that is, perhaps, one of the greatest challenges for Career Chicks with superwoman aspirations to overcome. Men manage to live with it; you can, too.

Choosing what you truly need and want to do will give you the confidence that your time is being spent on what is most important to and for you. It's unrealistic to try to deal with every one of the multitude of demands that come at you – that approach comes at the cost of not being able to do anything well. Remember this insight and draw on it when you need the strength to say *"no"* to some things or leave some things that you could do for another time.

Career Chick Hot Tip: Make what's important your priority.

Keep It Simple

You may find that people use stereotypes and role models in the workplace to categorize behaviors and set unrealistic expectations. These can create work rather than facilitate career success. For example, women are seen as the queens of multi-tasking, being able to hold a conversation and type an email at the same time with little effort. Scientific studies now suggest that this may not be the most efficient way of working due to the downtime and effort that is required to swap between tasks.

However, the social conditioning persists and women often feel that they need to do everything. Supergirl, Wonder Woman and Lara Croft belong in comic books and movies, not in real life. (Although some super strength, super speed and even the ability to fly would be incredibly handy … and a little X-ray vision and power of the force wouldn't go astray either!) You may feel that you need to operate at superhero levels just to juggle everything that is expected of you on a daily basis. But you don't. The key is to simplify your expectations and work out how much you can realistically do.

Career Chick Hot Tip: Simplify your expectations; you don't need (or want) to do everything.

Time For Yourself

If you try to do everything, you run the risk of not doing anything well, and not having the time to exercise, eat right, or do any of the personal things that are important to you. Looking after yourself is absolutely essential to achieve and maintain career success. It's not a luxury. Men manage to prioritize what *they* want to get done, whether it's going to the gym, nicking out of work to get a haircut or taking time to attend a lunch. Whatever your personal circumstances, no matter how busy you are, you need to prioritize the things that help you look after yourself. This could be anything from maintaining your appearance to enjoying things that you would usually feel guilty about. Like having a manicure, spa treatment, a massage or attending a yoga class. When it comes to career success, these are necessities, not luxuries.

While men are more likely to notice the overall effect than little details like a manicure, women certainly will. It sends a message that you are well-organized and in control, so consider time taken for a manicure, pedicure or any other beauty treatment you need as an investment in your career. Imagine sitting across from another woman whose eyebrows haven't seen any wax or tweezers for a while. You may be wondering if she doesn't care or can't cope. This means that the time spent on your appearance is a legitimate career-management activity and there is no reason to feel guilty about it!

Others will also notice how you handle the pressures and stresses of the work environment. Spending time on stress-management techniques, such as yoga, meditation or even a hobby you love, will help your demeanor. Your reputation will be enhanced if you look well groomed, calm and organized, rather than flustered, out of control and frantic.

The other activity to prioritize is exercise. This is widely understood to be important for your general health and well-being for reasons that include disease prevention, weight control and increased energy and stamina – all of which are important for whatever you choose to do with your life. For a Career Chick these are essential: you need every bit of energy you can muster to be at the top of your game. There isn't much point being promoted if you then take time off work because you are worn out as you haven't taken care of yourself. Exercise will help manage stress, control your weight and make you feel good. It also gives you time to think, listen to music and either be on your own, or with others. Be sensible about exercising within any health considerations you may have and get a medical check-up before you start out. But do it!

And there's another career-related benefit: others will admire that you make the time to exercise *and* do a terrific job. They really will think you are incredibly organized and in control. It also provides a non-work, gender-neutral subject for small talk that men are likely to be interested in. Remember, networking and relationships are important to your career, so it's handy to have a topic of mutual interest to talk about. Of course, these work benefits are really the icing on the cake compared to the health advantages, not that icing and cakes are the best analogies in relation to exercise but everyone needs a little indulgence now and then!

Career Chick Hot Tip: Take time and look after yourself.

Have Some Fun!

You should also spend time on things that you enjoy. You may think that spending time away from the serious pursuit of your career is an indulgence, but it can also be an investment in building your network. Playing or watching sport, being creative, even learning about wine and food can make you a more interesting person and help you engage in the small talk that is such an important part of building relationships. Finding things in common with others will deepen your relationships, and you'll find that people are more willing to go that extra mile for you. You can be an attentive listener and ask lots of questions, but at some point you need to have something to talk about. And you never know what contacts you'll make either through these activities or through others who share your interests.

A successful athlete spends time cross-training to build physical fitness and to complement the core skills that are required in their discipline. Career Chicks also need to take the time to rest, refresh and re-energize, so that they are at the top of their game when it matters. This means that time spent on looking after yourself is a priority. Don't begrudge yourself time to spend on the things you love, as well as your career. Your passion and enjoyment will help fulfill you and, ultimately, complement your life and career aspirations.

So when it comes to managing 'Everything Else' for career success, prioritize what is important to you. Simplify your expectations. Spend time on what is important and be confident in what you do. In the next chapter you'll find even more Career Chick Hot Tips, including how to dress for the workplace and how to travel in style. Use all of these to show the world that you are competent, in control and successful. And you will be!

Career Chick Hot Tip: Do the things you love and have some fun!

Career Chick Hot Tips to prioritize what's important:

- Work out what's important to you.

- Make what's important your priority.

- Simplify your expectations – you don't need (or want) to do everything.

- Take time and look after yourself.

- Do the things you love and have some fun!

Chapter 21

Chick Tips

"Know, first, who you are; and then adorn yourself accordingly"
Epictetus, philosopher in Ancient Greece (c. 55–c. 135 CE)

Career Chicks have a fabulous range of choices, not only in how they work and shape their careers, but how they incorporate being a woman into their career persona. The options are endless ... clothes, accessories, shoes, hair, make-up (to name a few). However, this freedom can cause confusion when deciding how to present yourself to the business world.

As discussed earlier, the fact that there are more men in the workplace means the business culture is skewed towards male behaviors and expectations. The way that men dress, socialize and integrate their personal lives with work has become the accepted business standard. This standard doesn't always support the requirements, needs or desires of women. Until the rules are rewritten, it can help to understand how the boys incorporate 'being themselves' into their work persona. That way, Career Chicks can do the same. Here are some more Career Chick Hot Tips that include how to dress for success, and how to travel for work in style.

The Daily Quandary

How you look in the business environment plays an important role in how people perceive your competence and organizational fit. However you dress, your style will be noted and judgments will be made about your suitability and capability. It may not be right but it will happen, which makes how you present yourself as a chick and career-minded person a priority and a daily quandary to be solved.

At a Yale University commencement speech in 2001, Hillary Clinton gave the following advice: *"Your hair will send significant messages to those around you ... Pay attention to your hair, because everyone else will."*[1] Clinton was being ironic about the unfair attention and judgments that are made about women based on their appearance. It shouldn't be the case but, at this time, it's a reality that chicks need to be aware of. Whether you agree or not, this means that apart from

'*Everything Else*', chicks need to prioritize how they look and present themselves.

This doesn't have to be a chore. Looking appropriate can also be fun and enjoyable. Unlike men, chicks are not limited to wearing a suit and a different color shirt and tie each day. It's kind of funny when all the men turn up on the same day in a blue shirt ... you'd think someone had sent around a memo! But no, it's just bound to happen when the poor things have such limited choice. Fortunately, there are many more options for chicks. The trick is to know what is right for you and what is appropriate for the business environment.

The quandary is how to use your appearance to positively complement and reinforce your image, your *Operating Style* and, ultimately, your reputation. You need to determine 'the look' or image you want to be associated with your work style. If you are in a corporate environment where everyone, male and female, wears a suit you may want to conform ... or decide on a slightly more individual style. Or you may be in an office that has many different styles of dress, so choosing a conservative, corporate style will make you stand out and reinforce your professionalism. Or you could be in a creative field and need to demonstrate your style and taste through what you wear. It doesn't matter which category you fall into. Just be aware that you are sending a message with your appearance, so make sure it's in line with the image you want to project.

Career Chick Hot Tip: Define the look you want to complement your professional image.

Some Rules Of Thumb

Whatever your chosen look here are two little gems you can apply: aim to be the best-dressed person in the room, and dress for the job that you aspire to. When you're the best-dressed person, you look like you're the best performer. When you're dressed for the job you aspire to, you look like you're already working at the level of that role. If your goal is to be in a senior role in your company, take note of how the women in these roles dress and follow their lead. No matter how much of an individual you are, your success may be influenced by the judgments of others, so dress appropriately for your work environment.

The environment you work in could also determine aspects of how you dress. For instance, if you have a job that requires you to be out of the office and walking around customer premises all day, then pants may be the best option, particularly if you need to climb ladders or step over stock in a warehouse.

There are another couple of rules of thumb that could be helpful for you. High-quality fabrics and cuts make a difference not only to how you look, but how you feel and even how crumpled and in control you look by the end of the day. For instance, a linen suit can look crisp and fresh from the drycleaners in the morning, but by the end of the day it will be crumpled, making you look as if you've had a challenging day. You might not be old enough to remember the disappointment of women the world over when the soon-to-be Princess Diana got out of her carriage on her wedding day and the most anticipated wedding gown for years looked creased. If the look doesn't match the expectation, there can be disillusionment or at least disappointment. Wearing quality fabrics can help you appear in control.

If you are considering what color to wear, keep in mind that no matter what the marketers and fashion police claim: black is the only black. When Coco Chanel introduced the Little Black Dress in 1926, *French Vogue* likened it to a uniform for modern women. Not a lot has changed, and no wonder. It looks superb dressed up or down, with a jacket for meetings or with jewelry for dinner. It doesn't mean this is the only color you should wear, but when you want to look absolutely professional it's hard to beat.

Career Chick Hot Tip: Follow the established rules of thumb to dress well.

Three Wardrobe Essentials

Notwithstanding your personal preferences there are three essential items that are advisable for every Career Chick to have in her wardrobe. These are a high-quality collared shirt, an amazing suit and a business-casual outfit. You can have, or may even need, more than one of each of these, but at least one of each is a Career Chick necessity. A collared shirt may not be the first preference for your individual style, but if you have an interview, major presentation or situation where everyone will be in a suit, a collared shirt is completely appropriate.

It's the chick version of a shirt and tie. You can't go wrong with one. You may not want to dress in the style of a corporate uniform, but for some occasions it can give you the confidence and look you need to help you 'fit in'.

An amazing suit or outfit in your wardrobe is an absolute must to help you take on the world. One that you put on and know it looks perfect. With the cut, the fabric, and the fit, you feel like a cross between one of the world's most stylish women (Michelle Obama, Jennifer Aniston, Beyonce …) and the most powerful chief executive you can think of. You are invincible in this outfit. You almost have superhero powers. You may not be able to leap tall buildings in a single bound but you feel fantastic and exude confidence. Some days, for some events – an important presentation, an interview or even your annual review – you need that extra help. Boost your confidence with your fantastic outfit. It doesn't have to be expensive, but it does need to be the best quality, cut and style that you can manage. And, most importantly, you need to love it!

The third essential for your wardrobe is a business-casual outfit. Wearing business-casual may be your office's usual dress standard, or perhaps you get to wear it one day a week or only occasionally for conferences and seminars. Even if suits are the usual order of the day, it's a good idea to have a business-casual outfit ready for training days or off-site meetings. No matter how often you'll be required to wear it, you need at least one business-casual outfit in your wardrobe.

The problem with business-casual is that it is neither business nor casual. And the rules, particularly for women, are even less defined than the corporate standard dress code. You need to be guided by your company's interpretation of 'casual', but that often doesn't mean that you can wear jeans, T-shirts or anything you like. Even if it does, is that the image you want to project at work? Or is it something to save for the weekend? A reliable rule of thumb is to dress to the standard you usually would, consistent with your business image, just in different clothes. This may be your chance to wear pants, rather than a skirt, or something a little less conservative. Your appearance will be under as much scrutiny on casual days as it is on more formal occasions. If you maintain your quality standard and dress consistently with your look, you won't go wrong.

Career Chick Hot Tip: Include three essentials in your wardrobe: a collared shirt, an amazing suit and a business-casual outfit.

Accessorize

Accessories that you love can be fun and help define your look. Comfort may also be a priority, especially when it comes to shoes. As fabulous as the tallest stilettos look, they may not be practical for accompanying your client on a tour of their factory or a long walk through an airport. Instead, use accessories like shoes, handbags, eyewear, fragrances, scarves and jewelry to have some fun with your style, enjoy being a girl and follow fashion trends. And still be appropriate as a Career Chick. No one said you have to be boring to be successful.

A handbag is the perfect accessory to meld fun, fashion and practicality. Remember, the perfect bag needs to provide easy access to all your essentials – your cell phone, pen, security-access card or other paraphernalia – so you won't need to scratch around in the bottom of your bag while other people wait for you. You may need one bag that is big enough to carry files when you travel, another to go with your business-casual outfit, and then however many you require to match your work outfits. Ample justification for as many bags as you need! (The definition of the word 'need' is up to you, your budget and your affinity with handbags.)

Accessories are relatively inexpensive, compared to a new outfit, and you can keep them up-to-date with fashion trends. The only trick with handbags is to be careful when you change them over and make sure you transfer all of your important items from one bag to another. There is nothing more annoying than getting to work and realizing you don't have your security access card or pen when you are trying to appear confident and organized. This I know from personal experience!

And, like Hillary Clinton said, don't forget the importance of your hair. If you have your hair dyed or cut in a certain style, keep it that way. Otherwise, you may give the impression that you don't care or are too disorganized to make time to look after yourself. Time spent at the Hair or Beauty Salon is not a luxury in your busy lifestyle, but essential to maintain your career image.

When it comes to how people perceive you, your make-up can be as important as your hair. A hard day can show on your face. If you rub your eyes when you're tired, mascara streaks across your face are not a classy look; nobody looks good with panda eyes. Keep some basic make-up supplies on hand to look your best throughout the day. A couple of touch-ups when you go to the ladies' room will help you look refreshed. You may even run into some senior women doing the same thing and get the chance for a casual chat (and also work in some favorable messages about what you are doing). Not all elevator pitches happen in the elevator. It also gives you the chance to stretch your legs and give your eyes a break, particularly if you work in front of a computer. Just don't do it so often that people think you are completely vain or have some kind of bladder control problem!

Keeping an emergency kit in your desk is another clever idea to help you deal with a variety of unexpected problems. A spare pair of pantyhose for the annoying ladder that appears 10 minutes before a presentation, a clear nail polish (for pantyhose repair if the spare pair have already been used – dab the polish around the edges of the run to stop it getting worse), a nail file, deodorant and some sanitary items will cover most emergencies. And some chocolate. No explanation necessary.

Career Chick Hot Tip: Accessorize to complete your look and enjoy being a chick.

Travelling Chicks

Travel for work is often a frequent career requirement, but there are a few things for unwary chicks to consider. Men seldom need to think about night cream, hairdryers and make-up, so chances are you'll have more luggage. If you do travel frequently for work, make up an extra set of toiletries and keep them packed and ready to go. It'll save time and ensure that you actually have everything you need when you get to your destination.

If you travel with men who only take carry-on luggage you may want to do the same. You don't want the boys leaving you behind at the airport or getting impatient waiting around for the girl who packed too much luggage. If you're not sure, ask someone you're travelling with if they'll be checking in luggage. However, if there's stuff you can't live without, like gym shoes for a workout, then don't worry about them. Take what you need. You could even consider catching a different flight and score some time on your own. Also take some of your home comforts with you, like a book you want to read or your MP3 player. Use the travelling time to do some of the things you don't usually have time for. A plane trip is a perfect opportunity to listen to music, read a trashy novel or even play a mind-numbing computer game. Don't work when you're on a plane. The person sitting next to or behind you could work for a competitor and be able to read your confidential documents. This is not a risk you should take. Sit back, relax and enjoy the travel. It's a chance to take time out from your regular commitments. You can still work a very productive day and take the opportunity to go to the gym, take a walk, have a fabulous meal or watch some TV before bed. Meet up with friends or use the time to network. You don't have to be on duty 24 hours a day just because you are away from home. Men certainly aren't.

Career Chick Hot Tip: When you travel, take what you need, including some home comforts and time for yourself.

Work It!

As you can see, aligning the rest of your life with your career doesn't mean you need to compromise yourself to fit into a corporate stereotype, whatever that is. You don't need to wear a neck to knee outfit (literally or figuratively) and hide who you are or work yourself to the bone when you travel for work. So put on that fabulous outfit and be confident in the image you present. Show the world that this Career Chick is in control and successful … and you will be. You can be yourself, enjoy being a woman and still have career success!

Career Chick Hot Tip: Look in control and you will be!

Career Chick Hot Tips for being a chick:

- Define the look you want to complement your professional image.

- Follow the established rules of thumb to dress well.

- Include three essentials in your wardrobe: a collared shirt, an amazing suit and a business-casual outfit.

- Accessorize to complete your look and enjoy being a chick.

- When you travel, take what you need, including some home comforts and time for yourself.

- Look in control and you will be!

Chapter 22

Unlock The CODE

"It is better to light a candle than to curse the darkness"

Chinese proverb

Business is a competitive environment for anyone. For women there is an extra degree of complexity as the nuances of the business culture are skewed towards men. But no matter how competitive the environment, you can still be positive about your prospects. Rather than being frustrated by the challenges you can do something about it and, like the proverb says, start lighting candles. Don't let your future career success be limited by what has happened to other people in the past, or even what you (or people you know) may have experienced. Your ability to achieve and experience career success is up to you and the choices you make. The CODE for Career Chicks provides some background knowledge and practical tips to help you develop the skills to make the choices that are right for you.

It's your choice whether you achieve whatever it is you define as success. It's your choice whether you become the best 'you' that you can be and build on this to achieve what you want, or whether you work away and wait in the wings for success to come to you (hint: history has shown that this approach is a long and fruitless one). Only you can choose how much effort you put into being proficient at what you do and how much focus you apply to developing your career as a standalone activity. You get to choose how you define success and what you're prepared to do to achieve what you want. You can focus on continually improving your performance and pursuing your personal goals or begrudgingly compare yourself to others who seem to achieve success with the greatest of ease. Whatever you choose is absolutely okay, as long as it's what *you* really want.

It doesn't matter how others define success or what they think you should do. It does matter that you make your own choices. You are the person who needs to live with them. Success for you may be reaching a certain title or pay level, or owning a specific car. Or it may be working in a particular field, for a specific company or with certain people. It may be that you just want to enjoy what you do, feel pleased with yourself when you think back on your achievements and be energized by your plans for the future. If you can achieve all these things you'll have a level of career success that would satisfy many people.

Career Chick Hot Tip: Determine your definition of success.

The First Move

None of this happens without dedication, effort and a plan to take personal responsibility for your career. Women put effort into their careers and have done so for many years, but the results show that there are fewer women in senior positions than you'd expect. Despite being excellent at what they do, which business culture requires, this is not enough. The male-oriented work culture, whether purposefully or subconsciously, has worked against women. Those in the positions to determine who achieves success have not necessarily appreciated their work.

Like visitors to another country, it's up to Career Chicks to make the effort to communicate to ensure that their value is understood. But at this particular time in history, men and women in business communicate in different ways with different practices and customs, and the weight of power is still with men. It's not necessarily their fault – historically, there have just been more of them in business and they have had no reason to change. For women to succeed it's vital that chicks learn how to communicate and act in ways that are understood so that they are able to get their messages and contributions communicated effectively.

Career Chick Hot Tip: Make the first move and learn how to get your messages communicated effectively.

Understand The Context

If you walk down the shopping streets of Paris and see a shoe store with a sign that says *"Chaussures"* you may think it's the name of the store. When you see it a few times you may figure that you have seen a few stores from the same chain. But as you see all sorts of shoe stores, with all sorts of branding, featuring the same word it doesn't take long to work out that the word means 'shoes'. That's how children learn language, by hearing words in the appropriate context. Once you know the meaning, you can figure out how to use this insight. You can ignore it or, if you want new shoes, you can look out for the signs and hit the stores. Understanding a few words in French will certainly make your shopping more successful.

Similarly in business when you see the same communication and behaviors repeated in context, you can understand what is happening and why, and apply this knowledge for your own benefit. For instance, from reading this book, you now know that men have coffee together not just for the caffeine boost or to avoid work, but to share information and build relationships. Now you can choose whether to engage in this activity (you should!). Knowing the CODE for career success won't turn you into a senior executive or board member yet, but it will help you understand the environment and better inform you to make choices about how you act and communicate. The Career Chicks Hot Tips are very practical ideas you can use to apply your knowledge of how men and business work.

Career Chick Hot Tip: Learn how men work in the context of business and apply this knowledge.

Your Greatest Asset

The focus areas of the CODE – how you *Communicate*, your *Operating Style*, your *Career Development* and how you prioritize '*Everything Else*', as well as how capable you are at what you do – come together to build your most important asset: your career reputation. This is your greatest and most valuable asset, which is the foundation for building your career success.

Your reputation includes how confident and capable you appear, how you work with others, the results you achieve, your cultural fit and your future potential. Your reputation influences the opinions of others and impacts many decisions that can have a huge impact on your success, decisions ranging from the projects you are assigned to and your remuneration, to whether you are considered for new opportunities or promotions. Therefore, to be successful it's critical that your reputation aligns with your capability and aspirations.

Career Chick Hot Tip: Recognize that your reputation is your most valuable career asset and leverage it.

Project You

Men instinctively understand the importance of *Career Development* as a skill and area of focus. The weight of numbers of men in senior positions, higher salaries in equivalent positions and the continued dominance of male culture in the business environment suggest that this has been successful for them. You can achieve the same success through focusing on your career, as well as your job.

Developing your professional reputation requires and deserves the same level of focus and application of energy, effort and skills, as any work project. (Only your boss doesn't assign this project; you do.) If it helps, you can even give it a clever name, as you would a work project: The Me Files, Project Me, Me4CEO or whatever takes your fancy. Write a project plan, set deadlines and tasks, and take them every bit as seriously as you would any work project. (It was this advice that helped get this book on its way.)

The need to manage your career, as the most important project of your career itself, is the same for men or women. For chicks, there is that extra little challenge, 'Project You' needs to be implemented in an environment that's not necessarily intuitive and may not accommodate the female approach to business or working with people. No matter, a chick with a plan is a formidable force!

Career Chick Hot Tip: Plan your approach and implement 'Project You'.

Pre-requisites To The CODE

Fortunately the environment in which you are implementing your project is not in a galaxy far, far away ... just more like a foreign country. Things are different there. But you can be successful by using the Career Chick CODE to work out the language, culture and environment. By being aware of the communication and cultural norms of business you have an insight and appreciation of the environment and an edge to help you achieve your best. Now you can *Communicate* in the same language as others, develop an *Operating Style* that enhances your reputation, and work specifically on *Career Development* activities, while knowing how to prioritize '*Everything Else*' that needs to be done (and looking good while you do it). These four areas are absolutely critical to ensure that you maximize your potential and reap the rewards you deserve.

However, there are some underlying assumptions and existing requirements, pre-requisites so to speak, that you must have for the CODE to work. And to be truthful, without these fundamentals, men aren't successful either. You need to have value, potential and credibility for the CODE to work, so it's assumed that you always aim to be excellent at what you do, keep learning and developing your skills, and integrate what you learn into what you do.

It doesn't matter how well you communicate, manage up or impress others if you aren't competent at what you do. No amount of meeting with mentors, networking or impressive career plans is worth anything if you don't have the core skills and attributes to do your job and do it well. The CODE isn't a way to trick people into thinking you are capable if you aren't. Cream, as they say, rises to the top, but if you aren't competent at what you do you'll sink to the bottom. If you pretend that you have capability that you do not have, you'll eventually get found out. The only sure-fire way to avoid this is to develop your skills, learn, practise and become really competent at whatever it is that you do.

Career Chick Hot Tip: Be excellent at what you do.

Continue To Learn

There are many ways to do this and it often starts with your education and training prior to getting a job. Once you are in the workplace it's up to you to continually develop your skills. In some roles you'll have a manager who is a fantastic coach and contributes significantly to your development (grab these opportunities with both hands). But at other times you could well have a manager who doesn't add to your knowledge, either because they don't have those skills or are unable to communicate what they know to you. You can't afford your development to stagnate, so when that happens the answer is to keep working to improve yourself. Keep learning the skills that are relevant to your role, whether they are in finance, sales, marketing or administration, there is always an opportunity to improve. Understand what is happening in your industry, company and field. Read books, magazines and online material that's relevant to what you do. You may need to study formally if you need a specific qualification for your field. And make sure that you establish mentors and your network; they are two of the best sources to learn from.

As well as your core function, there are other areas where you need to keep relevant, particularly in the area of emerging technology where you must keep up with changes. In the last few years Wiki's, blogs and the web 2.0 have become part of accepted business use. No doubt there are more changes on the way. To keep pace with technology and its application for business it's vital to keep your skills relevant. A younger relative or co-worker may become your mentor in this area. Another way to keep your skills up-to-date is to spend time with young graduates who join your organization to see what they have been learning about and what they know. If you have worked in one organization for a reasonable period of time (two to three years or more) make sure you spend time with people in other organizations as part of your job or new people who join your company from other places. It's an opportune time to 'pick the brains' of these people while they are fresh from another company, so you can find out how things are done there. This is a no-lose situation as you'll either learn something new or benchmark what you do and be pleased with where you are. Either way it will help you to be good at what you do.

Being good at what you do is the foundation of your career and its potential success. Doing your best will set you apart from others. To be your best you need to prioritize what is most important for your time and your focus. Prioritize the three most important areas of focus for your job. If you find it hard to make this decision, you can always ask your manager, something like, *"If you had to prioritize the three most important things I need to deliver what would they be?"* This should give you the information you need to know about what to focus on. It also tells you what to include in your elevator pitch, which explains what you do and what you are achieving. Just make sure that it's short and succinct enough to be told in a very short elevator ride (one floor, preferably).

Career Chick Hot Tip: Keep learning and developing your skills.

Be Your Best

One of the major differences between those who are good at what they do and those who really get ahead is that they don't settle for less than their best and they are constantly looking for ways to improve. If a report is okay, but not as thorough as it should be, then it may mean a rewrite. If a customer brochure doesn't make an impact it may mean another draft before it goes to print. If all your customers haven't been followed up at the end of the month it may mean a very busy couple of days for you. Whatever it takes to be your best is what you should focus on, not only for your career reputation, but also your own confidence and sense of achievement. Being prepared to do a little more than others will give you an edge over your competitors, both in a business and a career sense. Focus on what is important for you to achieve to help you identify exactly what you need to be excellent at.

Being your best positively impacts your confidence and sense of achievement. It takes you into a zone where you're absorbed and totally engaged; which feels fantastic. This transforms into confidence about what you're doing, which is apparent to others. Ironically, this increased confidence in yourself gives them increased confidence in you.

Career Chick Hot Tip: Do your best. Don't settle for less than you're capable of achieving.

Integrate What You Learn

When you combine your abilities, attitude and willingness to learn and improve with the CODE for Career Chicks you have the makings of a successful career. However, knowing the CODE and learning new skills is only part of the secret to building your reputation and unlocking your potential. The most important thing is to actually use what you learn. If you know that you can adapt your *Communication*, develop an individual *Operating Style*, focus on your *Career Development* and prioritize the time you spend on '*Everything Else*', you can transform your career effectiveness. But only if you actually do it! Integrating new activities and tasks into your working life takes conscious effort, but doing it makes '*Everything Else*' so much easier.

There are a lot of tips for Career Chicks to remember, so try out a couple and see how they work for you. Play around with some of the words or questions that have been suggested. Say them out loud to yourself three or four times until you feel comfortable with them.

Adapt the words to your way of speaking. Use words that you're comfortable with, so that you're at ease with what you want to say. Don't worry: no one will know that you learnt them from a book. It's highly unlikely that your male managers or colleagues will have read *Hot Tips for Career Chicks*! And even if they have, they won't think that the new things you're doing or saying are strange; this is the way that guys behave.

Career Chick Hot Tip: Integrate what you learn into what you do.

Use The CODE

Using some or all of the Career Chicks Hot Tips does not require changing who you are. Your worth is in who you are, what you know and the values that guide you. This is your unique value. Don't give that up for anything or anyone. This is not about trying to be someone else or someone that you aren't comfortable with. Ask any successful woman in the business world what her number-one piece of advice to other women is and she'll invariably say, *"Be yourself."*

This book has aimed to help you understand the subtleties and nuances of how people operate in the business world. You can use the Career Chick Hot Tips to demonstrate how capable you are to those who need to know but can't or don't communicate with you in the same language (men and women who have learnt to communicate like men). The Career Chick Hot Tips will help you showcase the abilities and potential that you have, so that others who influence and impact on your success can recognize your worth. The tips also provide you with some ideas of how to present yourself and what you do in a way that is easily understood and valued in the prevailing culture of business and organizations.

A successful career has many potential benefits: it can be intellectually stimulating; you can meet wonderful people who you enjoy spending time with; and you can achieve things in the business world that make a difference. You may not be an inventor, a Nobel Laureate or make newspaper headlines for changing the world, but you can make a difference by what you do, how you treat others or even by financially supporting yourself or others. Not to mention the fact that a career can provide you with the opportunity to earn enough money to enjoy a good standard of living.

There are probably lots of other things on your wish list and whatever they are chances are a successful career offers you the potential to achieve them. This will take effort, which is more about applying yourself, focusing on your career and being willing to try new things (like the Career Chick Hot Tips for instance!), rather than the number of hours that you work.

Over time, the male-oriented business culture will change, and the behavior and communications that are required for success in organizations will represent all customers, employees, shareholders and stakeholders. This funnily enough includes women! How this change will happen is not unlike the often-quoted story about how best to boil a frog. The story goes that if you stick a frog in a pot of hot water it will jump out. Frogs aren't stupid. But if you put the frog in cold water and gradually increase the temperature the frog won't notice and will stay there until it's too late. There is some scientific dispute about whether this is actually the case, but it's a good story that's often used to illustrate how to implement change in different contexts.

The frog analogy holds true when you think about how people react to change in the workplace. When you make a lot of noise about the need for change, you'll find everyone has an opinion – and many object. You can get caught up in all sorts of philosophical arguments about the role of women, feminism and a whole lot of stuff that's related but clouds the issues and makes the debate emotive. Instead of moving forward and getting on with the changes that are needed, the focus is on managing the outcry. On the other hand, if enough Career Chicks understand the subtleties and blend with the environment, men will get used to women being in 'their' working environment. Just like turning up the water temperature on the frog. Eventually it will change – even if it's only because you are there, which will impact the actions and reactions of those around you.

As more Career Chicks learn how the male-oriented business culture works, the more influence they will have and the more opportunity there will be to explain to men how chicks work. Then they can learn to appreciate the potential benefits of working with capable women. Not that there isn't an important and legitimate role for activists to put the water straight on to boil and make a lot of noise. There is. But it does mean that even if your style is to take it slow and gradually raise the temperature, you, too can be successful in facilitating change to business culture. You never know, the guys may realize we understand them more than they understand us and try to figure us out. Wouldn't that be a turn-up? Regardless, what is important for you as a Career Chick is to make sure that you do your best to achieve the career success that your abilities and contribution deserve.

> *Career Chick Hot Tip:* Use the CODE, achieve career success and enjoy it!

Career Chick Hot Tips to unlock the CODE for career success:

- Determine your definition of success.

- Make the first move and learn how to get your messages communicated effectively.

- Learn how men work in the context of business and apply this knowledge.

- Recognize that your reputation is your most valuable career asset and leverage it.

- Plan your approach and implement 'Project You'.

- Be excellent at what you do.

- Keep learning and developing your skills.

- Do your best. Don't settle for less than you're capable of achieving.

- Integrate what you learn into what you do.

- Use the CODE, achieve career success and enjoy it!

Career Chick Hot Tips
to manage *'Everything Else'*:

- **Prioritize what's important** to you.

- Be confident in the image you present by following some **Chick Tips**.

- **Unlock the CODE** and use it to achieve career success.

Hot Tips for Career Chicks to unlock the CODE to success:

- Use your **_Communication_** skills to demonstrate your contributions and capability.

- Develop an **_Operating Style_** that supports the image and reputation you want to be known for.

- Prioritize your **Career _Development_**.

- Manage **'_Everything Else_'** to focus on what's important

... and, enjoy the journey.

Acknowledgements and Notes

Chapter 1: Knowledge *Is* Power

1. Kennedy, Chad. Cover – P!nk Interview. *Teen Scene Magazine*. Accessed 18 Jan. 2009. teenscenemag.com   http://www.teenscenemagazine.com/sections/cover/cover_pink.php

2. Reflects publicly available data obtained by the author from company websites April 2010.

3. Sealy, R., Vinnicombe, S. and Doldor, E. (2009) *The Female FTSE Board Report 2009.* Cranfield University, 2009 Cranfield, UK.

4. Based on the listings published by the Financial Post 500 as updated on March 3, 2010.

5. Equal Opportunity for Women in the Workplace Agency. *2008 Australian Census of Women in Leadership.* 2008. p 4.

6. U.S. Census Bureau. Monthly Postcensal Resident Population, by single year of age, sex, race and Hispanic origin, 11/1/2008. *2007 Monthly National Population Estimates.*

7. Source: National Statistics website: www.statistics.gov.uk.   Crown copyright material is reproduced with the permission of the Controller Office of Public Sector Information (OPSI). http://www.statistics.gov.uk/cci/nuggest.asp?id=1651. Accessed 7 Feb. 2009.

8. Statistics Canada. 2009. *Table 2 Population estimates by sex and age group as of July 1, 2009, Canada.* Canada's Population Estimates: Age and Sex. Version updated 27 November, 2009. Ottawa. <http://www.statcan.gc.ca/daily-quotidien/091127/t091127/b2-eng.htm> 25 April 2010.

9. Based on Australian Bureau of Statistics Data. Australian Bureau of Statistics. Australian Demographic Statistics. *Estimated Resident Population, States and Territories.* Cat. No. 3101.0 Table 4. March Quarter 2010.

10. Source: National Center for Education Statistics. Digest of Education Statistics. *Table 258: Degrees conferred by degree-granting institutions, by level of degree and sex of student: Selected years, 1869-70 through 2016-17.* (2007)   http://nes.ed.gov/programs/digest/d07/tables/dt07_228.asp

11. Source: Higher Education Statistics Agency. *Higher Education Student Enrolments and Qualifications obtained at Higher Education Institutions*

in the United Kingdom in the Academic Year 2007/08. Table 5. 2009. http://hesa.ac.uk/index.php/content/view/1356/161/

12. Based on Statistics Canada. *University degrees, diplomas and certificates granted by sex, by province, 2007.* Education, training and learning. Version updated 23 March, 2010. Ottawa. <http://www40.statcan.gc.ca/101/cst01/educ51a-eng.htm> 25 April 2010

13. Based on Australian Bureau of Statistics Data. Australian Bureau of Statistics. Education and Work. *Persons aged 15-64 years with a non-school qualification, Level and main field of highest non-school qualification-by age and sex.* Cat. No. 6227.0 Table 12. November 2009.

14. Based on Australian Bureau of Statistics Data. Australian Bureau of Statistics. Education and Work. *Employed Persons aged 15-74 years, Selected characteristics-by level of highest non-school qualification.* Cat. No. 6227.0 Table 11. November 2009.

15. Bureau of Labor Statistics. The Employment Situation: March 2010. *Employment status of the civilian population by sex and age.* Table A-1. April 2010. <http://www.bls.gov/news.release/empsit.nr0.htm>

16. Based on Australian Bureau of Statistics Data. Australian Bureau of Statistics. Australian Labour Market Statistics. *Employed Persons, Industry and Occupation: Original – February 2010.* Cat. No. 6105.0 Table 2.4. Apr. 2010.

17. Based on Statistics Canada. *Labour force and participation rates by sex and age group.* Labour Force Survey. Version updated 29 January, 2010. Ottawa. <http://www40.statcan.gc.ca/l01/cst01/labor05-eng.htm?sdi=women> 25 April 2010.

18. Bureau of Labor Statistics. Current Population Survey. *Table 11. Employed persons by detailed occupation, sex, race and Hispanic or Latino ethnicity.* Annual Averages 2009.

19. Source: National Statistics website: www.statistics.gov.uk. Crown copyright material is reproduced with the permission of the Controller Office of Public Sector Information (OPSI*). Labour Force Survey: Employment Status by occupation and sex, April – June 2009.* <http://www.statistics.gov.uk/statbase/product.asp?vlnk=14248> Accessed 25 April 2010.

20. Based on Australian Bureau of Statistics Data. Australian Bureau of Statistics. Australian Labour Market Statistics. *Employed Persons, Industry and Occupation: Original – February 2010.* Cat. No. 6105.0 Table 2.4. Apr. 2010.

21. Catalyst (New York. December 9, 2009). *2009 Catalyst Census of the Fortune 500 Reveals Women Missing from Critical Business Leadership*

(Canada). Press Release. Retrieved 26 April 2010 < http://www.catalyst. org/press-release/161/2009-catalyst-census-of-the-fortune-500-reveals-women-missing-from-critical-business-leadership>.

22. Catalyst (Toronto. March 6. 2009) *Women Still Largely Shut Out From Senior Ranks of FP500 Companies.* Press Release. Retrieved 26 April 2010 < http://www.catalyst.org/press-release/145/women-still-largely-shut-out-from-senior-ranks-of-fp500-companies>.

23. Sealy, R., Vinnicombe, S. and Singh, V. (2008), *The Female FTSE Report 2008: A decade of delay.* Cranfield University, Cranfield, UK.

24. Equal Opportunity for Women in the Workplace Agency. *2008 Australian Census of Women in Leadership.* 2008. p 10.

25. Equal Opportunity for Women in the Workplace Agency. *2008 Australian Census of Women in Leadership.* 2008. p 12.

26. Equal Opportunity for Women in the Workplace Agency. Gender Income Distribution of Top Earners in ASX200 Companies. *2006 EOWA Census of Women in Leadership.*

27. The Corporate Library (Portland, Maine. November 6, 2008) *Female CEOS Receive Lower Total Compensation than Male Counterparts.* Press Release. Retrieved April 26, 2010. <http://www.thecorporatelibrary. com/news_docs/631110608ceopay08_femalediff.pdf>.

28. United Nations Development Program. Human Development Report 2009. *Gender-related development index.* Table J.

29. United Nations Development Program. Human Development Report 2009. *Gender empowerment measure and its components.* Table K.

30. Based on Australian Bureau of Statistics Data. Australian Bureau of Statistics. Australian Labour Market Statistics. *Employed Persons, Industry and Occupation: Original – February 2010.* Cat. No. 6105.0 Table 2.4. Apr. 2010.

31. Bureau of Labor Statistics. Current Population Survey. *Table A-6. Employed and unemployed full- and part-time workers by sex and age, seasonally adjusted.* March 2010.

32. Bureau of Labor Statistics. Current Population Survey. *Table A-6. Employed and unemployed full- and part-time workers by sex and age, seasonally adjusted.* March 2010.

33. Based on Australian Bureau of Statistics Data. Australian Bureau of Statistics. Australian Labour Market Statistics. *Employed Persons, Industry and Occupation: Original – February 2010.* Cat. No. 6105.0 Table 2.4. Apr. 2010.

34. Bureau of Labor Statistics. *Current Population Survey. Employment Characteristics of Families.* "Table 6. Employment status of mothers with own children under 3 years old by single year of age of youngest child and marital status, 2007-2008 annual averages." (2009)

35. Whitehouse, G., M. Baird and C. Diamond (2006) *Highlights from The Parental Leave in Australia Survey.* December 2006. http://www.polsis. uq.edu.au/index.html?page=55767

36. Johnson, Tallese D., 2007. *Maternity Leave and Employment Patterns: 2001-2003. Table 8.* Current Population Report, P70-113. U.S. Census Bureau, Washington DC.

37. Johnson, Tallese D., 2007. *Maternity Leave and Employment Patterns: 2001-2003. Table 10.* Current Population Report, P70-113. U.S. Census Bureau, Washington DC.

38. Thanks to Peter Kelly, Managing Director Asia, Coca-Cola Amatil for his insights into and appreciation of the value of women to business.

Part 1: Communication

Chapter 2: Choose Your Words

1. Carroll, Lewis. Chapter VII A Mad Tea Party. *Alice's Adventures in Wonderland.* Accessed 26 April 2009. http://wwwen.wikisource.org/wiki/Alice%27s_Adventures_in_Wonderland/Chapter7

2. For further reading see Albert Mehrabian's website http://kaaj.com/psych/index.html

Chapter 5: Write Well

1. Churchill, Winston. *The Few.* House of Commons 20 Aug. 1940. Parliamentary material is reproduced with the permission of the Controller of HMSO on behalf of Parliament.

Part 2: Operating Style

Chapter 9: Work In Teams

1. Thanks to Peter Lancaster & Jo Keeler at Belbin Associates for their help in verifying the Belbin Team Roles. For further information on the roles see http://belbin.com

Chapter 10: Negotiate

1. With much love and a huge thank you to Katie McDonnell for her wise and knowledgeable words. Also love and thanks to her sister Cassandra for, amongst other things, her advice that "*No-one* looks good with panda eyes." Noted and included as a Career Chick Hot Tip!

Chapter 12: Lead

1. Appreciation and thanks to David Breashears for permission to use his analogy about Mt. Everest with the challenges of leadership. To learn more about David and his work visit http://www.davidbreashears.com.

Part 3: Career Development

Chapter 14: Plan Your Career

1. Carroll, Lewis. Chapter VII A Mad Tea Party. *Alice's Adventures in Wonderland.* Accessed 17 May 2009. http://wwwen.wikisource.org/wiki/Alice%27s_Adventures_in_Wonderland/Chapter6

Chapter 17: Know When To Move On

1. From Comedy Writing Secrets, 2nd Edition copyright © 2005 by Mel Helitzer with Mark Shatz. Used with the kind permission of Writer's Digest Books, a division of F+W Media, Inc., Cincinnati, Ohio. All rights reserved.

Chapter 18: Get The Job You Want

1. More wise words from Peter Kelly, Managing Director Asia, Coca-Cola Amatil.

2. Thanks to James Carpenter for this clear explanation of a complex topic.

Chapter 19: Earn What You're Worth

1. Dowd, Maureen. Insulting the Crocodile. *The New York Times* 30 July 1997. Accessed 10 Jan. 2009. <http://query.nytimes.com/gst/fullpage.html?res=9B0CEEDB113AF933A05754C0A961958260>

2. The Corporate Library (Portland, Maine. November 6, 2008) *Female CEOS Receive Lower Total Compensation than Male Counterparts.* Press Release. Retrieved April 26, 2010. <http://www.thecorporatelibrary.com/news_docs/631110608ceopay08_femalediff.pdf>.

3. Equal Opportunity for Women in the Workplace Agency. Gender Income Distribution of Top Earners in ASX200 Companies. *2006 EOWA Census of Women in Leadership.*

4. Bureau of Labor Statistics. Highlights of Women's Earnings in 2008. *Table 2. Median usual weekly earnings of full-time wage and salary workers, by detailed occupation and sex, 2008 annual averages.*

5. Bureau of Labor Statistics. Current Population Survey. Household Data Annual Averages. *Table 39. Median weekly earnings of full-time wage and salary workers by detailed occupation and sex.* 2008.

6. Source: National Statistics website: www.statistics.gov.uk. Crown copyright material is reproduced with the permission of the Controller Office of Public Sector Information (OPSI). *2009 Annual Survey of Hours and Earnings.* http://www.statistics.gov.uk/cci/nugget.asp?id=285 Accessed 26 April 2010.

7. Based on Australian Bureau of Statistics Data. Australian Bureau of Statistics. Average Weekly Earnings: Trend. *Average Weekly Earnings.* Cat. No. 6302.0 Table 1. November Quarter 2009.

8. Human Resources and Skill Development Canada. *Work – Weekly Earnings.* <http://www4.hrsdc.gc.ca/.3ndic.1t.4r@-eng.jsp?iid=18#M_2 >. Accessed 26 Apr. 2010.

Part 4: 'Everything Else'

Chapter 21: Chick Tips

1. Zernike, Kate. Commencements; At Yale, Mrs. Clinton Ponders Hair and Politics. *The New York Times*, 21 May 2001. Accessed 3 Jan. 2009. http://query.nytimes.com/gst/fullpage.html?res=9803E3DE143DF932A15756C0A9679C8B63

Thank You ...

At the end of a book I often read the acknowledgments to gain an insight into the author. Usually it's just a long list of names and few tidbits of new information. Now I know why. While it might only take one person to write a book, it takes many people to provide the support, encouragement and expertise to make it happen. With heartfelt gratitude, and in no particular order, I would like to thank everyone who helped make my dream of writing this book a reality.

To all the many talented business people who have generously have shared their knowledge and expertise with me; many thanks to Stacie Adamedes, Serena Beirne, David Casey, James Carpenter, Stephanie Carullo, Bill Dunn, Mike Foster, Gary Hooper, Rosemary Howard, Lisa Hudson, Peter Kelly, Holly Kramer, David Nash, David Rampa, David Thodey and Fabian Venter. Your expertise and willingness to share it throughout my career has been (and is still!) appreciated.

Also thank you to Kandy Shepherd for sharing her expertise, my lovely editor Kirsten Wilkins, Karen Cunningham and Cheryl O'Neill for the cover design, and Colin Williams who provided a fresh set of eyes as a proof-reader. (Any errors you find are mine!)

And to the many friends and colleagues who have supported me in the writing of this book and the launch of the first edition: Steve Ahn, Marty Allen, Dominic Beirne, Grace Burgoyne (unofficial marketing assistant), Helen Candy, Sandie McCabe, Steven McDonald, Brendan McDonnell, Sharyn McDonnell and their girls Cassandra and Katie who provided words of wisdom that were included in the book and many that haven't been, Andrea Molloy (you rock), Maureen Owens, Kate Southam and Liam Adamedes – and thank you to all the girls in book club.

Thank you all, not only for your faith in my ability to write this, but also for the many coffees, emails and pep talks it took to get me through! To Sandy Burgoyne – thank you for not reading this until it was finished and for 'everything else'. To Heather Swain – for the conversation at 'The Vanguard' that made me persevere. Jenny Morris was brilliant too. And to Nick at Maisy's Café, whose many coffees fuelled my efforts.

Thank you to all the 'Calendar people', who include my family, godchildren, nieces, nephews and an amazing and supportive collection of friends – you are all so important to me. To my original playmates, my brother David and sister Lisa who I still love to hang out with and to their partners Sue and Barry. Thanks also to the many colleagues, managers, customers and co-workers over the years who have all been part of my career so far.

Thank you to the many talented Career Chicks out there, both those I've had the privilege to work with and those talented individuals I may never meet. I hope this helps.

And to Peter – I'll try and finish my next project in a long weekend (but I can't promise).

Karen Adamedes
Sydney / Australia / June 2010

Hot tips for career chicks

Index

www.ingramcontent.com/pod-product-compliance
Lightning Source LLC
Chambersburg PA
CBHW062127280526
45788CB00001B/79